T0326233

The Case Writing Workbook

This book offers a modular set of chapters that focus specifically on challenges related to case writing. Exercises, worksheets, and training activities will help guide readers sequentially through the entire process of writing both a case and an instructor's manual (teaching note).

Designed as an individualized workshop to assist case authors to structure their writing, this book combines the easy-to-understand, student-focused language of the first edition with new material covering the latest developments and challenges in the world of case writing. These include:

- A section on writing cases in condensed time frames
- A new module on writing short cases in various formats
- A new module on turning research papers into teaching tools
- A section about growing communities of practice in a university
- An expansion of the student case writing module to include a section on case writing for graduate students
- Twelve new worksheets
- A complete index to facilitate use of the book

Finishing all the book's assignments will result in a complete case and instructor's manual that can be tested in the classroom and submitted to a conference or journal. *The Case Writing Workbook* is a must for the shelf of any academic or student conducting qualitative research and looking to enhance their skill set.

Gina Vega is founder and president of Organizational Ergonomics, USA.

"Gina Vega's *The Case Writing Workbook* is a generous book written to support academics in researching and writing robust, fact-based cases that engage students and accelerate learning. The new edition continues to share a 'how to' practice-based approach to case writing with useful tips, worksheets and examples. The new modules are valuable additions to this comprehensive guide. Readers from novice to experienced will feel Gina Vega's presence as they read and progress through the workbook, her support and encouragement are present throughout."

Rebecca Wilson-Mah, *Royal Roads University, Canada*

"This user-friendly, step-by-step guide for faculty new to case research, writing and publishing is also a handy refresher for experienced writers. It's chock-full of practical advice and insider tips as well as helpful new modules on compact cases and transforming published research into cases. It also has weekly guides for case writing during heavy teaching semesters or sabbaticals. We distributed it at a workshop to help faculty succeed with case writing and publishing."

Laurie Levesque, *Suffolk University, USA*

The Case Writing Workbook

A Self-Guided Workshop

Second Edition

Gina Vega

Routledge
Taylor & Francis Group

NEW YORK AND LONDON

First published 2017
by Routledge
711 Third Avenue, New York, NY 10017

and by Routledge
2 Park Square, Milton Park, Abingdon, Oxon OX14 4RN

Routledge is an imprint of the Taylor & Francis Group, an informa business

© 2017 Taylor & Francis

The right of Gina Vega to be identified as author of this work has been
asserted by her in accordance with sections 77 and 78 of the Copyright,
Designs and Patents Act 1988.

All rights reserved. No part of this book may be reprinted or reproduced
or utilised in any form or by any electronic, mechanical, or other means,
now known or hereafter invented, including photocopying and recording,
or in any information storage or retrieval system, without permission in
writing from the publishers.

Trademark notice: Product or corporate names may be trademarks
or registered trademarks, and are used only for identification and
explanation without intent to infringe.

Library of Congress Cataloging-in-Publication Data
Names: Vega, Gina, author.
Title: The case writing workbook : a self-guided workshop / Gina Vega.
Description: Second Edition. | New York : Routledge, 2017. | Revised
    edition of the author's The case writing workbook, c2013.
Identifiers: LCCN 2016039445 | ISBN 9781138210158 (hbk) |
    ISBN 9781138210165 (pbk) | ISBN 9781315455891 (ebk) |
    ISBN 9781351863315 (web PDF) | ISBN 9781351863308 (ePub) |
    ISBN 9781351863292 (mobi/kindle)
Subjects: LCSH: Case method. | Business writing—Handbooks,
    manuals, etc.
Classification: LCC HF5718.3 .V44 2017 | DDC 001.4/33—dc23
LC record available at https://lccn.loc.gov/2016039445

ISBN: 978-1-138-21015-8 (hbk)
ISBN: 978-1-138-21016-5 (pbk)
ISBN: 978-1-315-45589-1 (ebk)

Typeset in Utopia
by Apex CoVantage, LLC

For Robert, my coauthor in life since 1965

Contents ● ● ● ● ●

Module 11 Special Formats and Delivery Systems   *287*

Illustrations   ● ● ● ● ●

Module 4

Module 5

Module 6

Module 11

Introduction   • • • • •

HOW TO USE THIS WORKBOOK

• • • • •

Who Needs This Workbook?

Cases have been used in business schools for a century, and they have never been more popular than they are today. Requests from deans, instructors, and corporate trainers in the United States and internationally for case writing workshops have increased each year since 2000, as novice case writers and experienced authors alike continue to struggle with the basics of this writing technique. In this workbook, I aim to help you move forward in mastering a rewarding and satisfying writing experience.

This case writing workbook offers something unique in the world of case writing manuals. Designed in individual modules, *The Case Writing Workbook: A Self-Guided Workshop* provides eleven stand-alone modules that focus specifically on challenges related to the writing process. The book is meant for day-to-day use as a model of the case writing process, with exercises, worksheets, and training activities that will guide you through the entire course of writing both a case and an instructor's manual (teaching note). Brief explanatory notes will lead you step-by-step through the exercises.

The Case Writing Workbook serves as an individualized case writing workshop for those who cannot attend one, either due to financial or time and scheduling constraints. Case writing workshops can cost individuals from $100 to $2,500, depending on the duration of the program; short funding, especially in public institutions, can make participation in such workshops nearly impossible for many academics. In addition, many on-site workshops are offered during the school year, when academics are immersed in classwork. This book provides all the benefits of an individualized workshop without the expense or scheduling conflicts. It offers both convenience and a cost-effective solution to participation in an actual workshop by providing the same tools and activities used by workshop facilitators.

Authors who follow the outlined process will succeed in developing a case and its related instructor's manual with little stress. You will benefit most from this book if you count yourself in one of the following categories:

- ■ If you are an academic looking for a new kind of scholarly writing challenge, this workbook is for you.
- ■ If you are ready to revitalize your publication record, this workbook is for you.

- If you are particularly interested in experiential learning and innovative pedagogies, this workbook is for you.

- If you want to learn how to use your research data in a teaching format, this workbook is for you.

- If you are looking for a way to combine research, writing, and theory applications to enhance your basic academic skill set, this workbook is for you.

• • • • •

How the Workbook Is Constructed

The Case Writing Workbook: A Self-Guided Workshop is designed as a series of modules, each of which focuses on a specific aspect of case writing. It is written in "real" English and avoids, to the greatest extent possible, academic jargon, acronyms, and "insider" terminology.

The modules, ranging from 10 to 40 pages in length, are a mix of exercises and explanatory text. The goal is to provide a variety of usable worksheets to facilitate the writing process, supported by sufficient textual explanation to make the appropriate use of the worksheets clear—just as an instructor would explain concepts in a face-to-face workshop. The worksheet design allows you, the reader, to practice each case writing skill as you apply it to developing your case.

A major case writing task is assigned in four of the first five modules. Authors who finish all the assignments will end up with a complete case and instructor's manual that can be tested in the classroom and submitted to a conference or journal, if desired.

Elements from a published case and instructor's manual illustrate each major assignment. This case, "Ken Roberts: Master Mechanic," by Duncan LaBay (Salem State University), appears in *The CASE Journal* 6.1 (2009). The full case can be purchased for use in the classroom through www.thecasecentre.org.

At the end of each module, you will find a section labeled "References and Readings." This section provides citations for the module and lists additional sources that deal with topics in greater depth.

• • • • •

Major Changes from the First Edition

I prepared this second edition in direct response to your requests for "MORE." Along with updates to nearly every module, I have added the following:

- A section on writing cases in condensed time frames (Module 3)
- A new module on writing short cases in various formats (Module 4)

- A new module on moving from research to teaching—turning your research papers into teaching tools (Module 6)
- A section about growing communities of practice in your own university (Module 8)
- An expansion of the student case writing module to include a section on case writing for graduate students (Module 10)
- Twelve new worksheets
- A complete index to facilitate the use of the book

● ● ● ● ●

A Road Map through the Workbook

As you will see in the following section, I have also restructured the workbook to make it more logical to follow.

If you are interested primarily in researching, writing, and publishing your cases, Modules 1–7 are what you need. If you want to work with others, including students, on case-related projects and learning, both with and without technology, add Modules 8–11.

● ● ● ● ●

Module Descriptions

Here is what you will find in each of the modules.

Module 1. Getting Started: This module provides background about case writing. I describe teaching cases and discuss where to draw the line between reality and fiction in case writing, why and how to use cases in the classroom, and why you might want to write one yourself (five exercises/worksheets).

Module 2. The Research Process: Every case begins with research, and this module will get you started on finding case subjects, getting approvals, mastering the basics of qualitative research (including a refresher on applicable methodologies), applying interview techniques, and managing data with or without the use of technology (12 exercises/worksheets).

Module 3. Writing the Case: This module provides an extensive discussion of the key elements of cases and walks you through the entire case writing process, from the selection of an appropriate writing style to the identification and avoidance of common case writing hazards (13 exercises/worksheets).

Module 4. Writing Short Cases: In an effort to engage students in a valuable learning experience without requiring much out-of-classroom preparation, many instructors are turning to the shorter case. Here is how to develop, write, and use these shorter cases (five exercises/worksheets).

Module 5. Building the Instructor's Manual: Beginning with the purpose of an instructor's manual (IM), this module provides guidelines for establishing professional credibility, identifies and illustrates the key elements of the IM, describes and assists in the development of learning objectives, and focuses on preparing and answering discussion questions (eight exercises/worksheets).

Module 6. Transforming Research Cases into Teaching Cases: How to take your published or unpublished research papers and turn them into teaching cases for publication and use in the classroom (four exercises/worksheets).

Module 7. Getting Your Case Published and Reviewing Cases for Others: Once your case is written and tested, the next step is getting it published. In this module, you will learn the proper way to respond to reviews, embark on the publication process, and do case reviews for others. I focus on the characteristics of "good" reviews and "good" reviewers, the value of participation in case conferences, and the methods for establishing an institutional case writing mindset (seven exercises/worksheets).

Module 8. Working with Coauthors: Writing in teams differs from writing alone or with one partner, but do you know how? In this module, you will learn how to design interview guides for use by multiple researchers and develop knowledge management protocols to facilitate group case writing (11 exercises/worksheets).

Module 9. Teaching with Cases: Writing and publishing cases does not help much in the classroom if you are uncomfortable using the case method. In this module, I suggest a variety of methods and exercises for you to try, including role-playing, brainstorming, student presentations, traditional three-board format, structured controversy, instant jeopardy, mock trials, and others (nine exercises/worksheets).

Module 10. Student Case Writing: The Case Research Study Model for Undergraduates and the Graduate Student Model: This module combines case and IM for undergraduate students in a reflexive model, and a more sophisticated model for graduate students that takes into account their more advanced knowledge base. Both models are defined, and technical instructions and lecture material are provided (15 exercises/worksheets).

Module 11. Special Formats and Delivery Systems: All cases are not created equal—some case formats lend themselves to specialized situations. This module makes suggestions about how to write and use vignettes, A/B cases, critical incidents, and other innovative case formats (two exercises/worksheets).

The Case Writing Workbook: A Self-Guided Workshop is not like other case writing manuals. I believe that you, the reader, want to learn a specific writing approach and are looking for some help in meeting that goal. For that reason, I designed this workbook with an eye toward developing and producing *usable manuscripts* rather than helping you isolate and overcome personal writing blocks or other generic skills. You can use this workbook alone or as adjunct to one of the existing case writing manuals that offer background material and theoretical supports for the applications I provide.

However you use this book, I send my good wishes for your successful writing and welcome any comments or questions you might have. I look forward to hearing from you and will do my best to answer e-mails as I receive them.

Gina Vega
gina.vega978@gmail.com

Acknowledgments

Writing, like teaching, is a lonely business, people tell me. Where do they get that idea from? To me, both teaching and writing are a great social collaboration, and doing either of them alone becomes a much more difficult and less satisfying activity.

I do not write alone. Every time I sit down at the computer (or at the legal pad or the special expensive paper that I am so stingy with or at the wrong sides of photocopies), I bring a large contingent of coauthors with me. These people include the protagonists of cases, the future readers of my output, my evaluators and critics, and the group of professionals who see to it that I am not embarrassed by what ultimately gets published. Sometimes these different audiences argue, leaving me in the middle to determine a moderate course. Sometimes these audiences applaud me (those are happy times), challenge me (fun times), or have no response to my work (bad times). But always, writing is social, collaborative, and fulfilling.

Thank you to my daughter, Rachel, who keeps me current with language usage, and to my special coauthor, my husband Robert, for his support, guidance, and help, and for his continuing faith in me.

Module 1

•••••

Getting Started

•••••

What Is a Case?

Beginning with the very simplest definition, a case is a **story**. This story describes a **factual** series of actions that occurred in the **past**. When a case is written as a teaching tool (the main focus of this workbook is the use of cases as teaching and learning tools), the reader is expected to do one of two things: (1) make a **decision** or recommendation to the protagonist for a course of action to pursue, or (2) perform an **analysis/evaluative description** of the action that has already taken place. Any decision or recommendation will be preceded by a thorough analysis, of course, but the main purpose of a decision case is the formulation of a recommendation. The primary purpose of an analysis or evaluative description case is the *process* of analysis and evaluation. How were prior decisions made? What methods were used? How else might these decisions have been made? Were the outcomes foreseeable from the actions? What about unintended consequences of the actions? How might they have been mitigated?

The keywords in the description teaching cases are *story, factual, past, decision*, and *analysis*. Regardless of which type of case you write, each of the following terms will apply:

■ **Story.** A case is always a story. That means it must include a beginning, a middle, and an ending. It must involve narrative description and often benefits from dialogue and human interaction. A case needs to be interesting enough to engage the reader on an emotional level as well as an intellectual one.

■ **Factual.** A case is based on facts. It is true to reality. It is not a fictionalized tale created by the author. It must be supported by documentation, whether published in a credible source or derived from interviews. The author's opinion has no place in a teaching case.

■ **Past.** A case takes place in the past—not in the present and not in the future. If the case were to take place in the future, it would be fiction. If the case were to take place in the present, students would not be able to analyze it based on outcomes. It would be guesswork, and education is not based on guesswork. It is based on the application of theories and analytical perspectives to past situations.

■ **Decision.** A case often requires a decision to be made. The reader is in the protagonist's shoes and must either make a recommendation of action to be taken, or consider the actions already taken and establish a perspective as to their validity based on theory. Opinions play an important role in decision making; however, we are exclusively interested in *informed* decision making; that is, decision making that has the benefit of educated analysis supporting it.

■ **Analysis.** The ultimate goal of teaching with cases is to encourage critical thinking in students—a crucial step toward wise decision making. Cases require students to analyze situations and evaluate actions that have been taken, as well as to consider alternatives to the actions that were taken by the protagonist.

● ● ● ● ●

Two Main Kinds of Cases: Teaching Cases and Research Cases

We will be devoting our efforts exclusively to teaching cases in this workbook. A **teaching case** is a factual description of a real situation. It is intended to serve as the basis for discussion in a particular course or discipline and contains sufficient information for students to be able to carry out the desired discussion. Teaching cases often have a decision focus (there is a particular decision to be made by the student on behalf of the case protagonist), but many course topics do not lend themselves to decision making; instead, some cases are written specifically for students to develop their analytical and evaluative skills. This is especially true in ethics and organizational behavior courses. (See Module 3 for complete information about writing a teaching case.)

A teaching case encourages discussion and investigation, and is always accompanied by an instructor's manual (IM) to guide the user in leading the case in the classroom. The IM contains a full case analysis, a teaching plan, a series of case questions and answers, and an epilogue that describes the real-time outcome of the case decision that has been made. (See Module 5 for a discussion of Instructor's Manuals, sometimes known as Teaching Notes.)

Despite any potential similarity to situations in other organizations, each teaching case is unique and presents a set of circumstances that reflect the distinctiveness of an individual organizational challenge. Therefore, it is important to avoid the temptation to generalize the decisions in one case to a broad recommendation for action in seemingly similar cases.

Although we will not be focusing on research cases in this workbook, it is valuable to understand the role of these cases. A **research case** is a descriptive analysis of a real situation that reflects a particular theoretical perspective, either by supporting a new hypothesis or by offering an alternative perspective to an existing hypothesis. A research case may be an $N = 1$ study of a specific phenomenon, or research cases may be aggregated to identify patterns of behavior that help explain greater social, economic, or fiscal trends.

See WS 1:1 for a chart to help you differentiate between teaching and research cases.

● ● ● ● ●

Frequently Used Case Models

There are many different models of teaching cases. Here are the ones you will see most frequently:

- **Classical.** This is what we mean most often when we talk about cases. It is generally 10 to 20 pages in length and includes multiple exhibits, with the level of complexity determined by the potential audience for the case. Classical cases can be decision focused or illustrative in nature, and they can be based on field research or library research. (For more on the research process, see Module 2.)
- **Cliffhanger.** This is a case based on events that are current at the time of the case writing. Often the case situation changes before the case makes it into print, so student analysis requires additional Internet research to remain timely. Generally, however, no resolution of cliffhanger cases has taken place before the case is used.
- **Multipart.** These are A/B cases (or sometimes A/B/C cases). A decision point is reached at the end of the A case. Based on that decision, the B case is distributed and a second decision point appears. The A case can stand alone, but the B case will not have sufficient background for analysis by itself.
- **Critical incident.** This is a short description of a situation, often published in textbooks as within-the-chapter mini-cases or caselets. They provide very little background information and focus exclusively on one brief activating event meant to illustrate a specific problem.
- **Embryo.** This is a short outline of a case—the very beginning of a case idea. We will be developing the embryo case as the first assignment in the Case Development Exercise. (See WS 1:4 Case Writing Assignment 1.)
- **Ex post facto.** This case, named for a Latin phrase meaning "after the fact," is one that takes place after the action has been completed and the outcome is generally known. It is a case for analysis and

discussion, not for decision making. Historical cases and cases based on significant and familiar situations are the foundation of ex post facto cases.

● ● ● ● ●

Reality v. Fiction

I cannot emphasize enough that a case must be factual. The case author must not invent situations, actions, conversations, characters, or locations. This is a bright-line rule meant to simplify adherence to facts.

But, you may argue, how can I possibly know what was said in a conversation between case protagonists if I was not there and if the conversation was not taped? How can I create the appropriate narrative over time if I did not witness the events as they unfolded? How can I present a case situation through the eyes of an objective observer if there is no such individual available to me? Without these things, I have no story and, if the case is above all a story, I have no case.

And what if the case protagonists will not give me permission to use their names and/or the name of the company involved? If I cannot invent these things, once again I have no case.

Where to Draw the Line

A bright-line prohibition against invention does not prohibit the reasonable re-creation of conversations and events, especially if these re-creations have been approved by the participants.

Who really remembers every word that was spoken in a meeting? What people do remember is the tone of the meeting, the participants, the interactions, and the general sense of the conversational trajectory.

So, if the main parties to a conversation remember a comfortable, easy-going chat with an agreeable resolution to a problem, you can re-create the meeting reasonably accurately, even if the words you use were not the identical ones spoken. Or, if the participants recall an acrimonious exchange of accusations and defenses, once again you can re-create the scene satisfactorily (with participant sign-off). You will need to footnote the conversation and indicate it has been re-created with participant approval, but that is a straightforward matter.

A more complex challenge involves presenting the facts of the case using a disinterested observer, a convention we see frequently in cases. A common convention, and one to be avoided, is the invention of an intern, an administrative assistant, a new hire, or some other individual who is not actually part of the situation but acts as an observer and narrator. The use of this technique is unacceptable. If there was no intern, then there simply was no intern. There is no impartial observer in this situation. If you need to make information available to the reader, you must find another way to do so.

Why is it harmful to invent a character—one who does not really play a role in the case—to act as chronicler? Because it distracts the readers, who may find themselves more interested in the intern (to whom the students can relate) than in the real protagonists who have a problem to resolve. Remember, cases are *factual* despite reading like *stories*.

One significant exception to this rule involves disguising a company or the names of individuals within a company. The best-case scenario is when a company and the protagonists provide approval for you to use the company name and their names, but sometimes there are good reasons to avoid identifying the company and the players. Under the latter set of circumstances, you may be asked to conceal the company's name, and this is absolutely an acceptable practice, especially if not disguising it may cause harm to any of the participants.

Take care when you disguise a company to avoid inadvertently using the name of another similar company. (An Internet search can help you here.) If you decide to move the company to another part of the country to further disguise it, take care to be reasonable in the geographic shift. For example, moving a Hawaiian surfboard manufacturer to Minnesota or an olive oil processor to Norway in order to disguise the company makes little sense. The problems experienced by surfboard manufacturers may appear similar to those experienced by snowboard manufacturers and problems experienced by olive oil processors may appear to resemble those experienced by herring processing factories, but they are actually quite distinct.

If you decide to shift the genders of the players to disguise their identities, be sure that the interactions in the case remain logical. The disclaimer about disguising the company and the individuals involved to maintain confidentiality must appear on the first page of the case so that the diligent reader does not spend a lot of time trying to do additional research on a company that does not exist.

See WS 1:2 for examples of acceptable re-creations and unacceptable inventions.

● ● ● ● ●

How to Use Cases

Cases provide students at all levels of post-secondary education with exposure to incidents and companies that may be far from their everyday experience. Cases are effective learning tools in multiple ways:

■ In the classroom, cases provide for lively discussion and in-depth analysis of business situations. No matter where a learner enters the learning cycle, cases are likely to provide an effective means of facilitating the process. Much has been written about learning styles and learning readiness, and learners of all styles seem to benefit from the use of cases. (See "References and Readings" for sources about learning styles.) Cases have proved to be especially useful for specific kinds of learning—learning that focuses on analytical skills and on decision making. Additional benefits include practice in the application of skills and in the development of written and oral arguments. However, cases do not excel in information transfer, which is accomplished through other means.

- In the boardroom, cases offer examples of consequences experienced by other organizations and provide cautionary tales. Many organizational consultants use cases in their training programs to guide executives in decision-making processes and improve communication skills.

- In the community, cases encourage communication and connection between town and gown, allowing business leaders to participate in the activities of their local university and enhance student learning. The business and educational communities are often surprised to learn how similar their concerns are, and cases provide ample evidence of these similarities.

- For faculty, case writing can provide an engaging path into both experiential learning and publishing opportunities. Teaching with cases requires the instructor to keep current with theory, with practice, and with pedagogical methods. In a teaching institution, case writing is an excellent tool for faculty to build and maintain their academic qualifications, and learning together in workshops and seminars creates additional value in terms of collegiality and writing partnerships (see Module 8 for tips on working with coauthors and building communities of practice around case writing).

● ● ● ● ●

Why Write Cases?

There are many reasons to write cases, and they fall into three basic categories: improved teaching and learning, personal scholarship, and accreditation challenges.

Improved teaching and learning is the main motivator for an instructor to write a case. We may become motivated to write our own cases when we cannot find a case that addresses an important issue, when we are presented with a great opportunity to study the activities that go on in an organization, or when we are intrigued by a certain company or a situation. (See Module 2 for more on where to find case situations and case subjects.) But the most compelling of these motivators is to help our students learn. This is the incentive that will shift us from thinking that cases are a "nice idea" to thinking, "I have to write a case on this topic so my students can learn this concept."

Personal scholarship provides another impetus for our case writing activities. Academics pass through many identified stages in their careers, beginning at the graduate school level, moving through untenured "junior" faculty status, then gaining tenure, promotion, and well-established roles (with less need to prove themselves through scholarship). Sometimes, faculty move into administrative positions that keep them from their normal scholarly activities, and when they return to more traditional faculty status, they find their writing skills have grown rusty. Case writing can help faculty at any stage of career development jump-start their research agenda and reinvigorate their scholarship.

Where are you in your academic career? See WS 1:3 for a checklist to help you identify your current scholarship and whether case writing is for you.

The Association to Advance Collegiate Schools of Business International (AACSB) has played a significant role in extending interest in the use of cases for experiential learning and scholarly publication. AACSB, the largest business school accrediting agency globally, has updated its accreditation requirements to focus on issues of publication impact that relate specifically to the individual institution's mission and faculty composition. The ongoing pressure for business schools to obtain AACSB accreditation requires faculty even at so-called "teaching schools" to conduct scholarly work that results in publication, often in the area of pedagogy or the development of teaching materials. AACSB recognizes cases (with their accompanying instructor's manuals) as scholarly contributions that reflect your disciplinary expertise. This emphasis on scholarship creates a market for materials whose usage can be measured readily and whose impact is transparent. Cases support the development of research and publication skills, and usage data stands as evidence of impact for maintaining and extending academic qualifications. Case writing thus creates a welcoming avenue for development of the pedagogical materials to support your institution's accreditation efforts as you create useful learning opportunities for your students.

Note: Before you move on to the next module, be sure to complete WS 1:4, Case Writing Assignment 1.

● ● ● ● ●

References and Readings

Anderson, L.W., and D.R. Krathwohl, eds. (2001). *A Taxonomy for Learning, Teaching, and Assessing: A Revision of Bloom's Taxonomy of Educational Objectives.* New York: Longman.

Bloom, B.S., M.D. Engelhart, E.J. Furst, W.H. Hill, and D.R. Krathwohl, eds. (1956). *Taxonomy of Educational Objectives: The Classification of Educational Goals.* Vol. 1: *Cognitive Domain.* New York: Longmans, Green.

Fink, L. Dee. (2003). *Creating Significant Learning Experiences.* San Francisco: Jossey-Bass.

Frost, P.J., and M.S. Taylor. (1996). *Rhythms of Academic Life: Personal Accounts of Careers in Academia.* Thousand Oaks, CA: Sage.

Gardner, Howard. (1983). *Frames of Mind: The Theory of Multiple Intelligences.* New York: Basic Books.

———. (1993). *Multiple Intelligences: The Theory in Practice.* New York: Basic Books.

Kolb, D.A. (1984). *Experiential Learning: Experience as the Source of Learning and Development.* Englewood Cliffs, NJ: Prentice Hall.

http://www.aacsb.edu/~/media/AACSB/Publications/white-papers/wp-assurance-of-learning-standards.ashx (accessed November 29, 2016).

● ● ● ● ●

Worksheets

WS 1:1   Teaching Cases and Research Cases

WS 1:2   Acceptable Re-Creations and Unacceptable Inventions: Refining the Bright Line

WS 1:3   Your Current Scholarship

WS 1:4   Case Writing Assignment 1

WS 1:5   Case Writing Assignment Sample

WS 1:1

Teaching Cases and Research Cases

Use this chart to identify the kind of case you are writing by comparing the sample passages with your own.

Element/Samples	Teaching Case	Research Case
Presentation of Facts		
Karleen Johnson, CPA, had seen many unusual business problems during the past 10 years, but she had never been rendered speechless before today. Today was the day she saw her uncle's will and learned that he had left his business—a clinic—to her. She was stunned because he had never discussed it with her.	X	
~ Your presentation of facts here ~		
Descriptive Analysis		
Several times, the center has approached the phase state that exists when a business needs to make the transition from an entrepreneur-driven to a manager-run organization. At this point, a formal process of "letting go" by the owners must begin in order for corporate growth to continue.		X
~ Your descriptive analysis here ~		

Theoretical Perspective		
Each of the four cases reflects the complexity of managerial succession in the Russian context. All the owners pointed to pressures within the institutional environment that compelled them to view hired CEOs with caution—even suspicion. Personal mistrust and poor confidence in contract law forced most of the owners to intervene in business operations. In all cases, when transferring managerial responsibilities, the owners emphasized the risks of losing their assets because of illegal actions by hired CEOs. All these factors led to a situation where owners were more preoccupied with personality traits and the possibility of building trust in the hired CEO than with their professionalism and skills. As a result, the hired CEOs often did not improve business performance; instead, they merely fulfilled a narrow group of administrative functions. Typically, the owner or dominant shareholder set the course of business development and de facto acted as the top manager.		X
~ Your theoretical perspective here ~		

Distinctive Circumstances		
The three most critical of the many local concerns were intimately connected. Bevilacqua bemoaned the fact that as more and more high-tech companies found a comfortable, less costly home north of Boston in the Merrimack Valley, these same employers were discovering an unexpected shortage of skilled personnel for the many jobs they created.	X	
~ Your distinctive circumstances here ~		

Author Opinion Included		
Team building is one of the most challenging processes that a small-business owner addresses. It can be difficult for an entrepreneur to cede authority to others in the organization; nonetheless, working without a dependable team can make the business owner's life far more difficult than it needs to be.		X
~ Your author opinion here ~		

Identification of Patterns of Behavior		
One day, a sudden snowstorm surprised us all. As I was digging out my own car, The Man Who Drove Himself appeared beside me, digging out his vehicle as well. I offered to take him back to the community because I didn't like the idea of his driving in treacherous weather, but he refused. It turned out that both the students who had been working with him had also offered to take him home, but he refused. His need for independence caused all of us a lot of worry but, upon reflection, reminded us about the importance of autonomy regardless of age.		X
~ Your identification of patterns of behavior here ~		

N-of-1 Study		
Ching-Mia left Forest Products in 1973. For the rest of the decade, he managed plywood plants for three other Taiwanese companies. However, the oil crisis of 1970s devastated the Taiwanese export economy, and the plywood industry slowed down. Decades of overlogging pushed up the prices of the logs essential for plywood production. Suddenly, the Taiwanese plywood industry collapsed and Ching-Mia was laid off.	X	

~ Your N-of-1 study here ~		
Instructor's Manual	X	
Push to Make a Decision, Recommend Action, or Perform Analysis		
The big question Hartstein and Stemberg faced was whether it would be possible to reinvent the U.S. floral industry along the European model.	X	
~ Your push to make a decision, recommend action, or perform analysis here ~		

Remember: A teaching case always tells a factual story that has already taken place, resulting in an emphasis on making a decision or recommendation or presenting an analysis.

WS 1:2

Acceptable Re-Creations and Unacceptable Inventions: Refining the Bright Line

> Use this chart to differentiate between acceptable re-creations and unacceptable inventions.

Element	Acceptable Re-Creation	Unacceptable Invention
Dialogue	If all parties to the dialogue agree that it took place more or less as re-created	If one or more of the parties involved has not been asked to sign off or does not confirm that the dialogue took place
Timeline	Approximate dates are listed to clarify the flow of activities	Dates are invented or adjusted for convenience
Location of the business	If the business makes sense in the disguised location	If the resulting business seems out of place
Disguise of the characters and/or organization	The names of the characters and the organization must "make sense"	Using the names of real people and/or real organizations without prior written approval
Creation of a composite character	Never acceptable	Because cases are real situations, composite characters are always unacceptable
Things that "could have happened"	Never acceptable	As above
Gender shift	If it makes sense and does not create an additional factor for analysis	Gender is tricky; always have an additional reader confirm the appropriateness of the new gender

WS 1:3

Your Current Scholarship
Is Case Writing for You?

Where do you stand among potential case writers? Consider the following factors before you decide to write a case.

Career Stage	Scholarship over the Past Five Years	My Goals for the Next Five Years
Stage 1		
Graduate student Adjunct instructor Lecturer	• Writing my dissertation • Have published fewer than three papers • Have coauthored several published papers	• Establish a research agenda • Complete my dissertation • Publish three papers in academic journals
Stage 2		
Untenured faculty member Tenured faculty member (any rank)	• Have not published anything • I have several papers in review/revision stages • I have a steady and consistent publication record • I am a prolific scholar	• Refresh my research agenda/establish a new agenda • Participation in accreditation efforts that require me to publish • Reinvigorate my scholarly production with new formats • Share some interesting experiences from my consulting activities • Make a real impact on the literature • I need a challenge • Satisfy intellectual curiosity
Stage 3		
Department chair Administrator (dean, associate dean, assistant dean) Consultant	• My administrative duties are in the way of scholarship; I have not published anything • I have several papers in review/revision stages • I have a steady and consistent publication record • I am a prolific scholar	• My consulting activities would benefit from the development of cases • I want to be part of a movement toward production of pedagogical materials • I am returning to the classroom and need to maintain my academic credibility • I am interested in new outlets and different formats

WS 1:4

Case Writing Assignment 1

This first assignment is designed to help you get a running start on writing your case. You will be putting together an "embryo case" to use as the foundation for subsequent exercises. Please do not skip this step even if it feels unnecessary to you, as the case writing project requires building on each previous level of development as you go along.

Please spend a few minutes thinking about a real business situation, problem, challenge, or issue you have encountered personally or about which you have substantial knowledge from a student or other source. What could you teach using that situation as an example? With this learning/teaching objective in mind, draft a brief "embryo case" using the following form as a guide. Keep your embryo case to about two pages, and be certain to include all the elements outlined in the form.

Please keep this completed form and attach your one-to-two-page embryo case to it.

Working title of the case:
Source of case data:
☐ Library research ☐ Interviews ☐ Consulting ☐ Personal experience ☐ Other (specify)
Industry:
Main character's name or pseudonym and job title:
Theory you intend to illustrate or discipline in which you will use this case:

Specific case issues to be raised (for the Instructor's Manual/Teaching Note):

Biggest areas of concern about case writing in general and this case in particular:

WS 1:5

Case Writing Assignment Sample

> *This first assignment is designed to help you get a running start on writing your case. You will be putting together an "embryo case" to use as the foundation for subsequent exercises. Please do not skip this step even if it feels unnecessary to you, as the case writing project requires building on each previous level of development as you go along.*

Please spend a few minutes thinking about a real business situation, problem, challenge, or issue you have encountered personally or about which you have substantial knowledge from a student or other source. What could you teach using that situation as an example? With this learning/teaching objective in mind, draft a brief "embryo case" using the following form as a guide. Keep your embryo case to about two pages, and be certain to include all the elements outlined in the form.

> *Note:* This is a sample from the development of our featured case.

Please keep this completed form and attach your one-to-two-page embryo case to it.

Working title of the case:
Ken Roberts—Master Mechanic
Source of case data:
☐ Library research ☑ Interviews ☐ Consulting ☐ Personal experience ☐ Other (specify)
Industry:
Automotive service
Main character's name or pseudonym and job title:
Ken Roberts, CEO

Theory you intend to illustrate or use with this case:

Small business management

Specific case issues to be raised (for the Instructor's Manual):

Customer relations in a service industry

Biggest areas of concern about case writing in general and this case in particular:

1. Accuracy and relevance
2. Level of disguise re: names/places
3. Producing a case that works re: class discussions and learning

Module 2

● ● ● ● ●

The Research Process

● ● ● ● ●

What Is a Teaching Case?

This module focuses on teaching cases. Please see Module 1 for a full description of the different kinds of cases.

A teaching case is a factual description of a real situation. It is intended to provide the basis for discussion in a particular course or discipline (see Module 5 for a discussion of Instructors' Manuals, also known as Teaching Notes) and should contain sufficient information for students to be able to carry out the desired discussion. While a decision focus (a specific decision to be made by the student on behalf of the case protagonist) is preferred by many professors, various outlets also accept cases whose purpose is for students to develop their analytical and evaluative skills.

Field-researched cases require a written release from the protagonists; always obtain the release **before** submitting a case for review to any publishing outlet. Secondary source or library cases do not require a release because all the information included in such cases is publicly available, but they do require extensive citations. Disguised field-researched cases also require a release in the event that the disguise is penetrated.

● ● ● ● ●

Where to Find Your Case Subject

Cases are all around you, everywhere. In fact, you are your own best source of cases. You have had a wide array of experiences and have interacted with many different people and organizations over the course of your professional and private life. You have listened to many stories told by your students about their own work experiences. You have traded stories with friends, colleagues, relatives, and neighbors. You have been intrigued by newspaper articles or advertisements for local companies.

And you have thought about ways to use these stories in class to teach specific techniques or to practice specific skills.

Your first step in "finding" case material is to identify what you want your students to learn (see WS 5:3 for an exercise to help design your learning objectives); then think of all the contacts you have who may be able to share a good story with you (see WS 2:1).

●　●　●　●　●

How to Approach Potential Sources

Approaching friends, neighbors, colleagues, and relatives is easy: "Hi John. I'm trying to come up with a good story that I can use to teach my students how to make ethical business decisions. Can you tell me about a time when you were confronted with an ethical problem at work?" John will try to comply and will cast about for an appropriate story. You can then decide if the story is likely to be rich enough for your use.

But how do you ask people you don't know if they'll help you with a story, an interview, or a case? Suppose you drive past the local shopping mall and see a store celebrating its tenth anniversary? How did the owner survive through the economic downturn? Maybe you could learn something to share with your students about carrying on through hard times or persistence in the face of hardship. Or perhaps you see a restaurant going out of business. You used to eat there frequently. What happened? Is there a lesson to be learned from the owner's actions or attitudes?

One time, I saw an advertisement in a local newspaper for a company that sold job lots and oddities. I had been in the stores before, and they were messy and disorganized. How did this business continue operating for 30 years? Why did people keep going back? I simply had to know, so I wrote the owner an e-mail expressing my admiration and my curiosity. I told him briefly about myself and my case writing experiences, and I asked if he'd be willing to talk to me on the phone about writing a case about his business. A series of e-mails and phone calls resulted in personal interviews with the owner, his son, and several employees, along with attendance at team meetings and marketing sessions. I published an interview with the owner in one journal ("Good Things Cheap: An Interview with Jerry Ellis") and a case in another journal ("Business Succession at Building #19: Overall, It's Better to Be the Father Than the Son"). Ultimately, the two men enjoyed the process so much they were happy to visit several of my classes, participate in student discussions, and add to a local oral history.

I have never had anyone decline to talk to me; people love to tell their stories and rarely get the chance (see WS 2:2 for a contact sheet).

● ● ● ● ●

Getting Approval to Research and to Publish

Before you start your case research, you should be planning for approval to use your case for a variety of educational purposes. This is a two-step process that involves obtaining approval to research and, subsequently, final approval to publish (if that is your goal).

The process begins with an informed consent form, often required by Institutional Review Boards (IRBs) at U.S. universities prior to beginning any research that involves human subjects. Most IRBs allow case research without formal preapprovals, but it makes sense for you to formalize your research relationship with the organization being studied so as to avoid disappointment later on, especially if your contacts leave or the company goes out of business before you finish.

The basic elements of informed consent are:

■ identification of the principal investigator and a means to contact that individual;

■ indication of the format that the research will take;

■ statement of risks and benefits to the company;

■ clarification of the voluntary nature of the research; and

■ consent to proceed, dated and signed by the company representative.

It is best to be as global as possible in your description of the format that the research may take. This will provide you with the broadest possible access to the data you need.

The same general principle holds true when presenting a publication release. Make the following clear:

■ The signer has read the case and made any corrections of factual misrepresentation.

■ The signer authorizes you to use the case in any educational manner (publishing, presenting, or teaching).

The publication release should be as short as you can make it while giving you permission to do what you want to do with the case itself. (The Instructor's Manual [IM] does not need a release and should not be shared with the company representative. The IM is a pedagogical tool and is not published for general consumption; it is available only to other academics.) The goal is to avoid sharing your personal analysis with students or the company being researched.

There are many formats that informed consent and publication releases can take. It is best to keep them as simple as possible, indicating that the case is for educational purposes and was not designed to demonstrate effective or ineffective handling of management decisions.

Be aware that even though attorneys have not been invoked in this release process, you are asking your contact to enter into a formal agreement with you. You will be asked by any distribution outlet in which you intend to publish if you have obtained a release, so it is best to get this release before you submit your case to a journal or elsewhere.

You can find three sample forms in WS 2:3. You should adapt them to the requirements of your own university IRB. Present these forms on your university letterhead for best credibility.

Remember—if this is a library case, you do not need to get approvals at any level. Information drawn from the public domain is yours to use, as long as you cite properly.

● ● ● ● ●

Your Interviewee as Coresearcher

It is important to recognize that the person you are interviewing is **not** the subject of your case; she serves in a different capacity, that of coresearcher. This relationship is best formed by taking the time to build trust and a collaborative spirit between you and the interviewee. The goal of developing the coresearcher relationship is twofold: (1) As the primary researcher, you need to share the power that arises naturally from your role so that your ideas and perceptions are not privileged over those of your agent (the person you are interviewing); and (2) the interviewee must understand the research process if she is to participate intelligently in the project. If the person you are interviewing becomes your partner in the process of writing the case, she can confirm or deny your assumptions, approve the direction in which you are heading, and see value in the outcomes. The person will feel appropriately valued and respected and consequently will be more likely to provide you with relevant information and final publication approval.

● ● ● ● ●

A Refresher on the Basics of Qualitative Research: Observation

Qualitative methods of data collection take two basic forms: observation and interviewing. Both forms are designed to minimize researcher impact while recognizing the effect that the researcher has on organizational culture. Theories of qualitative inquiry suggest that the presence of an outsider will always have an impact on "natural" interaction and emergent culture; therefore, it is preferable to take as many precautionary measures as possible when conducting on-site research. Above all, it is important for you, the case writer, to be mindful of the tendency to put your own interpretive spin on the actions observed. Qualitative techniques appropriate for case writing research (and subsequent analysis) are described here briefly.

Observation is a basic means of corroboration or triangulation of data. It allows you to determine how well a system appears to work by comparing what actually happens with what you are told happens during the interview process. We need to look with narrowed eyes on the everyday activities that are reported by interviewees so that we can study our own social surroundings. But trained observation is not simply "looking at things": it requires preparation and practice to separate that which you should notice and record from the trivialities that you can safely overlook. Concentration, mental focus, and reliable and accurate observations will help you to write the rich descriptions you need in a teaching case.

Thick Description and Contextualization

Anthropologist Clifford Geertz (1973) suggested that the essence of thick and rich description was akin to recognizing the difference between a wink and a blink. Only after making this distinction would the researcher be able to provide an understandable and intuitive description of a culture to the reader. This skill is critical to the successful case writer, as the interpretation and subsequent description of an organization's culture far supersedes simple exposition, timelines, and transcriptions of interviews. Case writing offers the academic the rare opportunity to use adjectives (as long as we avoid imposing our own evaluations on the actions of others). Here's what to look for in the process of contextualization:

- **Artifacts:** When doing research on-site in an organization, pay close attention to printed memos, manuals, directives, bulletin board postings, and other documents. They offer the researcher an additional level upon which to build a credible description for the reader who seeks to interpret action in light of apparently objective evidence.

- **Content and context:** Activities that make up everyday life are the central elements of many on-site observations. They not only provide a way to describe communication processes but serve as "situated content," meaning the location in which the interactions occur plays an important role in the communication itself. These passive elements can help us understand the action and behaviors as they occur.

- **Symmetrical research:** In this process, the participants are coresearchers and perform analysis concurrent with the researchers. Validity is established through the coresearchers' review and ultimate acceptance, rejection, or reinterpretation of the researcher's initial interpretations. In other words, ask your coresearcher (the person you are interviewing) to confirm or disconfirm your interpretations before you allow those interpretations to drift into your writing.

Observation can be more daunting than you anticipate, but it becomes a much easier process if you follow these four rules:

1. Eyes open
2. Mouth closed
3. Don't touch
4. Don't translate

WS 2:4 is a fairly detailed observation checklist. Use it as is for practice (in your own environment, in the doctor's office, in a cafeteria or restaurant), and then refine it for use in your case-related research.

● ● ● ● ●

Real Conversation: The Art of the Interview

Some very effective methods of interviewing come from the oral history tradition, which employs a much more conversational style of interviewing than the standard interview techniques we tend to use in business. I call this process "Real Conversation" to differentiate it from fact-finding survey interviews and more impersonal forms of dialogue. Most of the interviewing for case studies will take this "real" format.

Real conversation is a 90/10 process. Ninety percent of the time, you will be listening. You will speak only 10 percent of the time. When you do this at business meetings, social events, and casual get-togethers, the people around you comment that you are a good conversationalist. Why? Because you are giving them space to speak.

The same theory works in case interviewing. What *you* have to say is not important; what matters is what the person you are interviewing has to say. Limiting your own input creates space for the input of others. As an academic, you are likely to find this difficult to do. I urge you to practice listening at every opportunity. WS 2:5 summarizes five basic listening techniques for collecting case data.

Begin at the Beginning: Do Your Background Research before You Contact the Interviewee

Do not even consider conducting an interview with the client without having done your homework. Prior to your first interview, find out everything you can about the person you are going to interview, about that person's company, and about the general topic that is driving the interview.

Your goal is to learn everything you can on an *informant* level beforehand so that you can move your interviews to the *person-centered* or *respondent* level. The interviewee is your partner in the process and is also an observer of his own experience. Person-centered interviewing is difficult for the interviewee because of these dual unarticulated roles; your job is to be prepared so as to avoid the simplistic questioning that can keep the interview stuck at a superficial level. Use the informant role to confirm facts and the respondent role to understand personal impacts.

Your early forensic research should focus on facts. One of my early mentors taught me that every case is comprised of four "Cs"—Causality, Conflict, Complications, and Characters. Some of these facts relate to the people (Characters) involved in the company; others relate to situations (Complications). If you are very fortunate, you may stumble over an identifiable Conflict or two in this search for background. Causality is for the reader to determine during the analysis phase.

If you are researching a larger corporation, it is easy to become overwhelmed by the sheer mass of publicly available information. Where do you start? What are the most important elements to find out about? These two questions are the stumbling blocks of forensic research. In WS 2:6, you will find a chart to get you started. It includes some frequently used (and generally necessary) research categories, some suggestions for research into specific areas (in italics), and blank rows for you to use for your own particular categories.

Establish a Relationship: Make the Interviewee Real and Make Yourself Real

The most effective interview process includes the significant cues that are provided through body language, facial response, and the general comfort level that exists between interviewer and interviewee. The work environment itself provides many behavioral and attitudinal clues that enrich the interviewer's understanding and subsequent writing. This is why most in-depth interviews are done in person. WS 2:7 provides 10 rules for conducting a successful interview.

How to Frame the Questions That Elicit the Information You Need

■ Start with the easy stuff—some biographical information, length of time with the company, current job title and responsibilities—but don't get carried away. It is very tempting to spend a lot of time making friends and talking about personal background, but all you're trying to do is set the stage for the meat of the interview.

■ Move from general questions related to the organization and the theme of the research to specific questions that this interviewee can address.

■ Avoid questions that start like this:

Can you . . . ?

Will you . . . ?

Are you . . . ?

Did you . . . ?

Have you . . . ?

Table 2.1 provides samples of questions that are likely to encourage conversation rather than push the interviewee into a verbal corner.

Table 2.1 General Question Types

	Type of Question	Sample Question
1.	Why	Why did this happen?
2.	How	How did you feel about that?
3.	Suggestive	You said . . . Can you tell me more about that?
4.	Reflective, to ask for more detail	What else do you think about . . . ?
5.	Descriptive	Could you describe . . . ?
6.	Definition	Would you explain what . . . means?
7.	Third person	What were other people doing?

Table 2.2 supports positive question design and suggests effective and ineffective ways to ask questions.

Table 2.2 Good Questions Are. . .

	Description	Example of the Wrong Way to Ask One	Example of the Right Way to Ask One
Open-ended	These questions cannot be answered with a yes/no response.	Were you involved from the very beginning?	When did you first become involved in the project?
Not dichotomous	Avoid backing the interviewee into a verbal corner.	Are you satisfied with the way the program has developed?	What has been your reaction to the way the program has developed?
Not leading	Remember that you are interested in the interviewee's answers, not your own opinion.	What was done wrong from the get-go?	How did things progress from the beginning?
Not dominating	You are not conducting an interrogation.	Did you try to make a change? Did the other organization cooperate? Can you explain why? Have you continued to pursue the change?	What kinds of things did you do to support the change program?

	Description	Example of the Wrong Way to Ask One	Example of the Right Way to Ask One
Validating	If the interviewee feels comfortable and safe from attack, he is more likely to tell the stories that interest you.	People seem to have told you only good things about the program. Why have you not solicited a more balanced response?	From your position within the company, what kind of feedback have you received from participants? Walk me through one of those feedback meetings.
Singular	Ask one question at a time, rather than combining two questions.	When you launched the project, how did you get started? What was your first objective?	What was your first objective upon launching the project?
Clear	A confusing question will lead to a confused answer.	Why did you think that you were doing the right thing when you decided not to move forward before getting upper-level approval and lower-level buy-in?	What approvals did you have to seek before starting this project?
Warm and neutral	The interviewee should feel safe from judgment.	Why did you move forward without being sure of internal support?	That was a tough situation to face. What did you discover was the best way to handle these problems?
Exemplars when appropriate	Sometimes, you can increase your question's clarity by providing an example of a similar situation.	What was the workers' response?	How did the workers respond? I am familiar with a similar situation where the workers responded like this . . .

Active Listening: Learn How to Listen

The quality of the interview depends more on the listening skill of the interviewer than on the answering skill of the interviewee. *Active listening* means listening for the intent as well as the content of an answer. It is a skill well worth developing (refer to WS 2:5). Active listening requires your full attention on three levels:

■ You need to listen for content—facts, dates, specific information that clarifies past or subsequent situations.

■ You need to listen for emotion—the unarticulated body and facial language that sheds light on the way the speaker feels about the content.

■ And you need to listen for flow of the interview itself—sense when the speaker is running out of steam or tiring from your questions.

Politeness demands that you allow the respondent some time to frame an answer, but what starts out as a simple pause for thought can easily turn into a distracted internal monologue that results in a negative interview experience. How long should you wait for an answer? As long as the interviewee remains attentive to you. When the interviewee loses focus (you know what this looks like from your classroom experience), move on to another question. The interviewee will appreciate this kind of empathic listening and sensitivity to her needs.

Know what questions you want to ask, but don't be afraid to let your informant go off on a tangent. This is often the precursor to the most interesting and illuminating stories because it's what the interviewee *wants* to talk about. You will want to take advantage of this opportunistic interview, so this is the time to let the interviewee take the lead; stay alert, however, because you must be able to relate this story to the information you are trying to learn. Once you understand and are able to repeat back to the speaker the gist of the story he told you, you can move forward to make connections with the topic of your research.

Follow Through with Probes

Probes are simply follow-up questions, and they tend to employ a series of consistent formats. Easterby-Smith, Thorpe, and Lowe (1991) suggest seven different ways to probe for further information:

1. The basic probe—repeat the initial question.
2. Explanatory probe—building onto vague statements by asking "What did you mean by that?" or "What makes you say that?"
3. Focused probes—for specific information.
4. Silent probes—just wait until the interviewee says something.
5. Drawing out—repeat the last few words the interviewee has said, and then wait expectantly.
6. Giving ideas or suggestions—ask the interviewee, "Have you thought about . . . ?" or "Did you know that . . . ?"
7. Mirroring or reflecting—expressing in your own words what the interviewee has just said.

Probes can be tricky, because they can easily turn into interrogation, which will both turn off the interviewee and violate the trust that you have spent time building. Your goal is never to invade someone's privacy, so you must respect that certain conversations are simply out of bounds.

It can be wise to prepare your follow-up questions before you begin your interview, but practice them often so they become a natural part of your conversational or dialogic style. Some of my personal favorites include the following:

- Hmmmm. . . Tell me more about that.
- So, then what happened?
- May I tell this back to you? You correct me if I've misinterpreted something.
- This is really interesting. Can you flesh it out a little?

Despite your best efforts, problems can arise during the interview process. Table 2.3 offers some ways to encourage interviewees to provide rich answers to your questions.

Two Recurrent Problems in Interviewing: How to Generate Stories and Narrative from Question-and-Answer Formats

Table 2.3 Problem 1: The Interviewee Does Not Tell Complete, Rich Stories

The Interviewee:	The Fix:
Doesn't understand what you are looking for.	Rephrase your introductory remarks about the purpose of the interview until you are certain that the interviewee understands.
Doesn't believe she has anything of value to tell you.	Be a good listener, using body language such as looking at the interviewee, nodding, and smiling to encourage and give the message, "I am interested."
Doesn't understand why you would want to interview her.	If necessary, use verbal encouragement such as "This is wonderful information!" or "How interesting!" Be careful, however, not to pepper the interview with verbal encouragement such as "uh-huh," said at the same time that the interviewee is speaking as this will distract her.
Doesn't remember.	Rephrase and re-ask an important question several times, if you must, to get the full amount of information the interviewee knows.
Has a series of stock stories that he has developed and is used to telling, almost according to a script. This interviewee is not about to let you deviate from his script.	Ask for specific examples if the interviewee makes a general statement and you need to know more. Or you might say, "I don't understand. Could you explain that in more detail?"
Is not used to telling her story publicly and needs much coaxing and reinforcement.	This person needs questions to get warmed up and more questions to keep going.
Meanders through the story, and not according to the beginning-middle-end model that you have in your mind. The memories have a form other than linear time.	You have to figure out how to allow the narrator to tell these memories in a way that makes sense to both teller and listener.
Is afraid to give private or personal information and thus gives you information that will preserve a public "mask."	Assure the interviewee that you will not use any material that is "off the record." It is not your job to "out" anyone.

(Continued)

Table 2.3 (Continued)

The Interviewee:	The Fix:
Prefers or is used to building and sharing a story with others in a group rather than telling a story solo.	You can do a general group interview; then do an individual one-on-one interview to "clarify the different roles" that the team members played.

Table 2.4 will help you identify your own stumbling blocks during the interview process and offers suggestions to solve that problem.

Table 2.4 Problem 2: I Cannot "Connect" with the Interviewee

I Am:	The Fix:
Too nervous to think calmly and clearly about what to say next.	Overprepare with questions, follow-ups, and probes. Remember to breathe and take your time—the interviewee is undoubtedly just as uncomfortable as you are.
Disorganized.	Be sure your questions are typed out rather than scribbled so you can read them easily. Leave space between questions so you can write the answers directly below them. Use the back of the page for observations.
Not really listening to what the interviewee is trying to say.	Be flexible. Watch for and pick up on promising topics introduced by the interviewee, even if the topics are not on your interview guide sheet.
Prepared to hear certain answers and have closed my mind to other avenues of inquiry.	Ask follow-up questions and then ask some more.
Presenting a critical attitude to the interviewee.	Learn to practice empathic neutrality—caring about the interviewee without judging his stories, perspectives, comments (Patton, 1990).
Behaving and speaking in a cultural "foreign language."	Ask for definitions and explanations of words that the interviewee uses and that have critical meaning for the interview. For example, ask a Xerox employee what is meant by a Dreaming Session. How is it used? What is its purpose?
Too pushy.	Learn to accept "no" for an answer. If you push too hard during an interview, you will wear out your welcome quickly. Let someone else take the lead on the questioning.
Afraid of silence.	Allow silence to work for you. Wait. Then, if nothing is forthcoming, move on.

When to Stop: Setting a Time Frame and an Interview Structure

How Long Should the Interview Take?

The only way to answer this question is on an individual basis, and it depends purely on your experience level and on the patience or focus of the interviewee.

■ How long can you pay close attention? Once you lose the ability to follow the trajectory of the interview, you need to end for the day. You do not want to waste your interviewee's time or your own, and you do not want to have to revisit the same questions at a follow-up interview.

■ When will the interviewee start drifting off or showing signs of impatience? Once the interviewee loses focus and you have tried unsuccessfully to bring her back to the topic, it is time to end the interview for that day. Any questions you ask beyond this point are likely to provide unsatisfactory returns, and you may alienate the interviewee by continuing an unwelcome conversation.

How Should I End the Session?

Be sure to take the following into account:

■ People who are being interviewed have the same need for closure as the interviewer. It is your responsibility to provide that closure by indicating how appreciative you are of the time the interviewee has taken out of his busy schedule to talk with you. You need to let him know that you are available should he have any further information he'd like to share, amplification of his comments to provide, or questions to ask. Leave your contact information (e-mail, phone) and an open invitation to future conversations, and briefly outline what you will be doing with the interview. And thank him again.

■ If you need to schedule a follow-up, this is the time to do so. After indicating your appreciation, conclude with a simple verbal request:

> *Thank you so much, Pauline, for your time this morning. You have raised some interesting questions in my mind, and I'd like to think about them a little more and then chat with you again. Can we schedule a follow-up interview for next Monday at 2:30 P.M., or would Tuesday morning be better? I anticipate that this interview will be much shorter, perhaps just half an hour, and will focus solely on the clarification of prior points.*

Taking Notes during the Interview: A Necessary Evil

It is important for each researcher to develop a personal system of note taking and follow it consistently. There are many methods of note taking, the best of which allow the interviewer to differentiate easily between her observations or thoughts and the comments of the person being interviewed (see WS 2:8, The Two-Column Research Notebook, for a sample excerpt and a blank form for your use). Here are several suggestions:

1. Establish a "cheat sheet" derived from your interview guide by numbering your questions and using only the numbers in your notes. This

cuts down on your writing and leaves you plenty of room on the page to take notes.

2. Then, divide your page in half, using one column for your observations and follow-up questions and the other column for the interviewee's responses. Be consistent in your note taking to avoid mixing up your personal critiques with responses.

3. Or, use the recto (right) side of the page for interview notes and the verso (left) for your comments, analysis, and observations.

4. Or, develop a code to identify your observations from the interview responses.

5. Or, if you tend to be a visual learner, use a mind map to track the interview. You can find extensive information about building mind maps at www.mindmapfree.com.

6. Be exuberant with punctuation (!! ???) and other personal codes to identify salient comments.

7. Be sure to use quotation marks around exact quotes so you can obtain approval for those quotes later.

8. For taped interviews: Regardless of how reliable the recording technology may be, **take notes** or you will risk having to recreate the entire interview if something goes wrong with the recording (for instance, if you delete it by mistake, or the sound cuts out, or the power fails).

● ● ● ● ●

Getting Out of Your Own Way

Some of the challenges that confront a case writer are problems that we make for ourselves: lack of awareness of the sensitivities of others (hot button issues); not capitalizing on our strengths; and operating under assumptions that we carry with us (even if we're unaware of them). I describe some of these challenges in the following list and offer some suggestions for dealing with them.

■ We talk too much. As academics, we spend most of our professional lives talking to others, too often in the form of lecture. We are the all-knowing and our listeners are the seekers of wisdom, especially in the classroom. The case interview turns that paradigm upside down: We must become the seekers of information, not the speakers of information, and we must learn to tolerate silence.

■ Triangulation gets overlooked. Sometimes, we have so much confidence in the person we are interviewing that we forget to confirm or disconfirm her claims. It is important to try to remove the interviewee's filter so that we can see and understand situations through a more objective lens. Trust, but cut the cards.

■ We interfere when we should just be listening. Linguists have claimed that there are male and female ways of listening. The male style of listening results in the development of solutions to the problems that are being discussed. The female style of listening encourages the speaker to talk more. Case interviewers need to use the female style of listening; our goal is not to solve problems, merely to surface them for others to analyze and resolve.

■ We are often in a hurry. As a result, we may rush to premature judgments, make snap decisions, inadvertently promote the early closure of interviews, or invest too much confidence in one perspective that limits our exposure to alternate ideas. Although decisiveness is a desirable quality in the business world, in a qualitative researcher speed and certainty may lead to incomplete or inconclusive findings. Take your time.

■ We are not prepared. There is simply no excuse for not being prepared for your interviews or your site visits. This preparation includes your forensic research but is not limited to it. Preparation includes setting yourself in the correct frame of mind to be observing, to be listening, and to be focusing externally. This process is much like what many of us do while traveling—we focus our minds on anything that is unrelated to our current situation. So . . . the screaming children, the long delays, the lukewarm coffee, and the uncomfortable seating disappear as we engage ourselves more deeply in our alternate activity of choice—an enticing novel, a video game, writing a poem. Personal preparation for your research involves the identical skills, but instead of focusing internally and ignoring our surroundings, we focus externally and absorb as much of the environment as we possibly can. And, please remember, if you don't record it or write it down, it didn't happen.

■ We fail to recognize our biases. We all have biases beyond standard research bias (procedural bias, response bias, reporting bias), and these biases can color our research and constrain our receptiveness to unfamiliar or uncomfortable subjects. It is very difficult to maintain a neutral perspective when faced with unsettling information, but failure to acknowledge such discomfort will restrict your ability to (1) record data accurately and (2) present your case in an evenhanded and honest way. Do the exercise about surfacing personal bias (see WS 2:9), and you may learn some surprising things about yourself. This self-knowledge is important to take with you to your interviews and site visits.

■ We fail to listen with a third ear. We forget to do this, spending most of our conversation time preparing what we want to say instead of listening and concentrating on both the words and the meaning of what our conversational partner is conveying. For practice with active listening, go to WS 2:10.

● ● ● ● ●

Handling Data: Data Are Perishable, So Transcribe and Upload Quickly

As you are aware, interviewing is hard work. At the end of the interview, the interviewee is tired and so are you. But there is one more task that must be completed, and that is your transcription of the interview tape and/or rewriting of your notes. If you do not perform this task soon after the interview, you will lose all sense of nuance, interpretation of body language, and memory of linguistic tics and pauses, along with your feeling of where you needed more information. The following model of transcription may prove helpful to you. Consistency in this process will make the actual case writing easier.

Step One

If you are working from *notes alone* (no tape, no video), you should proceed immediately to a location where you can think about the interview for a while. Flesh out your existing notes with comments. (Use a different color ink or add a column to the page to keep your own remarks separate from the interviewee's comments.) List the information that you still need to get or that you need to get because of what you have learned in the interview. Clarify any of your scribbles that may prove unreadable at a later date. Reflect on the interview and make notes of your perceptions. Fill in any blanks you may have left. Try to remember specific quotes that you had to paraphrase in your rush to get the notes written during the interview. If you are working with a writing partner, share your ideas and reflections at this time—do not wait until you both have time to get together. We both know that it will be too late, if ever, that you have a chance to really talk about the interview that was just concluded.

If you are working with *audio and/or video*, go back over the notes you took during the interview. (Yes, you did take extensive notes during the interview despite the digital recordings, because those recordings do not provide your ongoing reactions to the speaker.) There is no need to review the entire recording at this time, but you do want to get your own thoughts down while they are still fresh in your mind. For example, if the speaker tended to repeat herself for emphasis or gesticulated forcefully when making a point, this might be worth noting.

Step Two

This step is best performed when you have an uninterrupted block of time to work on it, but you should try to find that block of time within one week so the interview remains somewhat fresh in your mind. If working from *notes alone,* type them up in a three-column format, as shown in Table 2.5. My examples are in italics in the table:

Table 2.5 Three-Column Format

Question	Response	My Perceptions
Use the code from your list of questions	This is what the respondent said. If you have paraphrased, just type it as is. If you have quoted directly, be sure to use quotation marks.	This column is for your observations of body language, surroundings, interactions, behavior, etc.
Q17	*"I absolutely require that the people who report to me present me with their findings in a formal document. Although creativity is the route to product development, it has no place in finance."*	*The speaker seems angry about the issue of creativity and his role in the process. He is leaning forward and glaring at us.*
Q17 follow-up	*Everything in financial transactions has to be transparent, and creativity is not a transparent function.*	*I wonder what these responses are a reaction to. Follow up on this later.*

Note: Before you move on to the next module, be sure to complete WS 2:11, Case Writing Assignment 2.

● ● ● ● ●

References and Readings

Atkinson, P., and M. Hammersley. (1998). "Ethnography and Participant Observation." In *Strategies of Qualitative Inquiry,* ed. N.K. Denzin and Y.S. Lincoln. Thousand Oaks, CA: Sage, 110–136.

Easterby-Smith, M., R. Thorpe, and A. Lowe. (1991). *Management Research: An Introduction.* London, UK: Sage.

Geertz, C. (1973). *The Interpretation of Cultures.* New York: Basic Books, p. 6.

Golden-Biddle, K., and K. Locke. (1993). "Appealing Work: An Investigation of How Ethnographic Texts Convince." *Organization Science* 4, no. 4 (November), 595–616.

Handwerker, W.P., and S.P. Borgatti. (1998). "Reasoning with Numbers." In *Handbook of Methods in Cultural Anthropology,* ed. H.R. Bernard. Walnut Creek, CA: Sage, 549–593.

Holstein, J.A., and J.F. Gubrium. (1998). "Phenomenology, Ethnomethodology, and Interpretive Practice." In *Strategies of Qualitative Inquiry,* ed. N.K. Denzin and Y.S. Lincoln. Thousand Oaks, CA: Sage, 137–157.

Janesick, V.J. (1998). "The Dance of Qualitative Research Design: Metaphor, Methodolatry, and Meaning." In *Strategies of Qualitative Inquiry,* ed. N.K. Denzin and Y.S. Lincoln. Thousand Oaks, CA: Sage, 35–55.

Kahn, M. (1995). *The Tao of Conversation*. Oakland, CA: New Harbinger.

Kvale, S. (1983). "The Qualitative Research Interview: A Phenomenological and a Hermeneutical Mode of Understanding." *Journal of Phenomenological Psychology* 14, no. 2, 171–197.

Levy, R.I., and D.W. Hollan. (1998). "Person-Centered Interviewing and Observation." In *Handbook of Methods in Cultural Anthropology*, ed. H.R. Bernard. Walnut Creek, CA: Sage, 333–364.

Mitchell, R. (1997). "Oral History and Expert Scripts: Demystifying the Entrepreneurial Experience." *International Journal of Entrepreneurial Behaviour and Research* 3, no. 2, 122–137.

Patton, M.Q. (1990). *Qualitative Evaluation and Research Methods*, 2d ed. Newbury Park, CA: Sage.

Rae, D., and M. Carswell. (2000). "Using a Life-Story Approach in Researching Entrepreneurial Learning: The Development of a Conceptual Model and Its Implications in the Design of Learning Experiences." *Education + Training* 42, no. 4/5, 220–227.

Tannen, D. (1990). *You Just Don't Understand: Women and Men in Conversation*. New York: Ballantine Books.

———. (1994). *Talking from 9 to 5: How Women's and Men's Conversational Styles Affect Who Gets Heard, Who Gets Credit, and What Gets Done at Work*. New York: William Morrow.

Truman, C., D.M. Mertens, and B. Humphries. (2005a). "Arguments for an 'Emancipatory' Research Paradigm." In *Research and Inequality*, ed. C. Truman, D.M. Mertens, and B. Humphries. London: UCL Press, 3–23.

———, eds. (2005b). *Research and Inequality*. London: UCL Press.

Vega, G. (2000). "Good Things Cheap: An Interview with Jerry Ellis." *New England Journal of Entrepreneurship* 3, no. 1 (Spring), 5–8.

———. (2007). "Business Succession at Building #19: Overall, It's Better to Be the Father Than the Son." *Entrepreneurship Theory and Practice* 31, no. 3 (Spring), 473–492.

● ● ● ● ●

Worksheets

WS 2:1 Where to Find Your Case Subject

WS 2:2 How to Approach a Potential Case Contact

WS 2:3 Sample Informed Consent and Publication Release Forms

WS 2:4 The Observation Checklist

WS 2:5 Listening Techniques

WS 2:6 What Do You Want to Find Out?

WS 2:7 Ten Rules for Conducting a Successful Interview

WS 2:8 The Two-Column Research Notebook

WS 2:9 Surfacing Personal Bias

WS 2:10 Observation and Listening Exercise

WS 2:11 Case Writing Assignment 2

WS 2:12 Case Writing Assignment 2 Sample

WS 2:1

Where to Find Your Case Subject

What you want students to learn: _____

> (*Example:* Ethical business behavior)
> *List your contacts in the following categories.*

Category	Name	Contact Info	Comment
Example	Fred Friendly	ff@friendly.net	Knows a lot of developers
Consulting			
Previous employers			
Family			
Friends			
Neighbors			
Community organizations			
Professional associations			
Students			
Places you shop, repair your auto, get medical/dental care, local eateries, bistros, coffee houses			
Newspaper articles			
Online search, Facebook/LinkedIn/ other social media sites			

WS 2:2

How to Approach a Potential Case Contact

	Action	Example	Your Project
1.	**Spark**	*Clever advertisement*	
2.	**Response**	*E-mail request for an interview*	
3.	**Researching the company**	*Web search* *Newspaper search* *Visit a store (if retail)*	
4.	**Developing the relationship**	*Exchange of friendly e-mails* *Telephone conversation*	
5.	**Getting approval**	*Initial consent-to-research form*	
6.	**Boundaries and mutual goals**	*Clarify research process* *Explain your goals and identify their goals* *Not a consulting process*	

WS 2:3

Sample Informed Consent and Publication Release Forms

Adapt these forms to your needs.

Informed Consent Form

Case Study (name of company)_____

I am asking you to participate in a case study about your organization

The purpose of this study is to learn more about [*whatever you want here*]. If you agree to participate, I will [*observe you as you work during several morning or afternoon periods over the course of a month, will interview you several times, and will take notes on our conversations, or whatever you intend to do.*] Some of the interviews may be audio- and/or videotaped.

There are no major risks involved in this study.

No one other than the researchers will have access to your recorded interviews. Transcribed sections of interviews may appear in the case, and your name and company will be disguised if that is your preference.

The case study may benefit you.

Potential benefits to you are those associated with a collaborative research project—an opportunity to gain insight that can lead to improved conditions and effectiveness.

Your participation is totally voluntary.

You are free to terminate your involvement with this project at any time, for any reason. You can reach me at [*telephone number and e-mail address*]. I will be glad to answer any questions you may have.

I have read and understand the information above and consent to participate in the case study.

_____   _____   _____
Name (please print)   Signature   Date

Publication Release

Case Study (name of company) _____

Permission is granted to [*your name*] to include the material in the [*company name*] case for publication and dissemination on a world-wide basis. This case is to be used solely as a basis for class discussion rather than as an example of effective or ineffective handling of an administrative decision.

_____   _____

Your Name   Authorizing Signature

_____   _____   _____

Date   Title   Date

Or

Publication Release

I have read this case titled: _____

_____ and authorize the use of this material in case competitions, conference presentations, journal and textbook publications, educational and training programs, and in electronic formats for educational purposes.

This case is released without changes (or with the following changes, listed below).

Signature: _____

Name and Title: _____

Company:_____   Date: _____

WS 2:4

The Observation Checklist

Use the first three sections for practice; then design the last section for your own project.

1. Background Environment	What You Observed
Parking accommodations/public transportation	
Lighting of the workspaces, meeting places, break rooms, and waiting areas	
Color of the walls	
Temperature (a/c, etc.)	
Windows and their locations	
Size of the workspaces, meeting places, break rooms, and waiting areas	
Layout of the offices (draw diagram)	
Location of management offices in relation to worker offices	
Cafeteria accommodations	
Artwork or decorations	

2. Technological/Equipment Environment	What You Observed
Type of equipment allocated to individuals (worker and supervisor)	
Type of equipment for general/communal use	
Condition of equipment (age, etc.)	
Furniture in offices, break rooms, and waiting areas	
How communication is sent and received	

How the office is set up	
3. People/Interaction Environment	What You Observed
People's attitudes (laughing, scowling, friendly to coworkers, reserved, etc.)	
Items on people's desks	
How people are dressed	
How people answer the telephone	
Where people eat lunch	
Who people eat or take a break with	
Formality of communication with coworkers	
Formality of communication with supervisors (open/closed door management)	
How many share an office	
Proximity of workers	
Languages spoken	
Your Project Begins Here	**What You Observed**

WS 2:5

Listening Techniques

Action	*Purpose*	*Examples*
Neutral response	■ Show that you are interested and are listening closely. ■ This encourages the person to keep on talking.	■ Mm hmmm . . . ■ I see . . . ■ That's interesting . . .
Restatement	■ Make sure that you understand what is being said. ■ To check on the meaning of what the speaker has said. ■ To encourage the speaker to consider/reconsider what has been said both for accuracy and for intent.	■ So, as I understand it, your plan is . . . ■ You have decided to (do X) because . . . ■ If this is so, what do you think about . . .
Questioning	■ Get more information. ■ To make sure you understand what has been said.	■ Could you tell me more about . . . ? ■ Do you mean that . . . ?
Summarizing	■ Bring the whole discussion into focus. ■ Serve as a springboard for introducing a new topic.	■ These are the main points you have brought up . . . ■ If I understand what you have said, here's how you feel about . . .
Reflection	■ Show that you understand how the speaker feels about a topic.	■ So, you're saying that you feel . . . ■ That seems to show that you are pretty angry about . . .

WS 2:6

What Do You Want to Find Out?

Data, Information, Indicator	Level of Importance H = High M = Moderate N = Nice to know	Collection Method	Location or Source
All cases require these:			
Corporate history		Corporate website, handouts, and annual reports; newspaper articles; books	Internet; library; company archives
Industry note		Databases; newspaper articles	Internet; library
Easily identifiable problems		Interviews; newspaper articles; observation	
Less easily identifiable problems		Observation; interviews; public documents; internal documents	
Some cases require these:			
International factors		Observation, interviews	
Quality levels		Internal documents and observation	
Customer feedback/ stakeholder		Internal documents	
Work factors: Design, allocation, process		Observation	
Performance indicators		Internal documents	Finance, marketing, production
Employee morale		Observation, interviews	Turnover
In addition, your cases require these:			

WS 2:7

Ten Rules for Conducting a Successful Interview

	Rules	Your Job
	Rules	*Your Job*
1.	The interview is centered on the person who is being interviewed, not the person who is conducting the interview.	Put interviewees at ease, make them comfortable, and gain their trust.
2.	People are interesting, and their stories are interesting. When you find people interesting, they are more likely to share their stories with you. Nonetheless, people are likely to think that their stories are nothing special.	Make sure that people understand that their stories are not only special, but are worthwhile learning tools for students and others. I call this "revealing the ordinary," and I emphasize the value of considering people's everyday stories as important research.
3.	The theme of the research is the focus of the interview, not the general life history of the interviewee (no matter how interesting that part really is).	All the other questions you ask should culminate in the most important one of the interview. Do not ask it right up front; instead, work your way up to it by asking other, simpler questions.
4.	A good way to start your questions, to keep them specific, and to get the anecdotes you are looking for is to begin with: "Can you tell me about a time when . . . ?" and fill in that blank with the topic. For example, "Can you tell me about a time when your deliveries didn't come in and you had customers that you had promised items to?"	Ask open-ended questions.
5.	Keep the interview on the level of description, but listen between the lines—people rarely say everything they mean or mean everything they say. Try to understand the meaning of the words, pauses, facial expressions, body language, etc. when interviewing. You may make an incorrect interpretation, but if you have recorded the facts of the interview accurately and your own subjective assumptions parenthetically, you will be able to draw some fairly appropriate conclusions.	It is perfectly appropriate to confirm with the interviewee whether or not your assumptions are correct. Sometimes, this will even help the interviewee to reconsider his or her own assumptions.

6.	Develop a preferred method for taking your notes. I use a regular notebook with the pages folded approximately in half. On one side of the page, I record the answers to my questions, direct quotes in quotation marks, and paraphrased answers simply written down. On the other side of the page, I write my questions (or a code for the questions—like #1 when the question is the first on my list), my observations of the environment and of the way the interviewee behaves, looks, etc., and my interpretations.	Be careful to bracket or underline the interpretations, so you do not confuse them with facts or direct observations. Once you develop a system, stick to it!
7.	Be sure to differentiate opinions from facts.	Pay very close attention to cues.
8.	Determine your own presuppositions or assumptions—that is, opinions you may have about the subject or the subject matter before you have completed your interview.	This will require personal reflection, and personal reflection takes time. This investment of time is worth the effort, as you will see once you begin interviewing.
9.	Do as much of your archival research as possible before the interview. This will help you develop some sensitivity to the stories the interviewee is telling.	Show respect to the interviewee by your extensive preparation.
10.	Remember that the interview experience is supposed to be beneficial to both the interviewer and the interviewee. It is a rare occurrence for people to be invited to share their personal history, including triumphs and failures, with someone who is giving them undivided attention. The interviewee will value this process, and you must make it clear to him that (a) you respect his privacy as well as his willingness to share with you, and (b) you will benefit greatly from the time spent.	Remember to say, "Thank you!"

Sources: Kvale (1983); Mitchell (1997); Rae and Carswell (2000).

WS 2:8

The Two-Column Research Notebook

Sample Observation, Interpretation, Reflection	Sample Questions and Answers
Environment: There were rows of cubicles leading from the hallway ("main street") to the window at a 30-degree angle to the corridors. Each row seated some 15–20 people on each side, with their backs to each other. Pale colors dominated. All the workers at their cubicles, each with a computer monitor, could be observed by the people on the "bridge" *in the center of the workspace.* **Action:** Mike walked us through the hall to the bridge, where he explained the many screens on the main monitor, the call acceptance rate, and the number of calls taken on an average day (50,000 to 100,000). No one paid any attention to the five students and professor being taken on a tour. Mike spent a lot of time giving us numbers, statistics, and facts about the operation. **Reflection:** I guess there must be lots of tours and that's why people don't really notice us. The whole environment is kind of *Star Trek* futuristic, with the observation from the bridge and workers in their "pods" and very little apparent interaction. It all felt very "clean" to me—people dressed up in business clothes, working alone, no mess, no clutter—very little paper, a few pictures of family on desks. I like a little more noise and action—I don't think I'd be comfortable here.	**Q6 (refer to question list)** *Problems that occur:* "They lose touch with us—they make so many mistakes." "They have no interaction with different departments—you've got to be able to send to different departments to ask questions." Bernie used to take their leftovers and their questions, until she began to get 16–30+ items on her queue daily and had no time to do any other work except corroborate or reject. They started sending her everything and once she got 60+ items, her supervisor stopped it. Contractors are focused on what they do—sometimes *too* focused on speed and less on accuracy. When confronted with unexpected items, piece workers may say, "You killed my zone." The piece workers like to get into the "zone" of speed processing, and that's when they make many mistakes, so Bernie throws them some curves when she sees too many items too quickly in the quality control QC queue. Day and night staffs are in constant conflict because, for the day staff, accuracy is key; members of the night staff don't care if they make mistakes. The piece workers are getting better—there is less stress at home. B doesn't take a formal lunch period; instead, she takes small breaks throughout the day. "The biggest problem with the night staff is the training—they have too much general training and not enough specific training for the areas they are assigned to—and there's hardly anyone around at night to ask."

Record your interviews here.

Observation, Interpretation, Reflection	Questions and Answers
Environment **Action** **Reflection**	**Q#**
Environment **Action** **Reflection**	**Q#**
Environment **Action** **Reflection**	**Q#**

WS 2:9

Surfacing Personal Bias

Record examples that support your position in column two. Then record examples that support the opposite position in column three.

Topic	Support for Your Position	Support for the Opposite Position
All people are entitled to get a college education.		
Overweight people are fat because they lack self-control.		
We pay too much in taxes.		
Fidelity in marriage is highly overrated.		
Marriage is a relationship between a man and a woman.		
If I can do XYZ, so can you.		
People over 50 have trouble learning new technologies.		
Business is getting more and more unethical.		
Most people don't believe in God.		
Bankers are greedy.		

WS 2:10
Observation and Listening Exercise

For this exercise, you must recruit two helpers. They may be colleagues, storekeepers, relatives, neighbors, or friends. One of the two helpers will be the interviewee; the other will be an observer.

Tell your recruits that the person being interviewed will be asked to recall a business problem that was left to him to resolve. The problem might relate to dealing with a difficult person, organizing a complex meeting, preparing for a sales call, training a team in a new process—the specific topic is not important, as long as the person is prepared to be interviewed. The entire exercise will take an hour or less.

The second recruit who acts as an observer in the process should not speak but should take careful notes about (1) what worked well in your interview, (2) what did not work well, (3) the impact of your demeanor and body language on the interviewee, and (4) any questions that you should have asked but did not.

Ideally, you will conduct the exercise in the interviewee's place of business. If you cannot conduct the exercise at your helper's place of business, do Step 1 in a fast-food restaurant, a shopping mall, a pharmacy, or a supermarket.

Step 1

Invest 20 to 30 minutes observing the action around you. You may want to drink a cup of coffee or soda as "protective coloration" so you do not look obvious in your role.

Using WS 2:4, take extensive notes on the background environment, the technological environment, and the human interactions that occur while you are watching. Pay close attention to the details as well as the broad brushstrokes. Did you record the color of the smock that the cashier was wearing? Whether the pharmacist wears glasses? The noise level in the mall? The percentage of mothers and children in the supermarket? The behavior of the teenagers in the fast-food restaurant? What time of day did this take place? What was the weather like? Did anyone talk to you or ask you what you were doing? How did you feel observing and recording the action?

Step 2

Write up your observations in a narrative format, and share the narrative with someone who is intimately familiar with the location you were observing. Ask for that person's feedback. Did you portray the location accurately? Did you miss something major, like the policeman riding through the mall on a Segway? Would people be able to snap their fingers and say, "I know that place!"

If you have done your observation in your helper's place of business, ask that person what you missed and what needs to be included to give a richer picture of the location.

Step 3

Referring to WS 2:5 through 2:8, conduct your interview as if this were a "real" interview. Remember to take notes, even if you are taping the interview. Use probes to keep the interviewee talking as long as you can. The interview should continue for a minimum of 10 minutes, longer if possible. Even if you are not interested in the topic of the conversation, use all your skills to extend the interview, seeking depth and color in the answers.

Step 4

When you have completed the interview, ask the person acting as an observer to give you feedback about the interview process. You are likely to hear some very valuable information about your interview style that will help you in improving your technique when you have to do "real" interviews.

Step 5

Now, repeat the interviewee's basic story back to her. Ask her to tell you where you have misinterpreted something she said, where you have overlaid your personal perspective on her words, and where you have not been true to her words or her intent. What should you have asked that you overlooked?

Then ask yourself what the most difficult part of the interview process was for you. How can you make that part easier to manage? What additional preparation should you have done before your meeting? What worked well for you? How can you extend this strength to other areas? Jot down what you have learned in your research notebook for future reference.

WS 2:11

Case Writing Assignment 2

This assignment will move you one step closer to having a working case.

1. Using the embryo case that you developed at the conclusion of Module 1, do your preliminary archival research on both the company and industry involved. Be guided by the worksheets in Module 2 to do this research.

2. Then, using what you have learned in this module about interviewing, conduct at least one interview with the protagonist of your case.

3. Prepare the following two documents:

   ■ A two- to three-page summary of the case story, including the history of the organization you are writing about

   ■ A detailed outline of the material that the case will cover, including headings and subheadings.

Remember to base this outline on your specific expertise, disciplinary interest, and the learning outcomes you want your students to attain. (We'll talk about learning outcomes in Module 5–just use the ones you normally would use for your classes at this time.)

Note: Please complete this assignment before moving on to Module 3.

WS 2:12

Case Writing Assignment 2 Sample

A detailed outline of the material that the case will cover, including headings and subheadings.

Note: This is a sample from the development of our featured case.

Ken Roberts—Master Mechanic

1. Appearance of the mystery car
   a. Background
   b. Timing
   c. "The note"

2. Auto repair industry
   a. Independent shops
   b. Dealer networks

3. Ken's Haus
   a. Ken's personal history
   b. Business history
   (1) Description of the building

4. The car
   a. Origin/owners?
   b. Problems

5. What to do with the car
   Exhibits: Letter from the car owner
   How to find a good mechanic
   Online reviews of Ken's Haus

Module 3

• • • • •

Writing the Case

One last reminder before you begin to write: Did you get the Informed Consent Form or Permission to Research Form signed? Unless you are going to write your case solely from secondary sources, you must get permission to research from someone one level higher than the position held by your primary source. If you have not yet gotten formal permission to research the company, stop before you go any further.

Get permission or drop the project. Without initial permission, you risk investing a lot of effort in a project that may not come to fruition.

• • • • •

Selecting an Appropriate Writing Style

In the discipline of entrepreneurship, we teach our students that all you need to be successful is a customer. The product is not relevant, as long as someone will buy it. Your location is not relevant except for its proximity, availability, or ease of access to customers. Price does not matter; targeting the correct customer will hit a variety of price points. Novelty is not a factor; people like novelty but they also like reinvention of the old favorites. Customers buy what they want, not what you want to sell. The bottom line is: If you make your customer happy, you will be successful.

The same bottom line holds true when selecting your writing style for cases. You have two customers—the instructor and the end-user (students). As you will see in Module 5, the Instructor's Manual requires a different style from the case itself because the customer for each is different. For now, let's focus on the style to use when writing for students.

As academics, we are most familiar with formal, scholarly writing. At its worst, scholarly writing suggests long, convoluted sentences; complex structure; multiple internal citations; and passive voice. Avoid all of these when writing cases. Case writing requires a lighter hand, a more relaxed presentation, and the deft use of descriptive and evocative writing to stimulate the reader's imagination. Of course, case writing requires professional presentation of factual material, clear exposition of data and relationships, and thorough background and references. But it also requires something more—elegance and style.

You can differentiate among styles of writing by thinking about music. Scholarly writing for journal articles resembles classical music in terms of form, formality, rules, and complexity. Case writing is more like ballroom music with the elegance of a fox-trot, the excitement of a rumba, and the speed of a mambo.

Use the following examples of scholarly writing and case writing to help you determine which style will connect best with your target audience. Remember that certain styles will appeal more to some readers than others; you will write differently for an MBA class than you will for a traditional-aged entry level undergraduate class. Practice this skill using WS 3:1.

● ● ● ● ●

Examples of Three Writing Styles

Scholarly Writing

Business ethicists typically focus on honing individuals' moral awareness (their sensitivity to the impact of their actions on others; e.g., see Gautschi and Jones 1998; Morris 2001; Williams and Dewett 2005) and moral judgment (their ability to apply moral philosophical frameworks to make decisions that are ethically sound; e.g., see Jones 2009; Meisel and Fearon 2006; Morris 2001; Sims 2002). But widespread reports of misconduct in the private, nonprofit, and public sectors (see Ethics Resource Center 2008a, b, c, respectively) underscore the inadequacy of enhancing moral recognition and reasoning.

Note the multiple internal citations, parenthetical references, and the long and complex sentence structure.

Case Writing for MBA Students

The cyclical nature of the electronics industry created brutal consequences during the downturns. In the "bubble-building" years of 1997–1999, Teradyne had roughly 38 percent of the ICT market, to 37 percent for Agilent. This followed the profitability of the 1980s, when inventories were built in anticipation of steep demand. However, when the market changed, the result was overcapacity and large amounts of warehoused product. This experience was mag-

nified by the implosion of the 2000–2001 Internet bubble which spread through the computing industry, and by extension through the ICT companies whose market shrank by roughly two-thirds between 2000 and 2002. Teradyne's market share declined every year from 1997 to 2003 (except for small gains in 2002), then recovered somewhat in 2004 when it regained some ground compared to its major competitor, Agilent. (Appendix C). Agilent had managed to keep its market share during this period and in the post-bubble years of 2002–2004, it averaged 37 percent to Teradyne's 28 percent. Moreover, despite the vicissitudes of the electronics business cycle, this period saw the growth of yet another competitor, Aeroflex, which went from a negligible market share in 1997 to almost seven percent in 2004.

Note the assumption of knowledge inherent in reference to sophisticated economic trends.

Case Writing for Undergraduate Students

Since its founding in 1964 in a warehouse in Building 19 in the Hingham, MA, shipyards, the company had grown to four warehouses and 15 stores in Massachusetts, New Hampshire, and Rhode Island, each named Building #19 and a fraction. The company's naming standard was changed after they opened Building #19 15/16. Jerry and his wife, Elaine, used to do radio and television commercials together. When faced with "15/16," Elaine's lisp got in the way, and the store was re-baptized Building #19 1/5. In a casual environment of free-wheeling displays, odd collections of merchandise, and semi-squalor, Jerry Ellis sold millions of dollars a year worth of off-price goods to customers eager for a bargain and a laugh.

Note the informal language and anecdotes that make the characters real to the reader.

● ● ● ● ●

The Past Tense—Always

Cases are always written in the past tense. Always. Even when it makes you feel a little uncomfortable, you need to use the past tense. The only exception to this rule is when using direct quotes or in dialogue.

Why? Because the action in cases has already taken place, even if it is unfolding as you write the case. By the time students get the case, everything that you have written about has already occurred.

It is tempting to try to place students in the heart of the action and make them feel like they are solving a problem in real time, but the conventions of case writing prohibit this fantasy because cases are real, not fictionalized. As emphasized in Module 1, a teaching case always entails a factual story that has already taken place, resulting in an emphasis on making a decision or recommendation or conducting an analysis or evaluation.

● ● ● ● ●

The Four Cs of Case Writing

A valued mentor once told me that all cases have four main components, each of which is critically important to the success of the case: Characters, Conflict, Complications, and Causality.

Characters

It is hard to imagine a case without characters. The characters in a case move the action forward and create a sense of engagement with the reader. Without characters, a case becomes a mere report of activities—factual, but flat.

Conflict

A case is generally about some conflict—perhaps between people or between choices of action or behavior. Without conflict, there is no story, and without a story, there is no case. Again, there is only a report.

Complications

Complications or side issues are not added to a case simply to confuse or distract the reader. As we know, life is messy and that messiness belongs within the case, requiring students to evaluate the relative importance of facts provided. This is a critical learning takeaway of the case method.

Causality

Something, or some combination of things, has caused the problems in the case. It is useful for students to be able to identify not only how things have gone wrong, but why they have gone wrong. They may be able to synthesize this information from application of theory, but subtle suggestions of possible causes improve the analyzability of a case.

Refer to WS 3:2 for examples and characteristics of each of the Four Cs.

● ● ● ● ●

Key Elements of Cases

All cases contain some variation on the following eight elements. Of course, these elements rarely use as headings the didactically descriptive topic headings presented here. Instead of "The Opening Hook," a case is likely to begin without any heading at all. "The Company Story" or "History" is often headed with the company name. "The Industry" normally carries a heading that describes the content; for example, "Candy Manufacturing" or "The Auto Industry, 1950–1995." "The Actors" points not to film, theater, or television but to the protagonist's name. "The Situation," "Additional Information," and "The Closing Hook" simply use headings that describe the content to follow. "Appendices" are headed "Appendices" (or "Exhibits").

The Opening Hook

This is the grabber—the piece that is going to make people want to read more. In the fly fishing lexicon, this involves the initial cast. In the salt- or freshwater fishing lexicon, it involves jigging the bobber. Either way, the target—whether fish or reader—becomes fully engaged. The fish wants to escape, while the reader is drawn in despite himself.

We are familiar with famous hooks from literature:

- "Aujourd'hui, maman est morte." (Translated into English as "Mother died today"; *L'Etranger*, Albert Camus)
- "It was the best of times, it was the worst of times." (*A Tale of Two Cities*, Charles Dickens)
- "He was an old man who fished alone in a skiff in the Gulf Stream and he had been gone 84 days now without taking a fish." (*The Old Man and the Sea*, Ernest Hemingway)
- "In an old house in Paris that was covered with vines lived twelve little girls in two straight lines." (*Madeline*, Ludwig Bemelmans)

These hooks are unique for their brevity and their memorability. Case hooks are a little different.

Case hooks may include a clever one-liner, but such sentences will be preceded or followed by sufficient information to foreshadow the problem that will be outlined in "The Situation" section.

One traditional option for the hook is humor or a play on words. For example, in a case about a hospital, you may select language like: "Doctors and Nurses Hospital was suffering growing pains . . . "

Or a case hook may evoke emotions from the reader through an instantly recognizable scenario. A case about a small business owner might begin: "Tom sighed heavily as he thought about his newest hire—his soon-to-be son-in-law."

A successful case hook might create excitement or alarm in the reader: "Maria cradled the teenager's head in her arms as the ambulance's siren split the night air."

The hook can be the hardest element of the case to write because it needs to be short, snappy, interesting, and relatable on a personal level. Hooks generally serve as the introduction to the case protagonist, and they must create the desire in the reader to help or hinder the protagonist's goals.

One important cautionary note: Do *not* succumb to the temptation to fictionalize the case narrative in order to make the hook more attractive. We already know from Mark Twain that "truth can be stranger than fiction."

See WS 3:3 for an exercise on writing hooks.

The Company Story/History

Stories make no sense without context. Think about the way things get done in your own university. Without knowing the history and background, none of it would make any sense. Often, even knowing the history and background, a lot of it may not make sense!

So, the reader needs to know when the company was founded, who works there, how large the company is, what the corporate structure looks like, and so on. But aside from facts, be sure to describe the corporate myth. The corporate myth is the epic story that guides the culture, celebrates the founders, or describes company values (Gabriel, 2000). Provide enough information to get a full representation of the organization so that the reader will understand the situation more clearly when you get to that stage.

Language informs the reader about context, so be sure to use colorful and descriptive language as much as possible to build a picture for your audience. Use the protagonist's language when you can so that the descriptions are genuinely rich and evocative. Compare the two descriptions in Table 3.1 to see which one suggests more about the organization:

Table 3.1 Evocative Organizational Description

The company was registered in New York State in 1994 and in Massachusetts in 1997.	The graduate student registered her business in 1994 as part of her doctoral program activities. Later, when she had relocated to take advantage of the job offer that would propel her to success in her chosen field, she registered her company once again, in Massachusetts this time.

See WS 3:4 for an exercise on writing the company story or history.

The Industry

Most of the people who read your case will be unfamiliar with the industry represented in the story. Without some industry knowledge, it is very difficult to contextualize the action within the case and to understand the role the company plays within the industry. It is your responsibility as case author to provide the requisite information to the reader so that your case makes sense.

One way to do this is to write a miniature industry note, an in-depth look at an industry (energy, banking, automobiles) or a country or region (Russia, the Pacific Rim, Wyoming). This note should include sufficient historical background to provide a frame of reference for the reader, and often features social, environmental, and economic data. The importance of the industry or region for understanding the case will dictate the amount of space within the case taken up by this note. You may decide that a significant amount of information is necessary for the reader to analyze the case properly. In this situation, you may consider writing a stand-alone industry note that can be distributed to your readers and attached as an appendix to the case.

At the very least, you need to site your case situation within the broader framework of the industry or region you are addressing so that your readers are working with some knowledge of, say, cell phone technology or the shortage of trained nurses or the increasing rejection of genetically modified foods internationally.

See WS 3:5 for an exercise on writing the micro-industry note.

The Actors

Readers of cases don't care about situations, theories, or problems. They care about people. For that reason, case writers must really strive to represent the protagonist and other case actors clearly and graphically. The reader must feel empathy for one or more of the case characters in order to participate in helping that character to solve the case problem.

To help the reader develop an emotional response to the case characters, these characters must exhibit personality, they must have a physical description, and the reader must get a sense of why the character is in conflict. A six-foot-three bald body builder who is under the influence of steroids will evoke different responses than will a petite dark-haired dental hygienist who is picking up her lunchtime salad at the deli, so please be generous with your descriptors.

If you want to be confident that your readers will seek out positive recommendations for the problem presented at the conclusion of the case, be sure to paint your case characters as they really are. Avoid stock characters such as the greedy executive, the sleazy salesperson, or the hair-in-a-bun librarian—unless, of course, these descriptions are truly accurate. The characters in the cases you write may exhibit stereotypical characteristics, but they should be presented with some degree of nuance and layering. The reader must be able to recognize the character as "real."

See WS 3:6 for an exercise in writing about the actors.

The Situation

Typically, the most interesting part of a story is the story itself—the narrative. Although some people read stories for the character development or the rich descriptions, most people read stories for the action. However, the story is not exactly the heart of a case; the case problem as developed in the telling of the story is the true core. The most interesting cases read like fiction, but they are *not* fiction. "Once upon a time . . . " has little relevance for cases.

The situation is the section of the case in which you present the buildup to the problem, the problem itself, and various potential solutions being considered by the protagonist. Objectivity is the key to writing this section of the case. The biggest challenge case authors encounter when describing the problem is the tendency to inject their own evaluations, judgments, feelings, or personal conclusions; all of these must be left to the reader. The case writer's opinion has no place in the case. Save your perspective for the Instructor's Manual.

This section is all about action. Don't tell the reader about what happened—show the reader what happened. As the Russian playwright Anton Chekhov is rumored to have put it, "Don't tell me the moon is shining; show me the glint of light on broken glass."

This is your opportunity as an academic to use adjectives! This is where you have the opportunity to move the reader to an emotional response as well as an intellectual one. Even though you may have learned that emotions have no place in business writing, emotions do belong in case writing. We carry our emotions with us, and so do the characters in our cases and the readers of our cases. The reader should be moved to find a solution to a problem being experienced by a real person in a real dilemma.

The situation does not have to be long, but it has to cover the subject. Remember your audience. The problem itself should be sufficiently intricate to challenge the reader intellectually (you will write the case differently for an MBA class than you would for an undergraduate class), but not so complex as to overwhelm the reader.

See WS 3:7 for an exercise on writing the case situation.

Additional Information

Life does not follow a straight line, nor should a case narrative. Life is messy, with lots of side trips and occurrences that do not relate to an individual's overarching life story. Cases are also messy, containing extraneous information and peripheral issues that distract even the most careful reader. This is a good thing, as your students will never be confronted with a business challenge that follows a straight line from problem through analysis to conclusion. It is our job to prepare students for career-related challenges in the most realistic way we can. Adding non-essential information to our cases is one way to do this.

Just don't give away the ending!

See WS 3:8 for an exercise on including additional information in your case.

The Closing Hook

Returning to the fishing metaphor, this section sets the hook—it is the sharp jerk that motivates action or response from the reader.

There is an art to knowing when to end your case. You want to be sure that the reader will be motivated to help the protagonist solve his problem. However, you don't want to give away the "answer" in an analysis case or the decision in a decision-based case. You have to confirm that there is enough information within the case for the reader to be able to perform an analysis, but not so much information that the solution is obvious and little effort is needed to come up with a viable recommendation.

The closing hook is like the opening hook, in reverse. It must harken back to the beginning of the case and transfer the case problem to the reader. The protagonist's problem becomes the reader's problem, and the reader feels compelled to help.

Leave the reader hungry for more and eager to participate in the solution.

See WS 3:9 for an exercise on writing closing hooks.

Appendices

Appendices are all those things that didn't fit within the narrative but that provide data students will need for analysis. It is important to make references within the case to the relevant appendix or exhibit needed to illustrate the point you are making in the case. Readers will not know, for example, that you have provided for them a product list or demographic records unless you encourage them to "See Exhibit XYZ for further information."

Appendices may include:

- Organization charts
- Maps
- Product lists

- Financials
- Timelines
- Thumbnail descriptions
- Tables and formulae
- Statistics, demographics, and other data

See WS 3:10 for an exercise on selecting appropriate appendices.

The Title

I have left for last the element that readers see first. The title is the wriggling worm on the end of the hook that attracts the fish in the first place, but it can be difficult to come up with an appropriate title before you have completed the case. It is wise to bear in mind several hints:

- The title should be **descriptive**. If the case is about quality control in a hospital, for example, you might consider a title like: *Metropolitan Hospital: Sick of Errors.*
- The title should include the **name of the company** if familiar. Any *Fortune 500* company has a recognizable name, and this name may attract readers by its very familiarity.
- The title should tell the reader at a glance what the case is about. The academic colon is very useful to accomplish this goal. Simply follow the colon with the **case topic**, such as *Big Company Name: The Challenge of Globalization* or *Joe's Diner: The Search for a Head Chef.*
- The title should be **appealing**. No one wants to read a boring case, so it pays to avoid tedium right from the start.
- The title may reflect the **key decision** that the case focuses on: *General Motors Corporation: Too Big to Fail?*

● ● ● ● ●

Writing a Case and IM in a Condensed Time Frame

The job of an academic comprises three main elements: teaching, scholarship, and service. Depending on our individual institutions, these three elements are weighted differently. A research institution may require the instructor to teach only one course per given period, but will expect that academic to publish multiple papers in top-quality journals. A teaching institution may require the instructor to teach as many as four sections per semester and thus will downplay the importance of scholarship (and may, consequently, define it differently). The element of service also varies from institution to institution, but generally absorbs less of the academic's time than the other two elements. I do not know of any college or university that does not expect its faculty to produce some sort of scholarship. Module 1 and WS 1:3 will help you determine the sometimes opaque scholarship expectations your institution may have. In this section, we will focus on the demands of publication in a teaching institution.

The demands made on you as an academic in a teaching institution can be challenging, depending on your teaching and service responsibilities. Regardless of these responsibilities, it is still possible for you to conduct scholarly activity and produce something of value to add to the body of knowledge we share. We will look at ways you can write a full-length case and Instructor's Manual in two different kinds of time frames: "The Heavy Semester" and the "Sabbatical Semester or Summer."

The Heavy Semester

Typically, instructors in teaching institutions teach three or even four courses a semester, with two or three separate preps required. This is a lot of work! It takes a great deal of time to prep a course properly, to design or update teaching plans, to correct or comment on assignments, and to evaluate student accomplishment. All of this work takes place outside the classroom or meeting periods and is often not acknowledged by others as part of our workload. But we know how much time we devote to these activities. Add to that the 9–12 hours we spend in face-to-face meeting (or even more contact hours in online classes) and our service to the institution itself or to our academic disciplines, and we discover we are scrambling to find time to conduct any other activities in our lives. How can we squeeze out the time needed to write a case and Instructor's Manual in the midst of all this overwhelming activity?

The sample schedule in Table 3.2: Writing a Case and Instructor's Manual in One Heavy Semester and Worksheet 3.12 with the same title will help you to schedule the time in increments to accomplish this challenging task. I have designed the schedule to accommodate a 12-week period, even though most semesters are 14 weeks long. This built-in flex will allow for Thanksgiving weekend in the fall, spring break in the spring semester, or other possible non-working weeks or very busy exam weeks.

Throughout this section, I will refer to the modules, tables, and worksheets within this book as handy tools and templates to facilitate your work. You will notice that writing in a condensed time frame demands that you turn some of the writing process on its head, and begin with elements of the Instructor's Manual, writing the case to fit them as you go along.

Please be aware of two things before you begin.

1. During the heavy semester, there are a number of activities you will have to undertake prior to the term in order to implement fully this

table. These include some basic tasks that you can perform in the preceding semester or during the summer (see Table 3.3: Writing a Case and Instructor's Manual in a Sabbatical Semester or Summer).

2. The column in Table 3.2 estimates the number of hours each task might take you. This estimate is the number of hours the tasks take me, having performed them numerous times. They may take you a little longer.

Table 3.2 Writing a Case and Instructor's Manual in One Heavy Semester

Week #	Activity	Number of Hours
1	Go to WS 1:4 and WS 1:5 for a template and sample, then *draft* a very rough, simple version of the case situation. See Module 7: Getting Your Case Published and Reviewing Cases for Others, then *select* your target for this case: conference or journal. Which venue will give you the most bang for your buck?	3–4
2	Using WS 5:2 and WS 5:3, *identify* the audience, course, and placement of your case for the Instructor's Manual and *write* the learning objectives. This will help you situate the content and design your writing approach, as well as keep your Learning Objectives in mind as you begin. You have now completed two of the eight elements in the IM.	2
3	Follow the sample provided in WS 2:12 to *write* a detailed outline of your case, including headings and subheadings. This will make writing your case a straightforward matter of filling in the blanks.	2–3
4	See WS 3:3 and *write* your hook. Some people prefer to write this after completing the case, but I find that it gives me direction to draft one version as an early step in the writing process. Then, use WS 3:4 and 3:5 to *write* the "easy" parts—the industry note and the company story or history. Because you have already collected the data in your pre-semester work, these elements are uncomplicated to write.	4
5	*Write* the case situation (WS 3:7), *include* any additional information (WS 3:8), and *draft* the closing hook (WS 3:9).	4
6	*Share* the untitled case with the company and get a publication release from them (WS 2:3). With WS 5:4 and WS 5:6, return to the IM and *write* the literature review/theory/readings section, discussion questions and their answers.	4
7	Read the case again and using WS 5:5 and 5:1, *design* your teaching strategy and your synopsis. *Write* the epilogue (WS 5:7). Take a deep breath.	4
8	*Share* your case and IM with a trusted colleague inside or outside your institution. Ask for commentary on the case, IM, and the quality of the research and writing. Meet with the person, if at all possible, to go over the commentary.	3
9	*Revise* case and IM based on the comments.	3

Week #	Activity	Number of Hours
10	*Decide* on a title for your case. *Test* the case with live students in a colleague's class. Pay close attention to the way the case "works" and where it fails. Collect feedback on the case from the students and on the IM from the class instructor.	3–4
11	*Make the changes* that became obvious to you when teaching or observing the case analysis. Do trust both the student feedback and the instructor comments when making your revisions. Remember— they are your final audiences.	3
12	*Send* the case and IM to a conference or a journal. Be sure to follow the specific guidelines requested by the outlet (refer to Module 7). Check this twice. Do not shoot yourself in the foot!	2

The pre-work that is missing from Table 3.2 includes all the research elements of the case: selecting the company, making contact with them, obtaining a signed "consent to research" form, doing the background research on the company and industry, conducting interviews at the company, doing any relevant observation, and in general getting all your research ducks in a row. If you are writing a case from secondary sources, some of these activities (such as informed consent, interviews, observation) can be disregarded.

The Sabbatical Semester or Summer

When you have the fourteen weeks of a summer break or a sabbatical semester before you, with few professional demands or deadlines to meet, the research and writing process will be easier to manage. But watch out for the quicksand of procrastination—postponing your work until it is too late to meet your own personal deadline. As mentioned, if you are writing from secondary sources, the only major decision to be made before you begin is the selection of a company problem that intrigues you. As always, you begin with your Learning Objectives. What do you want your students to learn from the case? If you are clear on this, you can jump right into the research process. If you are performing field work, please refer to Module 2 for the appropriate steps to take.

This entire process is easier if done with colleagues in a writing community. Please see Module 8 for instructions about setting up such a community. The timelines I have provided and their related worksheets (3:12 and 3:13) are not written in stone—they are meant to be helpful guidelines and provide you with a writing trajectory. However, you may find a different system more comfortable for you. I hope that you will try this system out for size, and then revise it to meet your own needs.

Table 3.3 Writing a Case and Instructor's Manual in a Sabbatical Semester or Summer

Week #	Activity	Number of Hours
1	Using WS 2:1, *identify* your case subject. *Contact* the subject and obtain a consent to research form (WS 2:3) at your first meeting. *Conduct* background research on the company before your first interview.	8
2	*Continue* your background research on both the company and the industry, as well as any information you can find about the person you are going to interview. *Visit* the company and *conduct* interview #1. Refer to Module 2 for hints about successful interviewing and observation. WS 2:4 may be especially helpful here.	8
3	*Conduct* interview #2 as well as a secondary source, if available.	6
4	Go to WS 1:4 and WS 1:5 for a template and sample, then *draft* a very rough, simple version of the case situation. See Module 7: Getting Your Case Published and Reviewing Cases for Others, then *select* your target for this case: conference or journal. Which venue will give you the most bang for your buck?	3–4
5	If needed, *pursue* additional interviews or other research. Let the material you have collected percolate in your mind until you are comfortable with the focus you have determined.	6
6	Using WS 5:2 and WS 5:3, *identify* the audience, course, and placement of your case for the Instructor's Manual and *write* the learning objectives. This will help you situate the content and design your writing approach, as well as keep your Learning Objectives in mind as you begin. You have now completed two of the eight elements in the IM.	3
7	Follow the sample provided in WS 2:12 to *write* a detailed outline of your case, including headings and subheadings. This will make writing your case a straightforward matter of filling in the blanks.	3
8	See WS 3:3 and *write* your hook. Some people prefer to write this after completing the case, but I find that it gives me direction to draft one version as an early step in the writing process. Then, use WS 3:4 and 3:5 to *write* the "easy" parts—the industry note and the company story or history. Because you have already collected the data in your pre-semester work, these elements are uncomplicated to write. *Write* the case situation (WS 3:7), *include* any additional information (WS 3:8), and *draft* the closing hook (WS 3:9).	8
9	*Share* the untitled case with the company and get a publication release from them (WS 2:3). With WS 5:4 and WS 5:6, return to the IM and *write* the literature review/theory/readings section, discussion questions and their answers. Do not share the IM with the company (see Module 2).	4
10	Read the case again and, using WS 5:5 and 5:1, *design* your teaching strategy and your synopsis. *Write* the epilogue (WS 5:7). Take a deep breath. *Share* your case and IM with a trusted colleague inside or outside your institution. Ask for commentary on the case, IM, and the quality of the research and writing. Meet with the person, if at all possible, to go over the commentary.	7
11	*Revise* case and IM based on the comments. *Decide* on a title for your case. *Test* the case with live students in a colleague's class. Pay close attention to the way the case "works" and where it fails. Collect	7

Week #	Activity	Number of Hours
	feedback on the case from the students and on the IM from the class instructor. (You may have to wait until the new semester begins to complete this piece, unless you are willing to spend part of your sabbatical to attend someone's class.)	
12	*Make the changes* that became obvious to you when teaching or observing the case analysis. Do trust both the student feedback and the instructor comments when making your revisions. Remember—they are your final audiences. *Send* the case and IM to a conference or a journal. Be sure to follow the specific guidelines requested by the outlet (refer to Module 7). Check this twice. Do not shoot yourself in the foot!	4–5

> *Note:* Before you move on to the next module, be sure to complete WS 3:11, Case Writing Assignment 3.

● ● ● ● ●

References and Readings

Comer, D.R., and G. Vega. (2011). "The Relationship between the Personal Ethical Threshold and Workplace Spirituality." *Journal of Management, Spirituality & Religion* 8, no. 1 (March), 23–40.

Gabriel, Y. (2000). *Storytelling in Organizations: Facts, Fictions, and Fantasies.* New York: Oxford University Press.

Hung, H., N. Hunt, G. Vega, L. Levesque, H. Arslan, and C. DeLaunay. (2009). "Teradyne: On the Road to China." *The CASE Journal* 5, no. 2, 37–53.

● ● ● ● ●

Worksheets

WS 3:1 Writing Style and the Target Audience

WS 3:2 The Four Cs

WS 3:3 Writing the Opening Hook

WS 3:4 Writing the Company History

WS 3:5 Writing a Micro-Industry Note

WS 3:6 Writing About the Case Actors

WS 3:7 Writing the Case Situation

WS 3:8 Including Additional Information

WS 3:9 Writing the Closing Hook

WS 3:10 Appendices

WS 3:11 Case Writing Assignment 3

WS 3:12 Writing a Case and Instructor's Manual in One Heavy Semester

WS 3:13 Writing a Case and Instructor's Manual in a Sabbatical Semester or Summer

WS 3:1

Writing Style and the Target Audience

Write a paragraph in each style listed below using the information provided. Select a perspective for each paragraph that you think might be most appealing to your target audience. For example, global warming and its impact on financial markets, the economic effect of weather disasters on regional businesses, issues related to emergency planning (or a topic that you think of yourself).

Facts: Hurricane Irene made landfall in North Carolina on Saturday, August 27, 2011, as a Category 1 storm. As it progressed northward, it diminished in strength to a tropical storm by the time it hit Massachusetts, then headed straight into Vermont and on to Canada. Thousands of people were evacuated from North Carolina through New York City and the Rhode Island and Massachusetts coastal areas. Vermont suffered severe flooding of its streams and rivers. Hurricane Irene was blamed for 46 deaths in 13 states and had an estimated economic impact of $25–30 billion in losses. Experts warn that global warming can bring higher rainfall and raise the sea level, resulting in even greater losses from future storms.

Scholarly Style	MBA Case Style	Undergraduate Case Style

WS 3:2

The Four Cs

Following are examples and characteristics of the Four Cs.

"C"	Characteristics	Examples
Characters	■ Explicit traits (age, personality, unique information about the character) ■ Inferred traits (how a character is likely to act based on his/her explicit traits)	Ken, business owner and master mechanic, was close to retirement but continued to work hard (explicit). He was trustworthy (inferred). Laura and Matt, the mystery car owners, were strangers to Ken (explicit) and naïve (inferred). Brian, a trusted employee at Ken's shop, was not ambitious (explicit) but was a reliable worker (inferred).
Conflict	■ The heart of the story—why we care about the characters and want to help them.	A strange Volvo had appeared overnight and was parked directly in front of the repair shop's garage bay doors. Ken did not know the owners and had no idea what they expected him to do about the long list of problems they had outlined in their note to him. Was he supposed to fix them all? Price them out? Give the owners some other kind of information? Should he even consider working on the car at all?
Complications	■ Side issues ■ Additional complications ■ General information about the economy or the industry or the characters	For 20 years, Ken had several mechanics working for him, but they had left to start their own shops. Brian was working on a Toyota while Ken was trying to figure out what to do with the Volvo. The service department of auto franchises is a profit center that often puts car owners in conflict with the franchise owners, especially in warranty-related service.
Causality	■ What has caused the conflict or problem in the case?	Ken did not know the owners. There were many things wrong with the vehicle, and he could not guarantee that the vehicle would be safe when the problems were corrected. The Volvo was a luxury car and was mechanically complex. Ken could not afford to risk his reputation over this repair.

WS 3:3

Writing the Opening Hook

Following the example provided, draft an opening hook for your own case.
Use the material you developed in Modules 1 and 2 for inspiration.

Characteristics	Example	Your Sample
■ Interesting ■ Engaging ■ Introduces the protagonist ■ Foreshadows the problem to be addressed	It was 7:15 A.M. on the last Monday in February, and Ken could already sense that it was going to be an interesting week at Ken's Haus, Inc. He had arrived at work to find a mystery car parked directly in front of the overhead door into his repair shop . . . Ken had never seen this vehicle before. Luckily, among other notes and mail that had arrived through the mail slot over the weekend, there was a handwritten note from "Matthew" describing the car and its issues (see Exhibit 1), along with the keys . . . He did not recognize "Laura and Matthew" as customers he knew . . .	

WS 3:4

Writing the Company History

Following the excerpt provided, draft a company history for your own case.
Use the material you developed in Modules 1 and 2 for inspiration.

Characteristics	Example	Your Sample
■ Evocative language ■ Provides context ■ Rich description ■ Generous with organizational facts	Master mechanic Ken Roberts recognized the financial risks involved in his business venture. Even though he had a wife and young family to support, he left the dealership in 1979, rented a three-bay automotive service facility that had been vacated by a failed International Harvester dealership, and hung up his "Ken's Haus" sign over the door. More than 25 years later, he was still in the same location. In his office, a wall of four-drawer metal filing cabinets contained the repair orders of hundreds of satisfied customers. Over the years, Ken's business and reputation in the Newburyport, Massachusetts, area had grown. His first employee was a Volvo-owning carpenter and shade-tree mechanic who lived in the area, noticed the new business, and talked his way into a job with Ken as a mechanic. He worked for Ken for nearly 20 years, eventually leaving to start his own independent repair shop. In the 1980s, Ken also employed his brother-in-law as a mechanic, until he also left to set up his own repair facility. Throughout the 1980s and 1990s, Ken typically had either two or three mechanics working for him.	

WS 3:5

Writing a Micro-Industry Note

Following the excerpt provided, write a micro-industry note for your own case. Use the material you developed in Modules 1 and 2 for inspiration.

Characteristics	Example	Your Sample
■ Provides a frame of reference ■ Embeds the case situation in a broad industry framework ■ Contextualizes the action	In the automotive industry, new car dealers typically operated as franchises of the automobile manufacturer . . . Generally, a new car dealer had three profit centers: sales of new and used vehicles, sales of replacement parts and accessories, and vehicle service. The service department was an especially important aspect, given its expectation to contribute profit to the dealership, and at the same time to repair customers' vehicles in a manner and at a price that resulted in high levels of customer satisfaction . . . In general, among the higher priced European and Japanese vehicles, independent repair shops found successful market niches in metropolitan areas or in locales that were geographically distant from the nearest franchised dealer, as well as areas where the reputation of the local dealer service department was subpar . . . Auto repair remained one of the most difficult purchases for consumers to effectively evaluate. Many consumers seemed chronically unhappy with the level and cost of servicing their vehicles. Finding a good mechanic at times appeared to require equal parts of perseverance and serendipity.	

WS 3:6

Writing About the Case Actors

Following the excerpt provided, write about the protagonist of your own case. Use the material you developed in Modules 1 and 2 for inspiration.

Characteristics	Example	Your Sample
■ Character exhibits personality ■ Creates empathy for the protagonist ■ The reader "knows" this character	Ken had always been a car guy. Almost as soon as he got his license and was old enough to work, he took a job as a part-time car detailer at a franchised Volvo automobile dealership. He gradually rose through the ranks of its service department, eventually becoming service manager while still in his 20s. As he approached his 30th birthday, Ken wanted to try his hand at running his own business. He felt confident that he had the training and skills to succeed. Tow truck drivers often dropped uncooperative vehicles in front of his shop door and threw the keys through the mail slot in the passage door, knowing that Ken would go out of his way to help out stranded motorists, even those without scheduled appointments. As he approached an age where many small business owners would consider retirement, Ken showed no signs of slowing down.	

WS 3:7

Writing the Case Situation

Following the excerpt provided, draft the case situation for your own case.
Use the material you developed in Modules 1 and 2 for inspiration.

Characteristics	Example	Your Sample
■ Presents the problem ■ Ensures the reader can "see" the action unfolding ■ Calibrates the problem to the anticipated level of the reader	While drinking the hot coffee that one of his regular customers had brought in, Ken took another look at the content of Matthew's note. After 40 years in the industry, he had a pretty good idea of how to handle problem cars and problem owners, but this one was a puzzle. On the face of it, Matthew's note was exceptionally well detailed, but it described a shopping list of issues, many of which could become rather time-consuming and expensive to track down and resolve. Beyond that, who were Laura and Matthew? As he finished his coffee, Ken settled down to work on his scheduled morning appointments, figuring that by lunchtime, he might have further inspiration that would help him either to place the owners or figure out what their car needed. More fundamentally, he needed to decide whether he even wanted to work on their car.	

WS 3:8
Including Additional Information

Following the excerpt provided, draft some nonessential information for your own case. Use the material you developed in Modules 1 and 2 for inspiration.

Characteristics	Example	Your Sample
■ The information is not critical to the case analysis ■ The information sounds like it is important to the case ■ The reader wonders why the information has been included	Ken's building had a wide overhead door in the front, with a standard passage door to one side. Vehicles were driven in and backed out. The interior of the building was long enough so that two vehicles would easily fit lengthwise inside, and it was wide enough for either two or three across. As the shop was configured, hydraulic lifts were installed at the back of the left and right bays. For small, quick, in-and-out repairs that did not require a lift, two additional vehicles could comfortably be angled inside the door and in front of the hydraulic lift areas. Between the hydraulic lifts was a middle space where a vehicle could be parked without affecting the two working bays to either side. Ken reserved this space for inoperative cars with partially disassembled motors, for cars with complex problems that would require additional time to repair, and generally for nonroutine jobs. It was never a good sign for an owner to return to Ken's to find his car parked in the center bay.	

WS 3:9

Writing the Closing Hook

Following the excerpt provided, draft a closing hook for your own case. Use the material you developed in Modules 1 and 2 for inspiration.

Characteristics	Example	Your Sample
■ The problem becomes the reader's problem ■ You have not given away the answer or the decision ■ It is reasonably clear what you expect of the reader	By 5 P.M., only Matthew's Volvo remained out front. Ken went outside, pulled the car into the center bay of the shop, closed and locked the overhead door, and headed home. It would still be there in the morning, waiting for him. Ken knew that by the next morning, he would need to have a tactical plan for dealing with the owner and the potential repair of the vehicle, mindful of his reputation as one of the best independent shops in the area. As a service marketer, beyond providing competent repair work, he knew that word of mouth was critical to his business's continued success.	

WS 3:10

Appendices

Following the excerpt provided, list several appendices that make sense for your own case. Use the material you developed in Modules 1 and 2 for inspiration.

Characteristics	Example	Your Sample Appendices
■ Data that cannot fit comfortably within the case narrative ■ Information that is important or valuable for analysis	Exhibit 1: Matthew's note Exhibit 2: "Car Talk" Find a Great Mechanic search results for Newburyport, MA	

WS 3:11

Case Writing Assignment 3

This assignment will result in a completed full draft of your case.

1. Using the detailed outline that you developed of your case in WS 2:11 (Case Writing Assignment 2), "fill in the blanks" in that case outline.

   ■ Incorporate and expand the hook you drafted in WS 3:3.

   ■ Use the description of the company or organization you are studying (developed in WS 3:4) to guide your "Company" section.

   ■ Use the micro-industry note (WS 3:5) to build your "Industry" section.

   ■ Highlight the protagonist(s) and the primary issue based on WS 3:3, 3:6, and 3:8. Do your best to breathe life into the protagonist and to incorporate other characters into the story. Take care to make the actors as real as you can through thick description and dialogue.

   ■ Expand your closing hook (WS 3:9) so that it is comprehensive and compelling.

   ■ Identify and list at least two appendices to be included (from WS 3:10).

2. Share this rough draft of a case with a colleague and request constructive critical feedback. If at all possible, attend a case conference and present this draft at a roundtable discussion for comment.

3. Rewrite based on the input you have received.

WS 3:12

Writing a Case and Instructor's Manual in One Heavy Semester

Use this worksheet to set up your own schedule for writing your case and Instructor's Manual. Adapt it to your own needs and dates. At the completion of your case and IM, you will have developed a personal single semester model for case writing.

Week #/ Date	Activity	Number of Hours Proposed/Taken	
1/	Go to WS 1:4 and WS 1:5 for a template and sample, then *draft* a very rough, simple version of the case situation. See Module 7: Getting Your Case Published and Reviewing Cases for Others, then *select* your target for this case: conference or journal. Which venue will give you the most bang for your buck?	3–4	
2/	Using WS 5:2 and WS 5:3, *identify* the audience, course, and placement of your case for the Instructor's Manual and *write* the learning objectives. This will help you situate the content and design your writing approach, as well as keep your Learning Objectives in mind as you begin. You have now completed two of the eight elements in the IM.	2	
3/	Follow the sample provided in WS 2:12 to *write* a detailed outline of your case, including headings and subheadings. This will make writing your case a straightforward matter of filling in the blanks.	2–3	
4/	See WS 3:3 and *write* your hook. Some people prefer to write this after completing the case, but I find that it gives me direction to draft one version as an early step in the writing process. Then, use WS 3:4 and 3:5 to *write* the "easy" parts—the industry note and the company story or history. Because you have already collected the data in your pre-semester work, these elements are uncomplicated to write.	4	
5/	*Write* the case situation (WS 3:7), *include* any additional information (WS 3:8), and *draft* the closing hook (WS 3:9).	4	
6/	*Share* the untitled case with the company and get a publication release from them (WS 2:3). With WS 5:4 and WS 5:6, return to the IM and *write* the literature review/theory/readings section, discussion questions and their answers.	4	

7/	Read the case again and using WS 5:5 and 5:1, *design* your teaching strategy and your synopsis. *Write* the epilogue (WS 5:7). Take a deep breath.	4	
8/	*Share* your case and IM with a trusted colleague inside or outside your institution. Ask for commentary on the case, IM, and the quality of the research and writing. Meet with the person, if at all possible, to go over the commentary.	3	
9/	*Revise* case and IM based on the comments.	3	
10/	*Decide* on a title for your case. *Test* the case with live students in a colleague's class. Pay close attention to the way the case "works" and where it fails. Collect feedback on the case from the students and on the IM from the class instructor.	3–4	
11/	*Make the changes* that became obvious to you when teaching or observing the case analysis. Do trust both the student feedback and the instructor comments when making your revisions. Remember—they are your final audiences.	3	
12/	*Send* the case and IM to a conference or a journal. Be sure to follow the specific guidelines requested by the outlet (refer to Module 7). Check this twice. Do not shoot yourself in the foot!	2	

WS 3:13

Writing a Case and Instructor's Manual in a Sabbatical Semester or Summer

Use this worksheet to set up your own schedule for writing your case and Instructor's Manual. Adapt it to your own needs and dates. At the completion of your case and IM, you will have developed a personal sabbatical semester model for case writing.

Week #/ Date	Activity	Number of Hours *Proposed/ Taken*	
1/	Using WS 2:1, *identify* your case subject. *Contact* the subject and obtain a consent to research form (WS 2:3) at your first meeting. *Conduct* background research on the company before your first interview.	8	
2/	*Continue* your background research on both the company and the industry, as well as any information you can find about the person you are going to interview. *Visit* the company and *conduct* interview #1. Refer to Module 2 for hints about successful interviewing and observation. WS 2:4 may be especially helpful here.	8	
3/	*Conduct* interview #2 as well as a secondary source, if available.	6	
4/	Go to WS 1:4 and WS 1:5 for a template and sample, then *draft* a very rough, simple version of the case situation. See Module 7: Getting Your Case Published and Reviewing Cases for Others, then *select* your target for this case: conference or journal. Which venue will give you the most bang for your buck?	3–4	
5/	If needed, *pursue* additional interviews or other research. Let the material you have collected percolate in your mind until you are comfortable with the focus you have determined.	6	
6/	Using WS 5:2 and WS 5:3, *identify* the audience, course, and placement of your case for the Instructor's Manual and *write* the learning objectives. This will help you situate the content and design your writing approach, as well as keep your Learning Objectives in mind as you begin. You have now completed two of the eight elements in the IM.	3	
7/	Follow the sample provided in WS 2:12 to *write* a detailed outline of your case, including headings and subheadings. This will make writing your case a straightforward matter of filling in the blanks.	3	

8/	See WS 3:3 and *write* your hook. Some people prefer to write this after completing the case, but I find that it gives me direction to draft one version as an early step in the writing process. Then, use WS 3:4 and 3:5 to *write* the "easy" parts— the industry note and the company story or history. Because you have already collected the data in your pre-semester work, these elements are uncomplicated to write. *Write* the case situation (WS 3:7), *include* any additional information (WS 3:8), and *draft* the closing hook (WS 3:9).	8	
9/	*Share* the untitled case with the company and get a publication release from them (WS 2:3). With WS 5:4 and WS 5:6, return to the IM and *write* the literature review/theory/readings section, discussion questions and their answers. Do not share the IM with the company (see Module 2).	4	
10/	Read the case again and using WS 5:5 and 5:1, *design* your teaching strategy and your synopsis. *Write* the epilogue (WS 5:7). Take a deep breath. *Share* your case and IM with a trusted colleague inside or outside your institution. Ask for commentary on the case, IM, and the quality of the research and writing. Meet with the person, if at all possible, to go over the commentary.	7	
11/	*Revise* case and IM based on the comments. *Decide* on a title for your case. *Test* the case with live students in a colleague's class. Pay close attention to the way the case "works" and where it fails. Collect feedback on the case from the students and on the IM from the class instructor. (You may have to wait until the new semester begins to complete this piece, unless you are willing to spend part of your sabbatical to attend someone's class.)	7	
12/	*Make the changes* that became obvious to you when teaching or observing the case analysis. Do trust both the student feedback and the instructor comments when making your revisions. Remember—they are your final audiences. *Send* the case and IM to a conference or a journal. Be sure to follow the specific guidelines requested by the outlet (refer to Module 7). Check this twice. Do not shoot yourself in the foot!	4–5	

Module 4

●●●●●

Writing Short Cases

As we integrate cases into our classes, we are discovering an unan-ticipated challenge: students, undergraduate students in particular, rarely prepare cases in sufficient detail to make them valuable learning vehicles in the classroom. Even graduate students may avoid the deep preparation necessary for the intense evaluation and analysis of case problems. The vast majority of published cases, especially those pub-lished in journals are more than 10 pages of text supported by several (four or more) complex exhibits. However, when students have not pre-pared such cases thoroughly in advance of the class, class discussion falls flat and learning does not take place.

There are many solutions to this teaching challenge, some punitive and some corrective. This module focuses on a highly pragmatic solution—cre-ating cases that can be read and analyzed in one class or meeting session, with no prior preparation necessary on the part of the learners.

●●●●●

Creating Cases?

By "creating cases" I do not mean to suggest "inventing cases." Cases in short formats follow the same protocols as cases in full-length format; that is, short cases are:

■ factual stories;
■ that take place in the past; and
■ result in an analysis or a decision (see Module 1 for review).

Differentiators

However, there are differentiators between the full-length and short case models. As you will note in Table 4.1, although both styles of cases

Table 4.1 Differences between Full-Length Cases and Short Cases (Elements)

Full-Length Case	Short Case
■ A protagonist	■ A protagonist
■ A narrative (often with subplots)	■ A narrative
■ Information about the industry and the business	■ Information about the industry and/or the business
■ An actual situation/problem/challenge (or multiples of same)	■ An actual situation/problem/challenge
■ A focus (decision/analytical) requiring the application of specific tools	■ A focus (decision/analytical/or an application of a tool)

contain many similar elements, short cases require more than just abbreviation of length to make them viable learning tools.

Protagonist

An identifiable protagonist is always required. This protagonist provides a foil for the actionable decision to be made or a center for the evaluation of actions taken by the company. In a short case in particular, an explicit focus on the actions or behaviors of one individual as representative of a business dilemma allows the reader to relate more closely to the situation and its demands. As a reminder, most of us want to help *people*, but care far less about helping an anonymous corporate entity.

Short Case—Short Story

Because a case is at heart a narrative, a short case must contain a piece of a story. A full-length case will have a narrative with multiple subplots (as do situations in "real life"), but the short case can have only one plot. There is no room to travel down multiple paths in a short case.

Industry/Business Information

While a full-length case will include background information about the company and about the industry, a short case will include information about one or the other. If the industry is one with which we expect our readers to be reasonably familiar (fast food, health care, mobile phones, or banking, for example), we can spend our limited space on company background. If the industry is more esoteric, such as candy manufacturing or printing, the details of which are likely less familiar to most people, we need to dedicate some space to explaining the specifics of the industry that are relevant to the case decision.

Case Situation—One Problem

A case always has a problem/situation/challenge that needs to be addressed. In a full-length case, there are multiple such problems; a short case focuses on only one. It might be a piece of a problem that the longer case introduces or it might be a manageable smaller issue that you want students to address, always bearing in mind the limited space available.

A full-length case will require the application of multiple decision or analytical (or both) tools. A short case can require only one, or possibly two, such tools, as the limited information included in the abbreviated format will likely allow for limited analysis.

Length

Length does play a role, of course, in the development of a short case. It goes without saying that a short case is shorter, but how much shorter depends on your goals for the case itself. If you want the short case to be publishable in a journal, length requirements differ from requirements for case publication in book chapters or workbooks. If you are not interested in publishing your short cases, length is, of course, irrelevant. In all situations, if you are not seeking publication, none of the "rules" or protocols matter at all. Whatever will work in *your* classroom is the way you should put your case together. See the following section on suggested formats before you begin to draft your short case.

Table 4.2 offers some suggested technical differences in short cases from their longer cousins. You will note that, in most areas, the technical elements are identical. In every situation, however, it is best to consult the journal editor directly to find out if there are any specific refinements demanded by the journal in question (see Module 7). The key to writing a short case relates to a student's ability to read the case in class within, say, 15 minutes, and then proceed to the analysis using the data provided and the theories applied from that particular lesson.

Table 4.2 Differences between Full-Length Cases and Short Cases (Technical)

Full-Length Cases	Short Cases
■ 6–15 pages	■ 500–1500 words
■ Written in the past tense	■ Written in the past tense
■ Language appropriate for targeted readership	■ Language appropriate for targeted readership
■ Previously unpublished	■ Previously unpublished
■ Disguised cases OK, but NOT fiction or composite cases/characters	■ Disguised cases OK, but NOT fiction or composite cases/characters
■ Secondary research acceptable	■ Secondary research acceptable

Sources of Short Cases

Just as discussed in Module 2, cases are everywhere, just waiting to be written. Worksheet 2:1 (Where to Find Your Case Subject) offers a series of suggested sources of cases, including consulting, previous employers, family and friends, neighbors and community organizations, professional associations and students, the places you shop and the newspapers you read.

However, short cases have two additional sources that do not appear in this list: your existing full-length cases and your published or unpublished research cases. For the latter, please see Module 7: Moving from Research Cases to Teaching Cases. I will describe the process of abbreviating appropriately your existing full-length case in the section that follows.

● ● ● ● ●

Suggested Formats

The Prototypical "Short Case"

When I refer to the prototypical short case, I am really talking about a teaching case of shortest length possible sufficient to present a clear problem and provide data for addressing it. The most "traditional" short cases look like full-length cases and are researched, written, and taught in similar fashion. See the later section "On Teaching the Short Case" for some alternate techniques.

In general, choose a case focus that is manageable, select tightly focused learning objectives, write concisely, be selective about the data to include, be prepared to jettison your "favorite things," and finally, test the case with students. Three simple steps will get you started:

■ *Step 1: It's still about the Learning Objectives.* Before you write—even before you conceptualize the case—make sure you know exactly what you want students to learn from it. You can find a full description of Learning Objectives in Module 5 (Building the Instructor's Manual) and an abbreviated version in the section labeled "The Teaching Note."

■ *Step 2: Question the conventional.* Refresh your memory about all the protocols for case research and writing that you have used in the past (or read in this workbook). Consider each one individually and ask yourself, "Do I really need to do this? Is this information that the student needs in order to respond to the questions I am asking? What is of minimal importance and can be left out?"

■ *Step 3: Identify the "must haves" in your case situation.* How valuable is each element in the case? In a full-length case, you will have leeway to include some "nice to know" information, but a short case must be concise, and every word must have value. "Same old, same old" has no currency here, but it is critically important to include sufficient data to make the case teachable.

See Worksheet 4:1 for a sample short case.

The "Critical Incident"

The term "critical incident" can be misleading because it is used in so many different disciplines for a variety of purposes. The one common usage it has among its far-reaching descriptions is a dramatic event that makes one stop and think. When I use this term in relation to a form of short case, I mean specifically to describe a situation that either needs resolution or about which the learner can devote some thinking time. The critical incident does not provide background; instead, it is a stand-alone illustration of a concept.

Critical incidents are most often published in textbooks as boxed caselets or callouts. You can see samples in any textbook you use in your classes. When published in journals, critical incidents are often grouped in multiples with one related teaching note. Critical incidents are fun to write, because the writer is only structuring a situation rather than a complete narrative with data and potential depth of analysis possible. However, as a form meant for publication, there is less opportunity for academic scholarly publication and more for trade publication.

The "Instant Case"

One source of cases that we overlook frequently is the "Instant Case," a case derived from a class presentation by an invited speaker. The one requirement of this kind of case is that the speaker must be willing to answer questions put forth by the students in order to give some informal life to the case story. What is particularly inviting about instant cases is the ability of an entire class of students to write individual cases about the same presentation, giving you, as instructor, the opportunity to evaluate student learning on several levels—critical thinking skills, analysis, and communication technique.

The process starts with inviting a speaker whose experience is particularly relevant to class content, such as an entrepreneur for a small business class or an economist for a finance class. Each attendee takes notes on the presentation, which provides experience in observation and interviewing (see Module 2). The quality of the note taking will have a large impact on the quality of final product. This is a great way to introduce case writing to students and to give them some listening practice as a group.

The sample I have provided in WS 4:2 is a draft of an instant case about Lucy Dearborn, owner of Lucia Lighting. She visited my entrepreneurship/small business management class and spoke about her launch process and a "typical" day in the life of a small business owner. Students used my draft sample as a way to get their own instant cases started. Each student case was different, and it was a valuable learning experience for all of us to see how differently each person perceived the message that Lucy was sharing with us. See Module 10 for building the student-written cases.

Yes, you do have to obtain a release from the speaker if you have any intention of using the cases in a future publication (see Module 2 for sample publication release forms).

Distilling a Full-Length Case into a Short Version

You have written a traditional, full-length case and, whether published or not, you would like to use this case in an abbreviated format. The challenge is cutting down to the bone and still leaving enough meat to allow for a valuable analysis. In this situation, you need to work concurrently on the case and on the Instructor's Manual, beginning with the Instructor's Manual. You will be turning the Instructor's Manual into a Teaching Note format. Here's how you get started:

- *Step 1: In the Instructor's Manual.* Examine the Learning Objectives and select only one or two, both of which should be on the same topic. Delete any other Learning Objectives immediately. Don't look back.

- *Step 2: The Synopsis.* Remove any reference within the synopsis to topics that will not be included in the distilled case. It is important to be clear about the focus of the case, because the synopsis is the marketing piece targeted to instructors and a strong synopsis will sell your case; a weak one will not appeal to instructors. No one has time to review cases that appear unfocused.

- *Step 3: Adjust the Usage.* Adjust the intended use, including the description of the potential audience. Now that you have eliminated some of the Learning Objectives, the case will be used differently, in a more limited fashion.

- *Step 4: Discussion Questions.* Delete Discussion Questions that no longer reflect the more limited objectives of the case, along with their answers.

- *Step 5: Theory and Pedagogy.* Reduce the theory discussion and the teaching strategy to match the new case usage. The epilogue should remain untouched. Any new teaching strategy should focus only on the new Learning Objectives. If your strategy is simply a traditional discussion of the case questions, you can delete pedagogy altogether, as this section should add something new to the teaching process.

■ *Step 6: In the Case.* Remove any material from the hook that is not related to the new Learning Objectives. You may shorten the hook or leave it as is—this depends on the way you originally wrote your hook. Deletion of your own carefully structured wording can be painful; this is a good time to engage a colleague in your distillation.

■ *Step 7: Be Ruthless!* Go through the entire case, cutting out everything that does not fit within your new objectives. You will need much less background information, less industry information, and many fewer exhibits for your new, distilled case. Your well-crafted words will hit the cutting room floor with a thud. Swallow hard and move on.

■ *Step 8: Refine the Close.* Now that the case problem is different, the task of the reader has to be adjusted to match it. The rewritten Learning Objectives will help you redesign the closing hook. Make sure that the reader understands the task in the distilled case. A distilled case can be as compelling as the original as long as its purpose is clear and the reader knows how to assist the protagonist or evaluate the action.

■ *Step 9: Write a New Title.* The title of a case must reflect the content of the case, so the title of the distilled case should be narrower in scope than the original case title. Example: Instead of "General Hospital Suffers Chronic Shortages," consider "General Hospital Seeks an Injection of Nursing Talent" to indicate a narrower set of problems.

Worksheet 4:3 and Worksheet 4:4 are exercises geared to practicing the distillation process, as it is one you can use readily to create usable instructional materials for your classes and for general use. If you are distilling someone else's case, be sure to get a release from the original author if you intend to distribute the distillation widely.

From Research to Teaching in Short Order

Module 6 is a complete guide to turning your research case study or your basic research findings into a teaching case. The same concepts apply to the short case based on research findings, coupled with the preceding instructions about distillation, if you are using a full research case to begin with.

● ● ● ● ●

The Teaching Note

It is really simpler to write an entirely new short case from your research than it is to distill a full research case into a short format teaching case. By selecting one case story from among the many you will have collected during the research process, you can narrow the case focus sufficiently to limit the Learning Objectives and generate a useful and factual narrative. Your research material is chock-a-block with possible teaching material—the real key to identifying it is your ability to narrow your eyes and be critically discerning.

Module 5 is all about the Instructor's Manual or, as I would call it when written for a short case, the Teaching Note. What is the difference between the two?

The Instructor's Manual is truly a "manual"; that is, it provides an extensive discussion of the case, its usage, and theoretical supports; often includes an analysis, multiple discussion questions and their answers, and an epilogue—all of which are focused on several Learning Objectives featured in the beginning of the manual.

A Teaching Note is far less complex. It contains most of the sections mentioned in Module 5, but they are all compressed and minimized to provide specific guidance but little theoretical background beyond the simplest mention. The assumption is made that, because the short case is one that was not provided prior to the class session, students either will not have needed much theory to perform the analysis or that the theory has already been taught and this case is being used primarily for illustrative purposes.

As you can see from Table 4.3, both the purpose and the construction of the Teaching Note differ in several respects from that of the Instructor's Manual.

Writing a Teaching Note is not simply shortening what you might write for an Instructor's Manual. The focus of a Teaching Note is on the *teaching* elements. As a result, instead of providing a literature review and references, you should provide any creative ways you have developed (and tested) that will help students learn the material more effectively. See Worksheet 4:5 for a sample Teaching Note.

Table 4.3 Elements of an Instructor's Manual and Teaching Note

Full-Length Instructor's Manual	Short Teaching Note
Abstract/synopsis (250–300 words)	Abbreviated abstract (50–75 words)
Research Method (field or secondary sourced)	Topic (keywords only)
Intended audience, course(s), and placement	Intended audience
Learning objectives (3–5)	Learning objectives (1 or 2)
Discussion questions and answers (3–5)	Discussion questions and answers (2–3)
Teaching strategies	Teaching tips
Literature review and references	Activities to enhance learning from the case, if any
Epilogue	Epilogue

●●●●●

On Teaching the Short Case

Module 9 contains multiple suggestions for ways to teach cases in general. Teaching with short cases is a little different from the usual ways we teach, however.

Short cases are particularly suited for use in exams or other kinds of in-class evaluative exercises. Students have to have internalized theoretical material thoroughly in order to apply it on the fly, either in writing or in a more interactive manner (see WS 4:3 for an example of how to use a short case in an in-class exercise).

If used in a written exam, simply using the discussion questions as exam questions will result in a clear indication of students' ability to apply theory and to perform a relevant analysis without consultation with others.

Short cases do not lend themselves readily to the "sage on the stage" approach (Module 9) because their length and concomitant lack of complexity do not demand the kind of expertise you might add to the discussion. They are far more appropriate to use in a "guide on the side" mode, creatively engaging student collaboration and building a stronger classroom community.

●●●●●

Worksheets

WS 4:1 A Sample Short Case

WS 4:2 Sample of an Instant Case

WS 4:3 Distilling an Instructor's Manual

WS 4:4 Distilling a Case

WS 4:5 A Sample Teaching Note

WS 4:1

A Sample Short Case

Professor Rose's Frustrating Day

Professor Rose taught psychology to undergraduates in Ohio State University at Mansfield. She was very active in school governance and in her regional professional association, the Midwestern Psychological Association. She sat on multiple university committees and was the adviser for the local Psi Chi chapter. She taught two large intro to psychology sections and one small senior seminar for majors. A prolific researcher, Prof. Rose was a very busy academic. Despite a shortage of graduate assistantships at her campus, she was pleased to learn that she had been awarded a graduate assistant for the year to help with the administrative demands of her various activities.

Upon meeting Lakshmi, Prof. Rose was charmed. The young woman had all the technical skills she needed, was an excellent writer, and was eager to get to work. What she did not have was a social security number, and the university required her to obtain one before she could be put on the payroll. This took three weeks to accomplish, critical weeks at the beginning of the term. Prof. Rose began to fall behind.

Finally, all the details were ironed out, Lakshmi was added to the computer system, a work location and schedule (Tuesdays/Thursdays from 11:00 A.M. to 4:00 P.M.) was established for her, and she set to work designing the new bulletin board for the Psi Chi honor society and updating a newsletter for Prof. Rose's major curriculum project. One hour before her 1:00 P.M. Tuesday class, Prof. Rose asked Lakshmi to compile the results of a small survey she had distributed to the class the previous week. The survey was 16 Yes/No questions, and 47 students had completed it.

Prof. Rose	I know you are fast on the computer. Can you please put together the results of this survey so I can present them in class in an hour?
Lakshmi	Of course! I will type it out right away.
Prof. Rose	No need to type out the questions. I already have them on my computer. I just need the results. Just use columns: Q#, Yes, No, and fill in the results.
Lakshmi	OK. Right away.

At 12:50, Prof. Rose went to class without the results and decided to present them at the next class. When she returned to her desk, Lakshmi gave her a thumb drive with the survey results. Instead of a compilation,

she received a copy of the survey without data. She asked Lakshmi to correct this. "Oh, of course, right away," she replied.

The next iteration included each individual survey listed, without any tallies. Prof. Rose looked at the 47 pages of data, all in Word rather than Excel, all in narrative without numbers. How would she be able to use this? She explained the problem again to Lakshmi. Once again, Lakshmi took the file and began to work.

Finally, after two more tries, at 4:00 P.M. she delivered what Prof. Rose wanted, a simple list that looked like this:

Question	Yes	No
1	43	4
2 Etc.	26	21

Prof. Rose	Thank you, Lakshmi. This is exactly what I wanted.
Lakshmi	Don't you want all the back-up forms that I printed?
Prof. Rose	No. They are exactly what I had originally given you. Why would I want you to reproduce them? I do need to leave for the day, now. Have you completed the bulletin board that you started last Thursday?
Lakshmi	No. I had done it but I thought it looked too bright, so I took it down. I will figure out a better way to do it at home and will bring it in tomorrow.
Prof. Rose	You can't do that . . . I cannot pay you for tomorrow. The university has strict rules about the hours you may work. I really do need that bulletin board done quickly as the term is well underway and students need the information that they are used to getting from the board. I do not need perfection, Lakshmi, but I do need some things done quickly. Let's talk about this on Thursday when you come in.

WS 4:2

Sample of an Instant Case

Lucia Lighting (Based on a class presentation by the business owner. Additional information may be included in any/all of the elements listed.)

The Opening Hook	"Every day is like Christmas! It's the best thing I ever did, starting this business," said Lucy Dearborn, founder of Lucia Lighting. Lucy was talking to a group of entrepreneurship students when suddenly, she could no longer contain her enthusiasm about the home lighting business she had opened with her partner in Lynn, MA, several years earlier. Her energy and excitement drew the students toward her as she talked about her young business, her past, and her anticipated future.
The Company Story	After 15 years selling lighting for someone else, Lucy had the opportunity to open her own store in 2005. One of her customers was going to buy a building about 15 minutes from where she was working, and he offered to partner with her in a new lighting store venture. She jumped at the chance, even when she learned that the building had spent its previous life as a funeral home. As she explained to the class, "Funeral homes are the least likely places to be haunted."
The Lighting Industry	With millions of home and personal businesses throughout the country, the market for lighting seemed endless. Even in the relatively small North Shore region of Massachusetts, demand was high. There were half a dozen other small lighting companies within a 10-mile radius of Lucia Lighting, and there were also large national chains, like Lowes Home Improvement and Home Depot in the general area. Competition was stiff, but Lucy and her partner felt that they could compete based on their special competencies.
The Situation	Lucy loved her business. It was part of her, right down to its eponymous name: Lucia Lighting. Lucia, the goddess of light, was the business's inspiration and guide to Lucy's heart. "Love your business like a child," she was fond of saying. "Just be sure you know this: Your freedom disappears when you open a business." She wasn't saying this just for effect. Lucy worked 65–75 hours each week, and sometimes that didn't even include doing any of the design work that she loved or selling attractive fixtures to the young customers just starting their lives or the established, more financially robust customers who were her real target market. Sometimes, simply shoveling snow or cleaning the bathroom had to take precedence over her favorite work. She didn't get to see her family nearly as much as she wanted to. She missed seeing her nephew in the class play, she came late (if at all) to family parties, and hanging with her Mom or her husband became a thing of the past. She had to adjust her mindset and prioritize Lucia Lighting over all else. Missing things was getting to her after 2½ years of constant work.

| The Closing Hook | Lucy's smile dimmed a little as she thought about her young nephew and how much fun she had with him. The students wondered if they could manage to work so hard and give up what was important to them in order to make their own businesses succeed. Could they come up with some way for Lucy to "buy back" some time for family before that little kid grew up without her? |

WS 4:3
Distilling an Instructor's Manual

Select a full-length case that you have written and/or taught successfully. Using the Instructor's Manual for that case and following the instructions in Module 4 for Distilling a Case, use the following table to develop a Teaching Note for your own distilled case. Be ruthless in cutting out as much as you possibly can from the Instructor's Manual to create a Teaching Note to use in class (and to guide your creation of the short/distilled case in WS 4:4).

	Full-Length IM	*Distilled TN*
Synopsis		
Usage		
Learning Objectives		
Discussion Questions (List)		
Theory and/or Pedagogy		
Answers to Discussion Questions		
Epilogue		

WS 4:4
Distilling a Case

Using the same full-length case for which you distilled the Instructor's Manual into a Teaching Note, follow the instructions in Module 4 for Distilling a Case. Use the following table to develop your own distilled version of the full-length case. Be ruthless in cutting out as much as you possibly can from the long version of the case to create a narrower case to use in class, but take care not to eliminate material that you have indicated in the Teaching Note should be included.

	Full-Length Case	Distilled Case
Hook		
Background/Industry		
Character Development		
The Situation/Problem		
The Close		
Exhibits (list)		
Title		

WS 4:5

A Sample Teaching Note

Professor Rose's Frustrating Day

Synopsis

A professor and graduate assistant have communication problems based on cultural misunderstanding.

Key Words

communication, culture

Suggested Audience

UG, graduate, executive education

Learning Objectives

■ Students will become aware of and sensitized to the potential for misunderstanding and conflicting assumptions between people of different cultures
■ Students will practice interpersonal communication and develop communication methods that take into account diverse cultural backgrounds

Discussion Questions

1. What lessons in communication can we draw from this story?
2. Where did communication break down?
3. What should Prof. Rose focus on for the future?

Pedagogy

The case can be taught per Geert Hofstede's basic theoretical frameworks (see *Cultures and Organizations: Software of the Mind*, 1991, McGraw-Hill) or Charles Hampden-Turner and Fons Trompenaars' theories (see *Riding the Waves of Culture: Understanding Diversity in Global Business*, 1997, McGraw-Hill).

This case lends itself to role-playing, with the process outlined as follows. The instructions are based on an overall group size of no more than 20 students, divided into two teams. If there are more than 20 students involved, set up multiple groups of five for each role and run several concurrent role plays. The entire exercise can take 30 minutes.

1. Teams of Prof. Rose and Lakshmi meet for 5–10 minutes to:
   a. Establish their position (use the hints in the case to set up the characters).
   b. Figure out their goals.
   c. Set up an unwritten script.
   d. Select a representative to do the fish bowl role play (an alternate method is to have multiple role plays going on at once in groups of three. The third participant is an observer, as described in Step 3).

2. Representatives from each team come together in the center and play out the meeting between Prof. Rose and Lakshmi. The rest of the group take notes about the interaction, what works and what doesn't, what language and body movement is helpful, and other verbal and nonverbal cues.

3. Interpretation and debriefing of the action by the group, facilitated by the instructor, following the theories that the instructor prefers.

Discussion Questions and Suggested Answers

1. What lessons in communication can we draw from this story? Even when people speak the same language, it is easy for them to misunderstand one another. When they come from cultures with significantly different approaches to authority and power, the likelihood of misunderstanding increases.

2. Where did communication break down? Effective communication requires three main elements: encoding, sending the message, and decoding. Errors in this communication process occurred in all three steps.

Encoding: Prof. Rose did not make her demands clear to the student from India, whose expectations of directive instructions were unfulfilled by Prof. Rose's casual statements of what she wanted.

Sending the message: Prof. Rose did not itemize specifically how the deliverable she expected from Lakshmi should appear, its format, and the required time frame. By treating the request in a manner easily misinterpreted as casual by someone from a different culture, she received in return the wrong material.

Decoding: Lakshmi thought that the decisions were hers to make, and assumed that Prof. Rose wanted what she herself would have wanted. She did not inquire further as to the accuracy of the instructions or her interpretation of them.

3. What should Prof. Rose focus on for the future? She should state her demands as demands, not as requests. She should make sure that Lakshmi understands what is required in terms of content, process, and time frame. She needs to take this extra time to confirm understanding and allow Lakshmi space to ask questions. It is important to recognize the inherent power distance in their two cultures and find a way to account for it within their relationship.

Epilogue

Prof. Rose continued to be frustrated the entire academic year, while Lakshmi continued to deliver products that were just slightly wrong, a little too late. All attempts at explanation by Prof. Rose to Lakshmi resulted in verbal agreement between the two, followed by disappointment and poor outcomes. Both were happy when the year was over.

Module 5

• • • • •

Building the Instructor's Manual

• • • • •

The IM: Where the Rubber Meets the Road

The Instructor's Manual (IM), also known as a Teaching Note, is the least visible section of the case, the bottom two-thirds of the iceberg in the writing process. The IM is the element of case writing that makes cases acceptable scholarly presentations rather than simply good stories. Without the IM, the academic community can draw no conclusions about your professionalism, the quality of your research, or your ability to share your expertise with the rest of us. All academic journals require cases to have an accompanying Instructor's Manual and, although the IM itself is rarely published, journal editors will not even entertain submissions that lack this key component. The IM provides the instructor with invaluable assistance in class preparation and case analysis, turning even the most complex case into a "plug and play" classroom activity.

The IM provides the writer with two important benefits as well:

■ It helps you to conceptualize clearly what it is you want to convey through the case. It is easy to get carried away by telling the story of the case and consequently forget that the case exists to *teach* something. The IM will "keep you honest" in your case writing activities.

■ It establishes your professional credibility in the academic community. The instructors who use your case in the classroom can see at a glance that you are familiar with relevant theory, that you can contextualize learning, and that you are generous in sharing your knowledge with others.

The IM proves your scholarly mettle.

● ● ● ● ●

Who Will Use My IM?

Despite the fact that most of the users of your IM will be academics who are teaching their regular classes, you should write your IM with the fledgling user in mind. Some scenarios that magnify the importance of a comprehensive IM are listed here:

- The user/instructor has never taught the course before or is developing a new course altogether.
- The user/instructor is covering a class for someone else and has had little or no preparation time.
- The user/instructor has never used cases in the classroom before.
- The user/instructor has minimal knowledge of the case topic.
- The user/instructor is an adjunct teacher or a graduate student.

For anyone else, the Instructor's Manual is gravy; for the users just mentioned, the IM is a critical tool in bringing value to the classroom. Your IM needs to serve both groups.

Just as you calibrated your language carefully to engage the readers of the case, you need to remember that you are writing the IM for professionals, most of whom are very familiar with your topic and the theory that drives decision making in your academic area. For that reason, the IM is rarely as "friendly" as the case itself. It is a formal, scholarly document that follows a typical, although not universally consistent pattern.

● ● ● ● ●

Contents of a Typical Instructor's Manual

Instructor's Manuals generally share the eight components listed here. You should refer to the submission guidelines specific to the journal in which you want to publish your case for variations on these components, but you can be confident that at least these eight elements will be part of the requirement:

- Overview/Synopsis/Abstract
- Intended Audience, Recommended Courses, and Placement
- Learning Objectives
- Discussion Questions
- Teaching Strategies
- Literature Review, Theory, and Recommended Readings

■ Answering Discussion Questions

■ Epilogue

Overview/Synopsis/Abstract

This element serves as the hook for your Instructor's Manual. Remember the hook you wrote for the case, which was designed to grab the readers' attention and interest them enough to read further? The readers you were aiming for with the case hook were the end users, the students. But the readers you are aiming for in the synopsis are the instructors, the gatekeepers who decide whether or not to assign your case to their classes. It is a marketing effort, and this is your first and best chance to convince instructors to adopt your case.

In one paragraph, you must provide a brief overview of the case story, a list of critical case events, a description of the research methodology, the difficulty level, and the main problem focus, all while taking care not to give away any "answers."

The synopsis appears first in the IM, but it is often written last because it provides a high-level perspective on the case, and that distance is difficult to attain until your case thinking process is complete. See WS 5:1 for an exercise on writing a synopsis.

Intended Audience, Recommended Courses, and Placement

The potential users of your case want to know, right up front, if your case is written at a level appropriate for the class they have in mind. A case designed for undergraduates will be too simple for most graduate classes, and a case written for graduate students will be too complex for most undergraduate classes. A case written for an executive education program will not be suitable for either undergraduates (because of the complexity) or for graduate students (because of the inherent assumptions of work experience and job level held by the learners).

You must decide before writing the case which audience is yours and then design the case accordingly. Aside from complexity, other factors that play a role in matching the case with the audience include:

■ Language usage: Cases for undergraduates will avoid business and industry jargon, process and operational acronyms, and overly dense writing style.

■ Expectations of prior knowledge: The content of the case narrative must comport with the anticipated extent of the readers' content and skills knowledge. Undergraduate students rarely study advanced portfolio management, for example, while graduate students have long left behind the basics of designing functional spreadsheets.

■ Length: You will not be surprised to learn that undergraduates prefer shorter cases! If your case is 25 pages of text plus another dozen pages of exhibits, it is too long for most undergraduate students. Length is not a factor in cases for graduate students or executive education programs, although they, too, appreciate a concise presentation of facts.

■ Topical considerations: Again, this is a measure of life experience and academic background. You need to become familiar with the differences between various kinds of post-secondary programmatic offerings (graduate versus undergraduate offerings, for example) in order to calibrate your case properly and provide a useful IM to the instructor.

Once you have determined the academic level of your case, you need to identify one or more courses that might be enhanced by the inclusion of your case as a lesson or a series of lessons. Although it is tempting to suggest your case can work in multiple different courses, this is an unlikely expectation. It is the rare case that can be taught in, say, "Introduction to Management," "Entrepreneurial Finance," "Human Resource Management," "Marketing Communication," and "Business Policy." Select one primary area and perhaps a related secondary area, such as "Principles of Marketing" and "Introduction to Entrepreneurship" or "Financial Management" and "Personal Finance." You can always write another case to cover topics in "Human Resource Management" or "Managerial Accounting." If you have written your case specifically for a course that is uniquely titled at your own institution, such as "Creating Stuff" or "Living Your Work," it pays to use a more generic course title in your IM. Consider "Creativity and Innovation" or "Family Firm Management" instead of the more clever course titles used on campus.

It is also important to note for the user at what point in a given semester the case should be presented. Is this an introductory case—one best suited for use in the first third of the term? Which chapters in commonly used textbooks correlate best to the content of the case? Is this an end-of-term comprehensive case that requires broad topical knowledge on the part of the student? Is it a brief end-of-chapter style case to be used after a chapter devoted to a particular skill? The more information you can provide for the potential user, the more likely your case will be adopted broadly.

WS 5:2 will help you design the section on intended audience, recommended courses, and placement.

Learning Objectives

One key to designing a compelling, useful, and marketable case is a clear description of student takeaways, known more widely as Learning Objectives. These describe in detail what you want *students* to learn. Please note that these are **not** teaching objectives (the concepts that the *instructors* want to teach). Cases are the core of student-centered learning; therefore, the objectives must be focused on student outcomes.

Learning Objectives Describe Actions

This is your opportunity to state unequivocally what students should be able to *do* after analyzing the case you have written. Perhaps you want them to "identify the stages of life-cycle development of a small business." Perhaps you want them to "apply stakeholder analysis to a toxic waste site decision." Perhaps you want them to "design a program to implement organizational change in a multinational corporation." Each of these instances requires that students *do* something; there is some output required.

Learning Objectives Are Measurable

This demand for measurability can present a greater challenge than you might think. The evaluative words we use so often are rarely measurable (*easy, clear, large,* and *well written* are all understandable in comparison to something else, but as objective measures, they fail). According to the National Accrediting Agency for Clinical Laboratory Studies, "The following verbs cannot be measured or are redundant. They should be avoided when writing objectives: able to, shows appreciation for, awareness of, capable of, comprehend, conscious of, familiar with, shows interest in, knows, has knowledge of, learns, memorizes, understands, will be able to" (Waller, 2011). So what does the prohibition of these words leave us with? They leave us a necessity for specificity.

Learning Objectives Are Specific

We are left with the onus of focusing precisely on our purpose in writing a case. Bloom's Taxonomy suggests that skills in the cognitive domain center on knowledge, comprehension, and critical thinking. *Knowledge* deals with issues of recall, *comprehension* with issues of understanding, and *critical thinking* with the more advanced cognitive processes of application of knowledge, analysis of causes, synthesis of new alternatives, and evaluation of actions taken or judgments expressed. These activities are represented in a six-step hierarchy that begins with knowledge acquisition and moves sequentially through comprehension, application, analysis, synthesis, and evaluation. The six levels can be described in detail by using words that spell out exactly what we want to quantify: verbs such as *define, identify, estimate, paraphrase, compute, construct, prepare, illustrate, outline, compare, explain,* and *justify* require specificity in their usage.

In the interest of full disclosure, I love Bloom's Taxonomy. Yes, I know there are more current taxonomies, more modern expressions of Bloom's basic hierarchy of learning (Anderson and Krathwohl is one such current description), and more jargon-laden popular models, but I don't care. I love Bloom's Taxonomy the way I love tomato soup and a grilled cheese sandwich when I'm sick—just because it feels good. Benjamin Bloom's landmark *Taxonomy of Educational Objectives* has made pedagogical life easier for several generations of academics, and I strongly recommend you put it to work for you in your case writing activities. Here's how:

1. Visit some of the more credible websites that feature Bloom's work. You will find several helpful handouts that connect logical action words with the various levels of cognitive development to help you structure your own objectives. Try some of these:

   ■ Overbaugh and Schultz (2011) at http://www.stanleyteacherprep. org/uploads/2/3/3/0/23305258/blooms_new_handout.pdf (accessed November 9, 2016)

   ■ Forehand (2005) at http://epltt.coe.uga.edu/index.php?title=Bloom %27s_Taxonomy (accessed November 9, 2016)

   ■ Heer (2011) at www.celt.iastate.edu/teaching/RevisedBlooms1.html (accessed November 10, 2011)

2. Review your case. What was your initial goal in writing this case? Match that goal to a set of Learning Objectives developed after looking at the preceding websites. Do your Learning Objectives work in the context of Bloom's Taxonomy? If not, reevaluate the language in which you express your learning goals to fit more comfortably with Bloom's clear and succinct language.

3. When you design your Discussion Questions, be sure that each question relates to one or more of your Learning Objectives and that you have each of your objectives covered by one or more Discussion Questions.

Is it difficult to write solid Learning Objectives? Yes, it is. But once you get a good grasp of the goals behind writing them, you will find it a most worthwhile activity.

Practice writing Learning Objectives using WS 5:3.

Discussion Questions

The goal of the Discussion Questions is to focus student analysis and guide the classroom discussion in your chosen direction. These questions derive from the Learning Objectives. To reiterate, each Learning Objective should connect with one or more questions; each question, in turn, must relate to one or more of the Learning Objectives. (See WS 5:4 for a system that facilitates matching the Learning Objectives with the Discussion Questions.)

Discussion Questions have three primary characteristics:

■ They are open-ended; that is, they cannot be answered with a simple "yes" or "no."

■ They are analytical; they require students to think critically about the implications and consequences of various courses of action.

■ They pose a solvable problem that is neither too difficult nor too simple for the level of the students in your class.

The answers to Discussion Questions must be found within the text of the case; you may not include in the IM any additional material that does not appear within the case itself. If you discover that you cannot answer a given question from the case as it stands, you'll need to make some changes to the text. Consult the section titled "Answering Discussion Questions," which appears later in this chapter.

I call all those questions that have no answers grounded in facts from a case "Crystal Ball Questions." Some examples:

■ What will the CEO do?

■ How much profit will result from the introduction of a new product?

■ How popular will the new ISP be?

■ Why did the manager behave as she did?

These are interesting questions. Unfortunately, we would have to be mind readers to answer some of them and seers to answer the others. There are no facts—either in a case itself or available on the World Wide Web—that will tell us the future. There is no way we can peer inside the head of any of the characters in our cases to explain their motivations or actions. I know this and you know this. Yet, we sometimes succumb to the temptation to ask "Crystal Ball Questions."

Here's my advice on avoiding the tendency to slip into fortune-telling: Make a list of the questions you want to ask about your case, but do not answer them yet. Take the list to school and ask one of your colleagues to identify the specific data needed to answer the questions. (If you can get your students to do this, so much the better.) Then, take that list of elements back to your case and make sure that all the specified material appears somewhere in the case. If certain information is missing and you cannot add it into the case without compromising the flow of the prose, change the question. You can rewrite these same "Crystal Ball Questions" (as I have done in the following list) to make them answerable by the mortals who use our cases. For example:

■ If you were the CEO, what would you do? Why?

■ What is the potential profit that could result from the introduction of the new product? How would you calculate this forecast?

■ How can you measure the potential popularity of the new ISP? What data would you look for? Where can you find it?

■ What are some potential reasons that the manager behaved as she did? Support your answers with theory.

Suddenly, the student answers become richer, the learning becomes clearer and easier to identify, and the transferability of the response is improved greatly.

Teaching Strategies

Some cases are best taught by asking students the Discussion Questions; other, more complex cases lend themselves to specific teaching strategies and student preparation. You can find a complete discussion of teaching strategies in Module 8, but for the purposes of this section of the IM you should focus on two main topics: case preparation and teaching methods.

Case Preparation

Case Preparation relates to things that must happen *for students* before the case can be discussed. For example, what must students have learned before being assigned your case? You alluded to this in the second element of the IM, when you identified the placement of the case within the term and the books/chapters that relate best to the use of the case. Now is the time to be more specific, as in the following examples:

■ Students should have learned three different motivational theories.

■ Students should have developed a high comfort level with income statements and balance sheets.

■ Students should be familiar with the differences between teleological and deontological perspectives.

Equally important is the need to make sure that students have had the appropriate academic exposure to foundational concepts. Once again, specifics are key. Provide the full assignment:

■ Prior to class, review the chapters in your text on Maslow, Herzberg, and Vroom.

■ Read Chapter 7 in your accounting text and complete Exercises 4 and 7 on p. 278.

■ Write a two-page, double-spaced summary that outlines the differences between teleology and deontology. Be sure to include examples.

Teaching Methods

Teaching Methods is a broad term that relates to guidance and tips you'll be providing *the instructor* before teaching your case. You need to make two decisions at this time. The first is your recommendation for how students will gain the most from the case. Consider the following:

■ Is a lecture format appropriate? If so, provide the lecture outline in your IM.

■ Is a traditional three-board format your recommendation? If so, provide the board outlines.

■ Do you have a creative exercise to suggest? Provide the full instructions.

Your second decision involves ensuring that students will derive the planned benefits from your case. Again, specificity matters in terms of the clarity of your expectations. Sometimes, this can come in the form of follow-up assignments, a clearly outlined debriefing method, sharing the epilogue (see the section "Epilogue") with the class and leading a discussion about it, or some other means of confirming that students have learned what you want them to learn.

A great way to start a case discussion is through the use of **Icebreaker Questions**. Icebreaker Questions differ from Discussion Questions in their simplicity and in the near-total guarantee that students will be able to answer them:

■ How many of you have eaten pizza three or more times in the last two weeks?

■ Did you order something to drink with that? What did you order?

■ How much was your individual check the last time you had pizza? Raise your hand if it was less than $5.00, more than $10.00.

■ Who here owns a car? How much do you spend on gas weekly: less than $20.00, more than $35.00?

Questions like these will set the stage for an engaged classroom discussion. WS 5:5 provides a format for the section on Teaching Strategies.

Literature Review, Theory, and Recommended Readings

Remember the earlier examples of the fledgling users who would most likely benefit from the information in your Instructor's Manual? Here is where you get a chance to show true scholarly generosity—by sharing your extensive subject matter knowledge with your peers.

If the literature review or theory discussion is straightforward, as in several of the examples already given, it is a simple matter to outline basic theory. If your case is about motivation, a several-paragraph outline of the perspectives of three theorists will suffice. If your case is about a topic that requires considerable elucidation, you may have to write a bit more. A brief differentiation between teleology and deontology demands a set of clarifying examples in order for students to apply the theory properly. Performing this simple service for your colleagues will save a lot of time, effort, and frustration for instructors who are prepping this case quickly or who are unfamiliar with the theories.

Another way to handle this section in your IM is to prepare an annotated bibliography that provides full citations and a short description of the referenced material. This can be very useful for instructors who wish to assign additional readings to their classes or for instructors who want to learn more about a given topic before teaching your case.

Some case writers incorporate theory into the answers to the Discussion Questions (see next subhead), but this is not as helpful to instructors and may mislead less experienced instructors into anticipating that students will answer the questions with the same depth that you have provided.

The literature review section sometimes includes additional background material (often designed as a useful student handout should instructors wish to pursue the topic further with the class). This background material may take the form of an advanced industry note, a technical addendum, or an unfamiliar or less popularized business theory. These serve the same purpose as the exhibits that you prepared for the case itself—extended knowledge and information to be used as instructors choose.

Answering Discussion Questions

When writing the answers to Discussion Questions, you need to put yourself in the students' shoes. The questions should be answered from their perspective, using language *they* are likely to use rather than the traditionally more sophisticated style seen in academic writing. Two important points to remember when writing the answers to Discussion Questions:

■ Use the same language and complexity you would use to answer these questions for your grandmother (assuming your grandmother is not also a professor). Avoid writing, "A good student answer will include a discussion of several methods of financial analysis." Instead, provide the financial analysis.

■ Present realistic expectations of what an instructor might receive from a student. Even an A student is not going to answer the questions as fully as you would, but a less complete answer may still be acceptable for discussion purposes.

If you answer the questions and then discover that you based your answers on information that does not appear in the case, you have two choices: either go back to the case and incorporate the relevant information, or amend your answer in the IM. In order for students to perform a credible case analysis, they need information, facts, and sufficient understanding of the protagonist's past behavior to be able to anticipate his future actions or preferences.

It is often helpful to provide an A/C split in your answers, where "A" represents what an A answer might look like and "C" represents what a somewhat less inspired but still acceptable C answer might look like. Write out sample answers that meet the specifications for each grade. Users of your Instructor's Manual will thank you for making the effort to help them identify appropriate expectations.

WS 5:6 models the correct language and complexity to answer Discussion Questions for our sample case.

Epilogue

Students always want to know "what happened." At the end of every case discussion, even the most sophisticated attendees in executive education programs ask what the protagonists actually did. This is a natural response to the "tell me a story" style of learning that case writing encourages; so, as good storytellers, we must wrap up the case in an epilogue in the Instructor's Manual.

The epilogue provides information about the aftermath of the events in the case. It describes the decision that the protagonist made and allows students to compare their own recommendations to the actions actually taken. It completes the story and brings closure to the problem under analysis. It is one of the easiest pieces to write because it is a simple recitation of factual information, and it also provides closure for the case writer. Once the epilogue is written, you are done!

The epilogue brings the case up to date as of the time of publication, but, naturally, it can be updated further when necessary. This is a good assignment to provide for the analysis of classic cases—first assign the case and then assign the case update. More on this in Module 9.

Go to WS 5:7 for a sample epilogue on which to model your own.

Note: Before you move on to the next module, be sure to complete WS 5:8, Case Writing Assignment 4.

⦾ ⦾ ⦾ ⦾ ⦾

References and Readings

Anderson, L.W., and D.R. Krathwohl, eds. (2001). *A Taxonomy for Learning, Teaching, and Assessing: A Revision of Bloom's Taxonomy of Educational Objectives.* New York: Longman.

Bloom, B.S., M.D. Engelhart, E.J. Furst, W.H. Hill, and D.R. Krathwohl, eds. (1956). *Taxonomy of Educational Objectives: The Classification of Educational Goals.* Vol. 1: *Cognitive Domain.* New York: Longmans, Green.

Forehand, M. (2005). "Bloom's Taxonomy: Original and Revised." In *Emerging Perspectives on Learning, Teaching, and Technology*, ed. M. Orey. http://epltt. coe.uga.edu/index.php?title=Bloom%27s_Taxonomy (accessed November 9, 2016).

Heer, R. (2011). "A Model of Learning Objectives." Center for Excellence in Learning and Teaching, Iowa State University. Based on *A Taxonomy for Learning, Teaching, and Assessing: A Revision of Bloom's Taxonomy of Educational Objectives*, ed. L.W. Anderson and D.R. Krathwohl. New York: Longman, 2001. www. celt.iastate.edu/teaching/RevisedBlooms1.html (accessed November 10, 2011).

Overbaugh, R.C., and L. Schultz. (2011). "Bloom's Taxonomy." Department of Teaching and Learning, Old Dominion University. http://www.stanleyteach erprep.org/uploads/2/3/3/0/23305258/blooms_new_handout.pdf (accessed November 9, 2016).

Vega, G. (2010). "Crystal Ball Questions and Assumptions of Knowledge." *The CASE Journal* 6, no. 2 (Spring). http://www.emeraldinsight.com/doi/abs/10.1108/ TCJ-06-2010-B001?journalCode=tcj (accessed November 9, 2016).

———. (2011). "Dispelling Confusion about Learning Objectives." *The CASE Journal* 8, no. 1 (Fall). http://emeraldinsight.com/doi/pdfplus/10.1108/TCJ-08-2011-B001 (accessed November 10, 2016).

Waller, K.V. (2011). "Writing Instructional Objectives." National Accrediting Agency for Clinical Laboratory Studies, Announcements. http://www.naacls.org/ docs/announcement/writing-objectives.pdf (accessed November 10, 2011).

● ● ● ● ●

Worksheets

WS 5:1 Writing a Synopsis

WS 5:2 The Audience, Course, and Placement

WS 5:3 Learning Objectives

WS 5:4 Discussion Questions

WS 5:5 Teaching Strategies

WS 5:6 Answering Discussion Questions

WS 5:7 Writing the Epilogue

WS 5:8 Case Writing Assignment 4

WS 5:1

Writing a Synopsis

Following the excerpt provided, draft a synopsis for the Instructor's Manual for your own completed case.

Characteristics	Example	Your Synopsis
■ A brief overview ■ Critical events ■ Research methodology ■ Main problem focus	Ken Roberts, the owner of an independent automotive repair business in a small coastal city in New England, arrived early for work one Monday to discover an unscheduled and unknown vehicle awaiting repair in his shop's driveway. Ken needed to develop a tactical plan for dealing with the owner and the potential repair of the vehicle, mindful of his reputation as one of the best independent shops in the area. As a service marketer, Ken realized that the power of word-of-mouth recommendations could be just as crucial to his business's continued success as the high-quality repair work he provided his customers. Students are challenged to evaluate this situation and provide recommendations within the context of the marketing of services. This is a field-researched case. The author had full access to the owner of the business, meeting with him on numerous occasions.	

WS 5:2

The Audience, Course, and Placement

Following the excerpt provided, draft a description of the audience for your case, the course in which it should be used, and at what point in the term to use it.

Characteristics	Example	Your Sample
■ Who is the audience? ■ Which courses are most suitable? ■ When in the term should the case be used? ■ Which text(s) work well with the case?	The case is designed for undergraduate audiences in the business curriculum. Within marketing, it is well suited for use in a services marketing course or a small business course. The case has been tested in the author's upper-level undergraduate services marketing course, which consists of marketing and other business management majors. It should be presented midway through the semester. If used in a marketing principles course, the case works well in conjunction with the services marketing chapter found in most marketing principles texts (for example, D. Grewal and M. Levy, *Marketing*, 2d ed. [Boston: McGraw-Hill/Irwin, 2010], Chapter 12).	

WS 5:3

Learning Objectives

Following the example provided, draft a learning objective for your case at EACH level of Bloom's Taxonomy.

Level	Example	Your Learning Objectives
Knowledge acquisition	Connect a series of unrelated actions in a narrative to a set of marketing theories.	
Comprehension	Identify how consumers develop expectations for service provision, how consumer input helps businesses improve service quality and develop quality in services, and how they create a "zone of tolerance" for gaps between their expectations and perceptions of service delivery.	
Application	Apply consumer segmentation to a specific service industry.	
Analysis	Analyze the additional marketing mix elements that are specific to services (people, process, and physical evidence).	
Synthesis	Develop a tactical business decision regarding a specific consumer service request.	
Evaluation	Compare available options to potential outcomes.	

WS 5:4

Discussion Questions

Following the example provided, draft a discussion question for your case that relates to EACH learning objective.

Learning Objective	Discussion Question	Your Question
Knowledge: Connect a series of unrelated actions in a narrative to a set of marketing theories.	How is a customer likely to evaluate "quality" in the marketing of services—generally and specifically—with respect to automotive service?	
Comprehension: Identify how consumers develop expectations for service provision, how consumers help businesses service quality, and how they create a "zone of tolerance" for gaps between their expectations and perceptions of service delivery.	For typical auto repair customers, what are their expectations likely to be, and what is their "zone of tolerance" when things don't go as expected? What specific consumer segments exist with respect to auto servicing, and how do their "zones of tolerance" differ?	
Application: Apply consumer segmentation to a specific service industry.	Does Matthew appear to be a typical auto repair customer? What evidence do you find in the case to support your position?	
Analysis: Analyze the additional marketing mix elements that are specific to services (people, process, and physical evidence).	Which elements of the marketing mix (beyond a focus on consumers) do you find in the case? How might these affect service issues?	
Synthesis: Develop a tactical business decision regarding a specific consumer service request.	How should Ken proceed with the 1996 Volvo? Should he attempt the repairs or decline the work? Explain how he should deal with Matthew.	
Evaluation: Compare available options to potential outcomes.	As an independent auto repair provider, how can Ken effectively manage customer expectations? How can he apply the "service recovery" concept to enhance customer satisfaction?	

WS 5:5

Teaching Strategies

Following the example provided, design the section on teaching strategies for your case.

Strategy	Assignment	Your Sample
Pre-assignment	Students should understand customer requirements and gap analysis. Assign V.A. Zeithaml, M.J. Bitner, and D.D. Gremler, *Services Marketing: Integrating Customer Focus Across the Firm*, 5th ed. (Boston: McGraw-Hill/ Irwin, 2009), Chapters 4 and 5 on customer expectations and perceptions, and Chapter 7 on building customer relationships.	
Icebreaker questions	Who owns a car? How often do you take it to the shop? How do you decide which mechanic to go to? What do you usually spend on a tune-up?	
Exercise or activity	Divide the class into groups of three. Each group should have one person playing Ken, one person playing Matthew, and one observer. Role-play the conversation between Ken and Matthew. Have the players extend the conversation beyond the circumstances of the case. The observer should take notes about how Ken and Matthew conducted themselves, what worked well, and what did not work well. Debrief in the large group after small group discussion.	
Lecture focus or three-board discussion	One end board should be dedicated to facts about the case. These should include XYZ (be specific in your own section). The other end board should be dedicated to elements of service marketing theory that relate to this situation. The central board should connect the *facts* from one end board with *theory* from the other end board and list possible actions that Ken could take. Discussion about the potential consequences of each should follow.	
Final debriefing	Read the epilogue to the class. Ask the class if Ken made the right decision for the customer and/or for his business.	

WS 5:6

Answering Discussion Questions

Using the abbreviated example provided and drawing from your questions in WS 4:4, answer each discussion question for your case FULLY.

Discussion Question	Excerpted Answer	Your Sample
How is a customer likely to evaluate "quality" in the marketing of services— generally and specifically— with respect to automotive service?	In Exhibit 2 of the case, the information from consumers suggests that customers want honest, competent mechanics who can repair their cars the first time at a reasonable price. Other key characteristics they look for in mechanics include (1) a willingness to explain (in lay terms) the nature of the repairs their vehicles need, (2) a reputation for treating male and female customers the same way, and (3) safe neighborhoods/locations for their shops. Timeliness of repair, convenient hours of operation, and proximity to public transportation were also important, but to a lesser degree than the other characteristics.	
For typical auto repair customers, what are their expectations likely to be, and what is their "zone of tolerance" when things don't go as expected? What specific consumer segments exist with respect to auto servicing, and how do their "zones of tolerance" differ?	Vehicle owners want their car fixed right the first time, for the least possible cost, and with the least inconvenience and disruption to their daily lives. You can distinguish between those consumers who turn to an authorized dealer for servicing and those who patronize independently owned repair shops, gas stations, or franchised independent automotive service facilities.	
Does Matthew appear to be a typical auto repair customer? What evidence do you find in the case to support your position?	Matthew appears to be typical in his overall lack of knowledge about cars, but he is remarkably atypical in his willingness to simply leave his vehicle in front of an unfamiliar garage, toss the keys through the office mail slot, and expect that all will go according to his best interests.	

Which elements of the marketing mix (beyond a focus on consumers) do you find in the case? How might these affect service issues?	Ken continues with his normal activities and scheduled appointments until he has some free time to figure out how to handle the mystery car.	
How should Ken proceed with the 1996 Volvo? Should he attempt the repairs or decline the work? Explain how he should deal with Matthew.	The car may have appeared on his doorstep because of another shop's already having diagnosed the problems. We don't know, and part of the mechanic's sixth sense is to recognize these cases before they become a problem to him and cause customer dissatisfaction with his service. Time spent in this way may or may not be billed to the owner. It is more likely to be billed if the mechanic wants to fix the vehicle but the owner walks away. It's likely to be absorbed in the labor cost of doing business if the mechanic wants to fix the vehicle and gets the job. Note, however, that it is sometimes in a shop's best interest to decline work on certain cars.	
As an independent auto repair provider, how can Ken effectively manage customer expectations? How can he apply the "service recovery" concept to enhance customer satisfaction?	Ken has a customer base in a small community where both good and bad word-of-mouth recommendations travel quickly. A successful service provider is judged not only on his mechanical ability but also on his merits as a trusted personal adviser. Service recovery comes into play when the service delivery fails to meet the prior expectations of the customer. In the auto repair business, each customer encounter has the potential to either dazzle customers or send them running to find another service provider.	

WS 5:7

Writing the Epilogue

Following the excerpt provided, draft an epilogue for the Instructor's Manual for your own completed case.

Characteristics	Example	Your Sample
■ Summarizes case through a recitation of factual information ■ Completes the story ■ Provides the protagonist's decision ■ Updates the case when necessary	Ken test-drove the vehicle to verify the owner's complaints. He did not observe the "transmission slipping" as described by the owner. The "check engine light" was still on, and, indeed, the headlights were not working. Ken spent about half an hour assessing the car's electrical system, especially in the area of the transmission mode switches (Winter-Sport-Economy "W-S-E" mode switch). He observed rust in the area of the switch contacts, presumably from water that had leaked through the open sunroof directly onto the switch assembly in the center console. From the vehicle's condition and the owner's note, Ken had a feeling that another mechanic had already attempted to fix the various issues with the car but was unsuccessful. He suspected it was a "problem car" with many hidden defects. Ken called Matthew, the owner, to decline the job. He told Matthew he was unsure of the extent of the vehicle's problems and suggested the car might need considerable work before it could once again be considered a safe and reliable form of transportation. Matthew removed the car the next day. Ken did not charge Matthew for his time or expert opinion. As of the date the case was written (Fall 2009), Ken had not seen the car or its owner again.	

WS 5:8

Case Writing Assignment 4

This assignment will result in a complete draft of your Instructor's Manual.

1. Using the examples that you developed in the exercises in this module, extend each of the following sections until the IM is ready for testing, along with the case.

   ■ Overview/Synopsis/Abstract
   ■ Intended Audience, Recommended Courses, and Placement
   ■ Learning Objectives
   ■ Discussion Questions
   ■ Teaching Strategies
   ■ Literature Review, Theory, and Recommended Readings
   ■ Answers to Discussion Questions
   ■ Epilogue

2. Test the case in your own classes, if possible, and adjust the case and/or IM based on your students' responses.
3. Now, ask a colleague to test the case in his or her class, using your IM for guidance. Request permission to attend the class and observe how the discussion proceeds (without identifying yourself to the students as the author). You will learn a great deal watching someone else teach your case.
4. Rewrite based on the input you have received.
5. Prepare to submit your case to a journal or other outlet (see Module 7).

Module 6

• • • • •

Transforming Research Cases into Teaching Cases

The qualitative methods we use to conduct research often result in academic case studies. These case studies are "research cases." This module will help you transform those research cases into powerful "teaching cases" and will help you bring your valuable research directly into your classroom.

In research cases, the "answers" appear directly within the case studies themselves. In fact, the answers are threaded so tightly into the fabric of the case story that it can be a daunting process to unwrap the two. Instead of providing the answers within the case, this module provides a method for unwrapping the academic research case and repurposing it as a teaching case.

• • • • •

Why Consider Transforming Your Published Research into a Teaching Case?

As a qualitative researcher, you might like to transform your academic research case studies into teaching cases for three main reasons, one of which serves students, the second of which serves the institution, and the third of which serves you as author.

The first reason to transform your academic research case into a teaching case is for pedagogical purposes—to facilitate student learning. You have conducted some important research and want to share it with as many audiences as you can. Your peer academic audience will read your case study in journals or hear it at a conference. Students, especially undergraduate students, do not attend conferences nor do they read academic journals. Nonetheless, your research may be important for them. A teaching case is the most direct and practical method of sharing what you have learned with your students. If you teach only two classes, you are likely to introduce your research to more people than might otherwise become aware of it in a year or more.

The second motivation for transforming your research into a teaching tool is to be able to respond to the new AACSB standards and show the *impact* of your work. When we talk about research articles published in journals, impact is generally measured based on citations and journal quality. However, it can be more difficult to determine the impact of teaching tools such as cases because cases are not generally cited in research articles. When you bring your published case into the classroom and use it to help students learn, you elevate the learning process and can actually show how your research has made an impact on your audience by usage and learning that is measurable. You will be improving the pedagogy of your classroom by making your research accessible as well as strengthening your institution's academic status.

The third reason to transform your research case study into a teaching case is to gain an additional peer-reviewed publication from one single research dataset. This is not only a legitimate goal, but one which is to be applauded as you are clearly pursuing the real objective of scholarship: making learning accessible in as many ways as possible. AACSB and other academic accrediting agencies consider teaching cases valid intellectual contributions primarily because of the instructor's manual that is associated with them, and this instructor's manual incorporates the main learning from your research. The process is self-reinforcing, a virtuous circle.

● ● ● ● ●

The Differences between Academic Research Cases and Teaching Cases

Academic research cases and teaching cases are similar, with the former focused on theory that describes or explains empirical research and the latter focused on practical applications supported by theory. The development processes for each are closely related and the research process for both is the same. The two kinds of writing differ dramatically, however, in terms of purpose and format.

A note up front: If at all possible, the authors of the academic research study and the authors of the teaching case should participate in the interviews, research, analysis, and writing together from the beginning, with the specialist(s) in each type of study taking the lead at the appropriate times (see more about working with colleagues in Module 8: Working with Coauthors). When a teaching case author joins the team after the academic research has been completed, she may have missed some nuance during the data gathering research process that might have provided additional depth to the teaching case. If the author of the academic research case and the author of the teaching case are the same, concerns about nuance disappear.

Despite the usual situation of different authors taking the lead at specific times in the research and writing process, their counterparts have valuable input to provide throughout the development of the project. Particular skills in writing, in pedagogical methods, and in analysis are not reserved for people who have self-identified as case researchers or as case writers. It is important to recognize the contribution of each individual when conducting the transformation of research into teaching.

The Research Goal

Academic research case studies are descriptive analyses of real situations. These analyses test specific theoretical perspectives through hypotheses or create new theory by offering alternative explanations for existing hypotheses. Academic research case studies vary from $N=1$ studies through extensive panel studies or aggregated cases that describe or identify patterns of behavior in terms of social, economic, or fiscal trends. They demonstrate rigorous qualitative research with multiple purposes.

According to R.K. Yin (2014), "Whatever the field of interest, the distinctive need for case study research arises out of the desire to understand complex social phenomena. In brief, a case study allows investigators to focus on a 'case' and retain a real-world perspective—such as in studying individual life cycles, small group behavior, organizational and managerial processes, neighborhood change, school performance, international relations, and the maturation of industries" (4).

In contrast, a teaching case is a story that describes a factual series of actions that occurred in one organization or group, or to one individual, in the past. As a teaching tool, the purpose of a case is either to encourage the reader to make a decision/recommendation for action or to analyze the past action and offer alternative actions for the future. The learning points in a teaching case are generally "disguised" by or embedded in the narrative, or story.

Naumes & Naumes (2012) emphasize the importance of storytelling in the learning process and focus on the value of details to give a story "life, vividness, and memorability" (xviii). Stories help us understand actions, and it is through the actions of protagonists that students learn with TCs. According to Yiannis Gabriel (2000), "stories open valuable windows into the emotional, political, and symbolic lives of organizations . . . we gain access to deeper organizational realities, closely linked to their members' experiences. In this way, stories enable us to study organizational policies, culture, and change in uniquely illuminating ways . . . " (2).

The Research Process

When a qualitative researcher decides to use the academic research case method to collect and analyze empirical evidence, she has probably already identified a possible trend or has noticed a phenomenon that bears further investigation. The researcher is likely to have a hypothesis in mind before beginning the data collection process. Or, if using grounded theory, the researcher is curious about a phenomenon and allows the data to tell the story and the theory to arise from the data collected. The author of an academic case study often does not know ahead of time specifically what she is going to write about.

When an instructor decides to write a teaching case for classroom use, she is frequently motivated by one of two opportunities: a business may have offered open access to its operations, and the instructor likes the idea of taking a good look at this business; or, the instructor wants to provide students with an opportunity to apply theories learned in class and needs a vehicle for such purpose. In developing a teaching case, the author knows in advance what she wants to emphasize.

Not surprisingly, the research processes for these two divergent activities differ in several ways. Nonetheless, the data collected in the two processes are similar and mutually reinforcing. The academic case study requires a structured approach to data collection, whether purely qualitative or mixed method research involving more traditional quantitative techniques. Simply, the academic case researcher may investigate phenomena through observation, participation, the use of various types of survey instruments, or a wide variety of qualitative strategies including ethnography, phenomenology, grounded theory, clinical research, and others (for a full description of these methods, see Denzin & Lincoln, 1998a). In all circumstances, the researcher takes great care to ensure the legitimacy of the research process, the triangulation of data sources, and the awareness of the impact of her own involvement in organizational activities.

The research process for a field-researched teaching case focuses more heavily on observation and interviewing, although it is not uncommon for a participant observer or consultant to write a teaching case once the consulting assignment has been completed. Consultants are mindful of their responsibilities vis-à-vis the client and therefore avoid writing cases about current clients or current situations. Unassociated researchers need have no such compunctions, especially if they are writing from secondary data.

You may use research that you have collected in an academic case research process in a teaching case without too much modification. You have already collected the data, you have undoubtedly heard some interesting stories that can serve to transmit the data to your audience, and you also know the end of the story—what happened after the case protagonists tried out an intervention, a new process, a counterintuitive corporate strategy. You do not have to "go back to the well" for further information, other than to obtain a publication release. If you intend to publish your teaching case, you must be certain to obtain a publication release, an approval granted by the case protagonists in order to indemnify yourself and the publisher against lawsuits brought by a potentially antagonistic case subject (see Module 2: The Research Process).

Language and Technical Differences

Writing conventions in the two case models differ based on the purpose of the study itself. Because an academic research case is reporting and describing a set of phenomena that are of necessity incomplete, researchers often use the present tense as a means of suggesting ongoing change and willingness to entertain alternative explanations of the data presented. These researchers generously supply the reader with opinions, value judgments, evaluations, and ongoing analysis throughout the case study. They invoke various theories and hypothesize explanations of behavior. They carry on a pedagogical conversation with the reader, sharing their own ideas and providing space for the reader to agree with or refute them.

Teaching case writers, however, must use the past tense at all times (except in direct quotes) to indicate the action in the case has been completed and cannot change. This immutability of action is determined by the very description of a teaching case, which emphasizes that the action is in the past, and the role of the reader is either to serve as adviser for future actions or to analyze the described actions. These case writers avoid sharing their opinions or judgments with the reader, although they do provide them in the instructor's manual for the use of the instructor in class. They are careful not to suggest that the thoughts and motivations of the protagonists are transparent; the authors serve as careful and complete reporters of actions, not as analysts of motivations or other unseen forces. They also save that analysis for the instructor's manual. Remember that the instructor's manual is the real scholarly contribution, while the case is the learning vehicle or pedagogical tool (see Module 1: Getting Started).

Unwrapping the Academic Research Case Study

Academic case studies take different forms depending on the kind of data that are being presented. These types may include but not be limited to single-case studies, multiple-case studies, or a combination of the two, and may be reported in a variety of formats and styles. For an academic research case study to be valuable to the academic or practitioner community, it must be significant, complete, consider alternative perspectives, and be timely. (Please see Yin, 2014, Chapter 6 for a full discussion of the presentation of an academic research case.)

Regardless of the form or type selected, an academic case study contains some minor variations of the elements in Table 6.1 (elements drawn from Naumes & Naumes, 2012). WS 6:1 illustrates these with short excerpts from research I published in *The Journal of Management Education* about service learning metaprojects.

Table 6.1 Elements of the Academic Research Case Study

Elements of the Academic Research Case Study	
The title	The title should be informative, directed to the desired audience, and tempting to the potential reader (see Huff, 1999, Chapter 6).
1 Statement of the purpose of the research	This appears in the abstract, the statement of research purpose and hypotheses, or in the introduction and informs the reader of what to expect in the paper.
2 General description of situation being studied	This section lays out the sections to come in the paper and what is included in each section. It provides an anticipatory taste of the study's content.
3 Literature review and its relationship to the specific case	The literature review provides key citations that relate to the specific study in question, rather than providing an overview of all related literature. Restraint is important in this section.
4 Research hypotheses or conceptual model	What are you testing? What are you building? This is the section that presents this material.
5 Connect study to hypotheses	This section develops logically from the preceding section. It explains why you have chosen the specific field of inquiry and how the case in question relates to the hypotheses.
6 Data that support or fail to support hypotheses based on research questions	This is the basic presentation of data which can take many different formats.
7 Statement of methodology and data collection process	How did you go about performing your research? How did you validate your data? This is where you describe in full the research field, the collection process, the means of triangulation, and other relevant processes.
8 Analytical methodology	What means did you use to analyze your data? Was it an inductive or deductive process? Some tactics to include in this section are the processes of identifying patterns and themes, contrasting and comparing situations, and establishing coding protocols.
9 Analysis of the research	This is the meat of the academic research case study—what did you find? Were your hypotheses supported? Does your conceptual model work based on your findings?
10 Summary, conclusions, and limitations of the study	This section is a restatement of research objectives, how the case study limitations may provide boundaries for generalizability of the findings, and a re-emphasis on the specific links of theory to the study.
11 Results of the analysis and final outcomes	This is a reiteration of findings and suggestions for future research.

Unwrapping the Teaching Case

Compare the preceding with the comparable elements of a teaching case. A teaching case can also take many formats, depending on the learning objectives you design. Regardless of length (varying from the boxed one-paragraph incidents that appear in textbooks and end-of-chapter two-to-three page cases through the extensive 15–20 page teaching cases with multiple exhibits that many publishers provide) or general goal (decision-focused or illustrative/analytical), all teaching cases contain most of the elements described in Table 6.2. It is important to know that, even though the instructor's manual is not published for general distribution, it is considered an integral part of the teaching case.

Although I have supplied descriptive headings for the various teaching case sections, these headings do not appear within the case itself. Instead, the generally accepted protocol is to use informative subheads in the teaching case. For example, instead of using the subhead, "The company story/history," a more appropriate subhead in a case would be simply, "XYZ Company." The subheads do appear in the instructor's manual (see Module 3: Writing the Case and Module 5: Building the Instructor's Manual for a full description of teaching cases and instructor's manual presentation). The excerpts that appear in WS 6:2 are drawn from a teaching case that was developed out of the academic research case described in the previous example.

Table 6.2 Elements of the Teaching Case and Instructor's Manual

Teaching Case	
The title	The title should be descriptive, appealing, and should include the name of the company (if a public company). It may also include the topic or the key decision to be made.
1 The opening hook	This is the material that engages the reader. It is a forerunner of the case problem and is meant to draw the reader in.
2 The company story/history	This section provides the context for the case, including corporate background and general history. This section requires rich description.
3 The industry	The situation appears here within a broader context and provides a factual framework in which to embed the company described earlier.
4 The actors	Because teaching cases are about the problems that people in organizations experience, it is important to identify protagonists with whom the reader can identify. Readers will gladly help to solve the problems that people have, but are less inclined to solve problems that "organizations" have.
5 The situation	This is the actual case narrative—the story as you wish to tell it. It must be true and accurate; however, it should not be dull or boring.

Teaching Case	
6　Additional information	Some case writers like to include additional information that is not relevant to the case "solution" in order to give the reader an opportunity to differentiate between the necessary facts and the tangential ones.
7　The closing hook	If this is a decision case, the protagonist will conclude this section with some kind of request for assistance. It will be clear to the reader what kind of help the character needs. If this is an illustrative case, the protagonist's actions and, possibly, the outcomes of those actions will be described and will generate a response in the reader.
8　Exhibits or appendices	These include the data that are necessary for analysis but that do not fit within the case itself (spreadsheets, maps, organization charts, timelines, and similar items).
Instructor's Manual	
9　Overview/synopsis/abstract	This element is the hook for the instructor and provides a high-level perspective on the teaching case.
10　Intended audience/ recommended courses, and placement	This section describes who the case was written for, when in the term to offer it, and the topics/texts with which it works well.
11　Learning objectives	This is a description of student takeaways—what the students who are assigned the case will be able to do after having read it.
12　Discussion questions	These appear twice in the Instructor's Manual, once in a simple list and later with full answers.
13　Teaching strategies	Any unique methods you have developed for teaching the case, including case preparation for students and teaching methods for instructors.
14　Literature review, theory, and/or recommended readings	This is an outline of the basic theory that your teaching case illustrates, including references that relate specifically to the situation. It is not an extensive literature review, but rather a simple guide for the instructor.
15　Answers to the discussion questions	These should appear as a student would present them to help the instructor develop reasonable expectations.
16　Epilogue	What happened after the situation ended? What did the protagonist actually decide to do? What were the results of that decision?

You will note that *most* (but not all) of the material from the academic research case finds its way into either the teaching case or the instructor's manual. You will further note that *some* of the material in the teaching case does not appear in the academic research case. Refer to Table 6.3 for a generic look at how the two types of cases treat similar information.

Table 6.3 Moving from Academic Research Case Studies to Teaching Cases: Parallel Elements at a Glance

Purpose or Explanation of Section/Element	Research Case	Teaching Case	Instructor's Manual
1 Engage the reader	Statement of the purpose of the research	The "hook"	Abstract
2 Usage information	General description of situation being studied	Company story/ history The actors	Audience/courses/ placement in term
3 Describe relevant research, theory, and recommended readings	Literature review and its relationship to the specific situation		Literature review/ theory discussion
4 Narrative	Research hypotheses or conceptual model	The situation or problem (story)	Learning objectives
5 Contextualize and enrich the case study situation	Connect RC to hypotheses	Industry information Exhibits	
6 Focus the analysis	Data that support or fail to support hypotheses based on research questions	Additional (peripheral) information	Discussion questions
7 Frame the research method and establish validity	Statement of methodology and data collection process		Statement of methodology and data collection process
8 Ways to look at the situation	Analytical methodology		Pedagogy/teaching strategy
9 Application of theory	Analysis of the research		Answers to discussion questions
10 Provide closure and perspective (reprise purpose)	Summary, conclusions, and limitations of the RC	Closing hook	
11 What happened?	Results of the analysis and final outcomes		Epilogue

● ● ● ● ●

How to Get from the Academic Research Case to the Teaching Case

Getting from research case to teaching case is a five-step process, as described here:

Step 1: Select an appropriate research case to transform.

There are several "must-haves" to make the research case transformable:

■ The research must have an interesting backstory that may or may not be included in the research case as it has been published. Only you, as the original author/researcher, will know the backstory and be able to reflect on it.

- There should be at least one narrative-worthy anecdote that can drive the learning experience. This anecdote should appear in the hook to interest the reader and engage his attention.

- You must be willing to excerpt one learning-worthy element from your original work. Many of us believe that our work is gold—untouchable. It is not. Some of it is more interesting than the rest, and we must pan for this gold amid the academic dross.

- There must be an identifiable protagonist, as we know that students will work hard to help a person in trouble, but don't care nearly as much about the positive or negative outcomes for a company.

- You must be able to get permission from the company to pursue the rewrite of the original data. If you had permission to publish research data, you still need permission for this very different product. It is your only protection against legal action. Sample release forms are available from your institution's IRB (see Module 2: The Research Process).

Step 2: Identify the differences between the Research Case and Teaching Case

As described throughout this module, research and teaching cases differ in all respects except for the focus on facts without embellishment or creation. Whether written for research or for teaching, cases are "true." I cannot emphasize enough that teaching cases adhere to facts. Do not include invented protagonists, even if they are convenient literary devices. Do not invent situations or dialogue that are not approved by the original "actors."

Step 3: Deconstruct Your Academic Research Study

Following the format and explanations in this module, deconstruct the elements of your research case and identify where they will fit most comfortably into a teaching case and instructor's manual. Using WS 6:3, complete the blank column after reviewing the elements in both types of cases.

Sometimes it pays to take on an additional author to help with this process. This additional author should have a more distanced perspective and special skill, either in writing the instructor's manual or in bringing life to the research data. It can be very difficult to give up some ownership of one's work, but this can make all the difference between a so-so teaching case and a compelling and publishable one.

Step 4: Building the Teaching Case and Instructor's Manual

If possible, write these two pieces concurrently, using the template in WS 6:4. First, identify the learning objectives for the teaching case. Then, fill in the elements in the worksheet. Be sure to design the teaching case so that it addresses the learning objectives. It is important to be aware that you already know too much about the company, the situation, the actors, and the "solutions" to be fully objective, but do try to keep it fairly simple for the reader. You cannot possibly incorporate everything you know into the teaching case and still have a product from which students can learn without drowning in data.

Step 5: Test the Teaching Case

This is a critical step in the case transformation project. It is the only way you will get the honest feedback you need for improvement and refining the case. If you cannot test the case in your own classroom, ask a colleague to help you out (and allow you to sit in the back of the room while the case is being taught). In fact, having someone else test the case for you is likely to provide you with more information than teaching it yourself because the testing instructor will not have the benefit of the "inside information" that you have not included in the case but are tempted to use in class. Any changes that are needed will become apparent to you quickly. Before you submit the new case to a journal, fix those weak spots in the case and instructor's manual.

● ● ● ● ●

Wrapping It Up

Teaching cases are valuable pedagogical tools because they expose students to a variety of real-life situations and allow them to analyze and create business solutions within the classroom environment. Your research cases can be a rich source of teaching cases, providing you with an opportunity to develop two or more scholarly products from the same body of research. The process of deconstructing a research case and then constructing a teaching case will also provide you additional insights that can benefit your students.

The value of this work is not only the opportunity for you to earn credit for two publications from the same dataset; it also helps to satisfy your scholarship requirements. Moreover, it can help to achieve the publication "impact" requirement for AACSB accreditation. Further, it facilitates student learning, and increases your level of credibility with your students by teaching what you have learned in the field. Finally, it will also help research faculty to bring the research about which they are passionate directly into their classroom.

• • • • •

References and Readings

Some of the material in this module was drawn from Vega, Simendinger, & Thomason (2015).

Bansal, P., and K. Corley. (2011). "The Coming of Age for Qualitative Research: Embracing the Diversity of Qualitative Methods." *Academy of Management Journal* 54, no. 2, 233–237.

Denzin, N.K., and Y.S. Lincoln. (1998a). *Strategies of Qualitative Inquiry.* Thousand Oaks, CA: Sage Publications.

Denzin, N.K., and Y.S. Lincoln. (1998b). *Collecting and Interpreting Qualitative Materials.* Thousand Oaks, CA: Sage Publications.

Gabriel, Y. (2000). *Storytelling in Organizations: Facts, Fictions, and Fantasies.* Oxford, UK: Oxford University Press.

Huff, A.S. (1999). *Writing for Scholarly Publication.* Thousand Oaks, CA: Sage Publications.

Meyer, H. (1998). "My Enemy, My Friend." *Journal of Business Strategy* 19, 42.

Morris, M.H., A. Kocak., and A. Ozer. (2007). "Coopetition as a Small Business Strategy: Implications for Performance." *Journal of Small Business Strategy* 18, no. 1, 35–36.

Naumes, W., and M. Naumes. (2012). *The Art & Craft of Case Writing, 3/e.* Armonk, NY: M.E. Sharpe.

Thomason, S.J., E. Simendinger., and D. Kiernan. (2013). "Several Determinants of Successful Coopetition in Small Business." *Journal of Small Business and Entrepreneurship* 26, no. 1, 15–28.

Vega, G. (unpublished). *Pick-Ups: Business Students Can Change the World.*

Vega, G. (2007). "Teaching Business Ethics through Service Learning Metaprojects." *Journal of Management Education* 31, no. 3, 647–678.

Vega, G., E. Simendinger, and S. Thomason. (2015). "Research Cases to Teaching Cases: A Model Format." *The CASE Journal* 11, no. 1. http://dx.doi.org/10.1108/TCJ-04-2014-0027

Yin, R.K. (2014). *Case Study Research, 5/e.* Thousand Oaks, CA: Sage Publications.

Zineldin, M. (2004). "Co-Opetition: The Organization of the Future." *Marketing Intelligence & Planning* 22, no. 7, 780.

• • • • •

Worksheets

WS 6:1 Elements of the Academic Research Case Study, Illustrated

WS 6:2 Elements of the Teaching Case and Instructor's Manual, Illustrated

WS 6:3 Deconstructing Your Own Academic Research Case Study

WS 6:4 Building Your Teaching Case and Instructor's Manual

WS 6:1

Elements of the Academic Research Case Study, Illustrated

	Academic Research Case Study		Excerpt
	The title	The title should be informative, directed to the desired audience, and tempting to the potential reader (see Huff, 1999, Chapter 6).	*Teaching business ethics through service learning metaprojects*
1	Statement of the purpose of the research	This appears in the abstract, the statement of research purpose and hypotheses, or in the introduction and informs the reader of what to expect in the paper.	*The urgent messages of good business include the importance of ethical management behaviors, focus on corporate citizenship, recognition of principled leadership, moral awareness, and participation in social change. . .*
2	General description of situation being studied	This section lays out the sections to come in the paper and what is included in each section. It provides an anticipatory taste of the study's content.	*This article describes the service learning metaproject (a nested set of projects required of all students) and shows what students can accomplish to promote a better world.*
3	Literature review and its relationship to the specific case	The literature review provides key citations that relate to the specific study in question, rather than providing an overview of all related literature. Restraint is important in this section.	*Experiential learning has long been a mainstay of postsecondary pedagogy. Since its first recorded program at the University of Cincinnati in 1903 through both Democratic and Republican federal administrations . . .*
4	Research hypotheses or conceptual model	What are you testing? What are you building? This is the section that presents this material.	*Many undergraduates come into college with a variety of preconceived notions about the world (Dziech, 2004; Fitch, 2000; MKay, 1997; Ostrow, 1995) . . .Although we in America espouse a classless society and equal opportunity for all, that message is often misinterpreted as expecting equal outcomes for all (Ritzer, 2000) . . . Service learning provides opportunities to enlighten students about stakeholder needs . . .*

5	Connect study to hypotheses	This section develops logically from the preceding section. It explains why you have chosen the specific field of inquiry and how the case in question relates to the hypotheses.	*The four key objectives of the service learning projects described in the article are (a) making contact with diverse populations, (b) making conscious moral decisions and commitment to ethical action, (c) deriving meaning from everyday activities, and (d) developing adaptability and flexibility . . .*
6	Data that support or fail to support hypotheses based on research questions	This is the basic presentation of data which can take many different formats.	*Agreeable store owners/ managers are more likely than their skeptical counterparts to engage in trusting, mutually beneficial, and committed cooperative relationships . . .*
7	Statement of methodology and data collection process	How did you go about performing your research? How did you validate your data? This is where you describe in full the research field, the collection process, the means of triangulation, and other relevant processes.	*Table 1 provides an overview of four metaprojects, three of which were run by students in business ethics classes and the fourth which involved the entire first-year business class . . .*
8	Analytical methodology	What means did you use to analyze your data? Was it an inductive or deductive process? Some tactics to include in this section are the processes of identifying patterns and themes, contrasting and comparing situations, and establishing coding protocols.	*The overall learning objectives for all our business students appear as Appendix C. There are 12 such objectives, half of them related to General Knowledge and Abilities and half related to Business-Specific Knowledge and Abilities . . .*
9	Analysis of the research	This is the meat of the academic research case study—what did you find? Were your hypotheses supported? Does your conceptual model work based on your findings?	*One important lesson that most of the students internalized is that the world does not revolve only around them . . .*
10	Summary, conclusions, and limitations of the study	This section is a restatement of research objectives, how the case study limitations may provide boundaries for generalizability of the findings, and a re-emphasis on the specific links of theory to the study.	*. . . they understand that being in business gives them the opportunity to change the world. This particular bit of understanding is what will stay with them long after the service learning projects are completed and forgotten . . .*
11	Results of the analysis and final outcomes	This is a reiteration of findings and suggestions for future research.	*The future is in the hands of our students. The more tools we can give them, the more likely it is that the world will have a future worth living.*

WS 6:2

Elements of the Teaching Case and Instructor's Manual, Illustrated

	Teaching Case		Excerpt
	The title	The title should be descriptive, appealing, and should include the name of the company (if a public company). It may also include the topic or the key decision to be made.	*Pick-Ups: Business students can change the world*
1	The opening hook	This is the material that engages the reader. It is a forerunner of the case problem and is meant to draw the reader in.	*A dozen undergraduate students clustered nervously in the entryway to Room 112 of the Business Studies building at Shawsheen College at five o'clock in the afternoon of April 27th . . .*
2	The company story/history	This section provides the context for the case, including corporate background and general history. This section requires rich description.	*Shawsheen College, a Catholic college located in Massachusetts, was a small school with a business program that served 250 students. The college had made a college-wide commitment to service learning . . .*
3	The industry	The situation appears here within a broader context and provides a factual framework in which to embed the company described earlier.	*Students encountered some recurring issues as they developed the plan. For example, determining how much to charge for the service took a lot of research and discussion . . .*
4	The actors	Because teaching cases are about the problems that people in organizations experience, it is important to recognize protagonists with whom the reader can identify. Readers will gladly help to solve the problems that people have, but are less inclined to solve problems that "organizations" have.	*Most of the students at Shawsheen College came from middle-class backgrounds with parents who protected them from the seamier side of life. They knew nothing about poverty or the pain of doing without . . .*

5	The situation	This is the actual case narrative—the story as you wish to tell it. It must be true and accurate, however, it should not be dull or boring.	*The students designed Pick-Ups as a not-for-profit service organization dedicated to serving assisted living communities and people in need.*
6	Additional information	Some case writers like to include additional information that is not relevant to the case "solution" in order to give the reader an opportunity to differentiate between the necessary facts and the tangential ones.	*In the early 2000s, students were eager to distance themselves from the series of significant ethical lapses in the corporate world, and ethical awareness and social responsibility were becoming increasingly important to them . . .*
7	The closing hook	If this is a decision case, the protagonist will conclude this section with some kind of request for assistance. It will be clear to the reader what kind of help the character needs. If this is an illustrative case, the protagonist's actions and, possibly, the outcomes of those actions will be described and will generate a response in the reader.	*This new understanding is what made them so nervous. What were the weak spots in their feasibility study? How could they improve it? What questions might these important stakeholders ask them? . . .*
8	Exhibits or appendices	These include the data that are necessary for analysis but that do not fit within the case itself (spreadsheets, maps, organization charts, timelines, and similar items).	Marketing flyer, financial projections
	Instructor's Manual		
9	Overview/ synopsis/ abstract	This element is the hook for the instructor and provides a high-level perspective on the teaching case.	*This case documents the development of a feasibility study by a group of undergraduate students for a service learning project . . .*
10	Intended audience/ recommended courses, and placement	This section describes who the case was written for, when in the term to offer it, and the topics/texts with which it works well.	*This case is field research and is suitable for undergraduate small business or entrepreneurship courses in the final third of the semester . . .*
11	Learning objectives	This is a description of student takeaways—what the students who are assigned the case will be able to do after having read it	*1. Evaluate opportunity via industry analysis, identification of a target market, and determination of competitive advantage.* *2. Design a strategy that matches the company mission . . .*

12	Discussion questions	These appear twice in the Instructor's Manual, once in a simple list and later with full answers.	1. What are the weak areas of the feasibility study? 2. How can you improve them?
13	Teaching strategies	Any unique methods you have developed for teaching the case, including case preparation for students and teaching methods for instructors.	*Assignment of the TogetherWorks website prior to reading this case will give the students food for thought to be used in their analysis. An evaluation rubric (sample attached as Exhibit A) can be provided to assist the students in their evaluations . . .*
14	Literature review, theory, and/or recommended readings	This is an outline of the basic theory that your teaching case illustrates, including references that relate specifically to the situation. It is not an extensive literature review, but rather a simple guide for the instructor.	*A feasibility study is an examination of a business opportunity to determine if it has the potential to be profitable and if it makes sense in the current situation or environment . . .*
15	Answers to the discussion questions	These should appear as a student would present them to help the instructor develop reasonable expectations.	*Not provided here in this example.*
16	Epilogue	What happened after the situation ended? What did the protagonist actually decide to do? What were the results of that decision?	*. . . the Pick-Ups business itself failed to gain sufficient support to carry on after the students graduated. The college was willing to provide most of the needed materials and staff, but the insurance issues were significant and the lack of a sustainability plan undermined the potential of this program.*

WS 6:3

Deconstructing Your Own Academic Research Case Study

Use the third column for excerpts from your own research study. Include the first part of the section, then uses ellipses (. . .) and insert the final few words. The purpose of this exercise is to make it easier for you to identify the elements that will have to change in your teaching case. Follow the example provided in WS 6:1.

Academic Research Case Study		Excerpt
The title	The title should be informative, directed to the desired audience, and tempting to the potential reader (see Huff, 1999, Chapter 6).	
Statement of the purpose of the research	This appears in the abstract, the statement of research purpose and hypotheses, or in the introduction, and informs the reader of what to expect in the paper.	
General description of situation being studied	This section lays out the sections to come in the paper and what is included in each section. It provides an anticipatory taste of the study's content.	
Literature review and its relationship to the specific case	The literature review provides key citations that relate to the specific study in question, rather than providing an overview of all related literature. Restraint is important in this section.	
Research hypotheses or conceptual model	What are you testing? What are you building? This is the section that presents this material.	
Connect study to hypotheses	This section develops logically from the preceding section. It explains why you have chosen the specific field of inquiry and how the case in question relates to the hypotheses.	

Data that support or fail to support hypotheses based on research questions	This is the basic presentation of data which can take many different formats.	
Statement of methodology and data collection process	How did you go about performing your research? How did you validate your data? This is where you describe in full the research field, the collection process, the means of triangulation, and other relevant processes.	
Analytical methodology	What means did you use to analyze your data? Was it an inductive or deductive process? Some tactics to include in this section are the processes of identifying patterns and themes, contrasting and comparing situations, and establishing coding protocols.	
Analysis of the research	This is the meat of the academic research case study—what did you find? Were your hypotheses supported? Does your conceptual model work based on your findings?	
Summary, conclusions, and limitations of the study	This section is a restatement of research objectives, how the case study limitations may provide boundaries for generalizability of the findings, and a re-emphasis on the specific links of theory to the study.	
Results of the analysis and final outcomes	This is a reiteration of findings and suggestions for future research.	

WS 6:4

Building Your Teaching Case and Instructor's Manual

Using the information you identified in WS 6:3, fill in the blank columns in the following table with proposed ideas for inclusion in your teaching case and instructor's manual. Refer to WS 6:2 for illustration of the elements.

Research Case	Teaching Case	Instructor's Manual	Ideas for Inclusion
Statement of the purpose of the research	The "hook"	Abstract	
General description of situation being studied	Company story/ history The actors	Audience/courses/ placement in term	
Literature review and its relationship to the specific situation		Literature review/ theory discussion	
Research hypotheses or conceptual model	The situation or problem (story)	Learning objectives	
Connect research case to hypotheses	Industry information Exhibits		
Data that support or fail to support hypotheses based on research questions	Additional (peripheral) information	Discussion questions	
Statement of methodology and data collection process		Statement of methodology and data collection process	
Analytical methodology		Pedagogy/teaching strategy	
Analysis of the research		Answers to discussion questions	
Summary, conclusions, and limitations of the research case	Closing hook		
Results of the analysis and final outcomes		Epilogue	

Module 7

• • • • •

Getting Your Case Published and Reviewing Cases for Others

• • • • •

You've Written Your Case: Now What?

Your case is complete. Its Instructor's Manual is complete. You have tested the case in class at least once. You have asked a colleague to test the case and give you some feedback about how it worked. You want to move forward and share your hard work with others, but you are not clear on the next steps. You've heard of case conferences and you know that cases are sometimes published in journals. You've used cases from textbooks and maybe even cases from disciplinary casebooks. Which venue should you aim for? Of course, the answer is, "It depends."

Start with a Case Conference

If you learn best in the physical company of others, consider making a case conference your first step toward publication. Case conferences tend to have a similar format, which is both structured and collegially informal:

■ Submissions are accepted based on the reviewers' estimation of the likelihood that the case can be improved through open discussion.

■ The author receives written reviews prior to the conference and is expected to submit changes/improvements based on those reviews before the conference.

■ Authors are grouped by topic, discipline, or case content and are assigned to roundtables. All of the formal roundtable participants receive a copy of each case to be discussed prior to the conference, and all are expected to provide written reviews for the authors.

■ At the conference itself, authors present their cases informally and the roundtable participants each comment on the cases and present their suggestions to the authors. General discussion ensues at the table, and authors are encouraged to ask for clarification and additional commentary.

■ A table leader facilitates the process and presents a more formal review for the author.

■ The authors leave the conference with a wide variety of suggestions for improving their case and IM before submitting the case to a journal.

Case conferences are a great way to begin the publication process, as you will be exposed to many different cases, writing styles, and review styles. You will also have an excellent opportunity to network with experienced case writers, as well as with other novices like yourself. Most case conferences even include a so-called "embryo" session, where case writers present the germ of a case—an embryo—and request suggestions for how to move forward, along with a newcomer session where participants can learn the basics of case research and writing.

Finding an appropriate case conference to attend is not difficult. There are several major case conferences and numerous regional conferences held annually across the world. In addition, many academic conferences have a case track where you can present cases that focus solely on your own discipline. Once you begin looking, you will be surprised at how easy it is to find a place to present your work for feedback. See WS 7:1 for a partial list of some regularly held case conferences.

How to Select a Journal

Selecting the appropriate outlet for your writing is always a challenge. You will have to make decisions about the following nine issues before you submit your piece to any journal. See WS 7:2 for some guidelines to help you make these decisions.

1. Should You Aim for the Highest-Ranked Journal?

Many academic organizations and associations "rank" journals in terms of relative prestige based on a variety of subjective factors such as "quality" and objective factors such as "impact" (citations in the literature). Each organization or association maintains its own ranking system, and many college and university promotion and tenure committees adopt a ranking system or develop their own rankings to evaluate the scholarship of applicants.

Case journals are rarely ranked because teaching cases are not generally cited in research manuscripts. Therefore, the primary indication of market acceptance for a case is usage (adoption rates). These rates can be hard to come by because publishers are reluctant to provide public access to their sales figures. There is no universal ranking accepted by all postsecondary institutions.

2. Peer-Reviewed or Non-Peer-Reviewed Journals?

The journals listed in WS 7:3 are blind peer reviewed. This means that you will not know who is reviewing your case, and the reviewer will not know the name of the case author.

Most journals have some sort of editorial review prior to sending the submissions out to reviewers who specialize in the disciplinary area of the case. This gives the initial editor the option to desk-reject a case that does not meet a minimal standard for that journal or that does not fit the journal's mission.

Non-peer-reviewed journals are reviewed only by the editor. This limits the variety and quality of accepted manuscripts as well as the diversity of opinion by authors and acceptability by peers.

3. The Journal with the Fastest Review Time?

Review time refers to the length of time it takes for an editor to (1) receive your manuscript, (2) read it, (3) send it to at least two peer reviewers, (4) have the reviewers read and comment on your manuscript, and (4) receive the results. The editor then compiles the comments and sends you a detailed letter explaining the reviewers' requests and the journal's editorial priorities.

Naturally, this process takes time. Journal reviewers are volunteers with a regular course load and service/administrative responsibilities just like you. Editors are the same. Just when you are ready to submit your case because you have finished your grading for the term, the reviewers are likely ready to take a breather from their service duties as well.

To compound the complexity, editors need to select reviewers very carefully to make sure their disciplinary expertise matches the case content and their reviewing style comports well with the journal's overall style. It is not unusual for a first review to take six months or more. Second reviews usually (but not always) move more quickly. Unless a journal specifically states that its review process is short, you should be prepared for a long wait.

4. A Journal That is Geared to Your Discipline?

Disciplinary-based journals often publish a teaching case in each issue. These cases are evaluated partly on the quality of the case and partly on the quality of the match between case content and journal content. A highly specialized case may fare better in a journal devoted to that particular content than it might in a more generalized journal because the reviewers will truly understand the content and be able to evaluate it thoroughly.

5. A Journal That Focuses on Pedagogy?

Pedagogy journals usually focus on papers *about* teaching methods, exercises to *facilitate* teaching, and *how-to* pieces. If a case is about the process of teaching, it may find a home in a pedagogy journal, but if the case deals with specific disciplinary content, a pedagogy journal is probably not the right outlet.

6. A Journal That Publishes Cases and Case-Related Manuscripts Exclusively?

There are several journals that publish cases and case-related manuscripts exclusively. These journals accept cases in many different disciplines and sometimes have special issues devoted entirely to one topic such as corporate social responsibility or international business.

The reviewers for case journals are very concerned about the usability of the case in the classroom and therefore will spend considerable time and effort reviewing the Instructor's Manual. Be prepared for a very close read of this element.

7. An Online Journal?

Some journals are published exclusively online. According to journal publishers, this is the move of the future, because today's students are often happier using e-books and electronic delivery of course materials. A journal's delivery system, whether online or in print, has no bearing on the quality of the journal, its acceptance policies, or its review process. The impact is solely on the delivery of materials.

8. A Journal That Distributes through Library Databases?

Case journals rarely distribute their material through library databases; however, disciplinary journals do make their cases available through databases. The Instructor's Manual is never made available to students, even when the case can be accessed through the library. All journals take great care to limit access to the Instructor's Manuals to legitimate course instructors.

9. A Journal That Works through Distributors and Does Not Make Its Cases Available to Libraries?

Some journals partner with distributors to make cases broadly available to the academic world. You can see individual websites for this distribution information. If your case is handled through a distributor, you may receive a royalty.

WS 7:4 provides a partial list of non-peer-reviewed journals and case distributors.

● ● ● ● ●

Steps for Success: Aiming at Journal Acceptance

When you think you are ready to submit your case, these five steps can increase the chances of a favorable response:

1. Run grammar-check, spell-check, and have someone else proofread your case and Instructor's Manual. Remove any identifying artifacts, such as track changes, that could destroy the blind review process. After making several revisions, it becomes nearly impossible to locate your own errors, and you do not want to embarrass yourself by committing careless errors. If English is your second language, consider adding an additional coauthor who can localize your language usage.

2. Make sure you have an objective reader evaluate your case and IM before you submit. A colleague can alert you to subtle omissions, repetitions, or inadvertent contradictions. Have someone classroom-test your case before submission—students will let you know exactly what works and what does not work. It can be very enlightening to sit in the back of a classroom where someone else is teaching your case and see firsthand what you need to improve, eliminate, or change in some way.

3. All journals provide extensive submission guidelines. Some of them relate to the content and "fit" of your proposed manuscript and the mission of the journal. Other guidelines relate to the formatting of your submission. Read the submission guidelines carefully and follow them *exactly* to expedite the review process. Format your case and IM the way the specific journal requests, not the generic way this workbook suggests. Be sure to include all the requested elements.

4. Write a clear cover letter that outlines the disciplinary area of your case, the target audience, and the general situation. For example, "This case submission is geared toward the undergraduate marketing student. It challenges the reader to redesign the marketing plan for a large electronics manufacturer doing global business." Confirm that you have already obtained the necessary publication releases if your case depends on primary research.

5. Check the file one more time, then hit "send."

● ● ● ● ●

Five Easy Steps to Guarantee Rejection

Here are ways to guarantee rejection from most journals.

1. Take your case in early form to a conference and then disregard the subsequent advice and suggestions you receive. Be sure to emphasize

that the case was already presented at a conference and was deemed acceptable by the sponsoring association.

■ Why is this unacceptable? Because acceptance at a conference is much easier to obtain than acceptance at a journal. The standards differ significantly, as most case conferences accept cases that will benefit from development and revision rather than cases that are ready for publication. If you have not made the basic changes and improvements suggested at the conference roundtable presentation, your case is certainly not ready for journal review.

2. Submit to a journal in your preferred format, regardless of the published submission guidelines. When the editor contacts you and asks you to submit per the guidelines, argue or else resubmit with multiple variations on the requested guidelines.

■ Why is this unacceptable? Because journal reviewers become accustomed to seeing materials in a specific format, and they do not want to spend their valuable reviewing time reminding you (1) that they use APA (or some other) format for citations, or (2) that exhibits should be incorporated (or not incorporated) into the running text, or (3) that they require an IM (Instructor's Manual) rather than a TN (teaching note). Reviewers might recommend rejection merely because they are irritated at your stubborn refusal to follow the guidelines. Frequently, the editor will not even send an improperly formatted manuscript out to reviewers. This can result in the "8-minute rejection," or desk-rejection by an editor that is nearly simultaneous with your submission.

3. If you receive a request to revise and resubmit, return the case and IM without having addressed all the changes requested. Do not provide any documentation as to what you have or have not done to your manuscript.

■ Why is this unacceptable? It is simply disrespectful to assume that the reviewers have time to try to locate your changes within the case. It requires that they reread the original alongside the new version, an activity that is both time-consuming and unnecessary if you do your job properly.

4. Insist on being "right." After all, you know more than the reviewers about your case, case situation, industry, and protagonists, right?

■ Why is this unacceptable? From time to time you have to make choices. Sometimes, the choice is between being "right" on the one hand, and getting the desired outcome, such as a publication, on the other. At most journals, the reviewers are generally "right."

5. Wait a year before resubmitting and then get irritated when the re-review takes more than a month to be completed.

■ Why is this unacceptable? Do you really have to ask this question?

● ● ● ● ●

Three Possible Outcomes

There are three possible outcomes from your case submission: acceptance, rejection, and revise and resubmit.

1. *Acceptance* without revision is rare. Very rare.
2. *Rejection without review* may result from submission to the wrong outlet or it may result from limited interest in your case situation at the journal in question. You can avoid submission to the wrong outlet by carefully reading several issues of the journal before submitting. Does this journal publish cases? Does it publish cases in your field? Are the cases featured in the journal teaching cases? Is your case topically appropriate?
3. *Revise and resubmit*, the most frequent response, provides you the opportunity to make recommended changes that will likely lead to final acceptance and publication of your work.

● ● ● ● ●

What Does "Revise and Resubmit" Really Mean? Responding to the Reviews of Your Case

You are far more likely to receive an editorial decision of "revise and resubmit" than "Congratulations, your case has been accepted"—especially on your first attempt. The way you handle your revision will determine the final disposition of your case submission.

People address their reviews in disparate ways:

■ Some people get angry, convinced that the reviewers did not understand what their goal was in writing the case. They reject all editorial and reviewer suggestions and simply leave their case to fester virtually in their computer's dead-letter file.

■ Other people read their reviews and ruminate over them until they find they cannot even identify what they are being asked to correct. They dither until they find a direction, then they move reasonably straight in that direction.

■ Still others set to work immediately, trying to juggle the often conflicting reviews without destroying the integrity of their original work.

■ When I started writing, I couldn't even bear to look at the reviews. I'd read them fast, get angry and (sometimes) hurt, and put them away in a drawer for a couple of days until I got past my first reaction. This was back in the days of typed and mailed reviews, before electronic submission processes. After a few days, I'd take them out again and mark them up, identifying what I would definitely do, what I would refuse to do, and what was still on the table. I prioritized my revision tasks, set to work, and resubmitted.

All of these approaches (and others) work for some people, so I will not advocate for any particular method. The only real failure is leaving the case in that virtual desk drawer and not addressing the revision at all. This is a waste of your good first effort. Remember your sunk costs and please don't allow yourself to leave a case or other writing project unfinished or unrevised.

What is really important to a good revision:

- Address the changes and return the case and IM within three months (or the time frame offered by the editor), or else let the editor know when to expect your revision. Don't let the case just sit around . . . deal with it!

- Pay close attention to the suggestions of the reviewers; at peer-reviewed journals, editorial decisions depend on the input of reviewers. *Your job is to make the reviewers happy.*

- In 1844, Senator Henry Clay famously declared, "I'd rather be right than president." Result? He was defeated three times for the office. Would you rather be right or be published?

- Respond to *all* reviewer suggestions, whether you like them or not. Responding means letting the reviewers know that you have considered their comments and suggestions carefully and have decided to take a specific action regarding each comment. It does *not* mean that you have to follow all the suggestions; sometimes, it is even impossible to do so, especially when the reviewers have conflicting advice.

- Respond to the editor's comments in your cover letter. If you are unsure of what the editor wants or have received ambiguous advice or conflicting instructions from the reviewers, be sure to ask. Then indicate in your cover letter exactly which changes you have made. Don't make the editor or the reviewers search for the change; make it easy for them to approve your work. See WS 7:5 for a sample cover letter and responses to reviewers for your revised case.

- Follow the formatting instructions required by the journal you are targeting. Every journal is different, and you don't want your work to be rejected simply because you formatted it incorrectly.

- If you think you have received a lot of help in revising your case, it doesn't hurt to thank the reviewers and the editor. It won't get your case accepted, but it will be appreciated.

The goal is to show the reviewers that you value their evaluation and suggestions and that you paid attention to their concerns (*all* of their concerns).

The goal is *not* to show how much smarter you are than the reviewers. Although it is good to have confidence in your own skill and abilities, remember that the reviewers are evaluating your work, not the other way around. You need to acknowledge the quality of their input and the help they are giving you in getting your case ready for publication and distribution.

●●●●●

Roles of the "Journal Gatekeepers"

The Editor

The editor sets the tone and vision for the journal. A journal's vision is likely to change when there is a change in editorial leadership, so it pays to find out who the current editor of your targeted journal is.

If this person has been editor for a year or more, you can simply read the editorial letters for the past few issues to gain some insight into the journal's current focus. If the editor is new, you can write a query letter asking if your submission is likely to be welcomed or if the journal's focus would preclude acceptance of your case. The editor is your champion in the publication process, serving as a buffer between you and the reviewers. An editor's decisions are final.

The Reviewers

A journal is only as good as its reviewers, and the editor depends heavily on their wisdom and skill. The reviewers see their role as protecting the quality of the journal while helping to develop and improve submissions to publishable status. As a result, reviews are often complicated, shifting from disciplinary content to case structure to pedagogical value to basic writing skills. The best reviews provide feedback in all these areas and more.

A few years ago, a colleague came to me in tears, holding a review of a paper she had submitted. I will share with you (with her permission) an excerpt from this review:

> . . . *It's clear to this reviewer that the author does not know what he's [sic] talking about. This is just a laundry list of facts without anything tying them together. He says he wants to use qualitative research, but there is no indication that he knows what that is. He can't form a hypothesis . . . start again.*

I looked at her paper and, it was true—the manuscript was no good. She really DID need to start again. But where was she to begin? The rest of the review continued in the same vein as it began, telling the author in broad and unpleasant generalities that her work was a waste of time, but the reviewer did not provide any guidance for this inexperienced academic to help her revise her paper to make it more acceptable and potentially publishable.

Joining the Society of Reviewers

One of the best ways to learn how to write better cases is to review the cases of others. Journals and conferences will welcome warmly your offer to review cases and will provide you with appropriate reviewing guidelines and suggestions. The following list is meant as a set of generic principles to govern your reviewing process.

The 10 Commandments of Case Review

1. People Like (and Need) to Hear the Good News

There is no such thing as a case that doesn't have *something* good to offer the reader. Find it and comment upon it. In writing. Right up front.

2. Be Generous with Your Praise

It doesn't cost you anything, and it is a good investment in the case writer's future. Every item that receives a favorable comment is one that the author will repeat in future cases. This is a great opportunity to plant the seeds for quality cases and case reviews in the future.

3. Assume That Your Words of Criticism Sound Harsher Than You Meant Them to Sound

People read your critique without hearing or seeing your personal style of delivery, your wink, your smile, your intent. In order that you not be misunderstood, it is useful to moderate your comments wherever possible so as not to sound cruel to the author.

4. Remember the Golden Rule: Do Not Treat Others as You Would Not Like to Be Treated

Keep in mind those first reviews you received on your article submissions early in your career. Did you cry? Do you wish to make others cry? Your self-evaluation should be about the level of *constructive criticism* you were able to provide to the case author. If it's not constructive, it's not valid.

5. You Are Not Judging the Author, Only the Quality of the Author's Work and Its Appropriateness for Your Venue (Conference, Journal)

If, like me, you get impatient with multiple grammatical errors (I think they show enormous disrespect for the reader), learn how to say, "Multiple grammatical errors (see p. 11, lines 3, 6, 9, 14, and 22) detract from the quality of the case and distract the reader's attention" rather than something more flippant, such as, "Don't waste my time with this quality of writing."

6. It's Not All About You

The purpose of the developmental review is not to show how much you, the reviewer, know. It is to help the author understand how to improve the case so that it is publishable according to your standards. It is your knowledge that helps the author attain those standards, so your goal is to share that knowledge in a modest way and not to humiliate the author. If you cannot set aside your ego, do not become a reviewer.

7. Be as Specific as You Can with Your Suggestions

Instead of saying, "Eliminate jargon," try, "Eliminate jargon. Specifically, on page 16 you write about connecting jumpers to the MDF without a floor plan. Instead, you could discuss insuring that floor plans provide the information necessary to connect the main distribution frame to the temporary wiring frame. Unless the case is designed only for telecommunications technicians, people will not understand the MDF and jumpers comments." This will allow the author to understand the extent of the jargon that has been used, seek it out, and replace it with clearer language.

8. Help the Author Locate the Sometimes Elusive Key Decision

Does the case have a decision focus? Not all cases have them, but if the goal is to make a case publishable, it is preferable (not required) to conclude with a decision point. Sometimes the case author is too close to the case to find the decision point, but you, at a distance, may see that the case needs to end earlier so that the decision can be made by the reader. Point out the appropriate spot and explain **WHY** that is the place to end the case. It can be very hard to understand this concept, and authors will make the same mistake again and again in subsequent cases if they are not given proper instruction.

9. Keep the Goal in Mind

Case writing is a process, not an end point. Your role will differ depending on the quality of the case you are reviewing and the experience level of the case writer. New case writers need *very gentle* handling and significant guidance, just as our first-year students do. More experienced case writers will grasp your suggestions more readily and require less explanation, but they will provide you with great opportunities to set stretch goals. You need to be prepared for this; it's not always easy for the reviewer to offer suggestions for a case that is pretty good to begin with. The most difficult task you will have is to offer a good, developmental review for a case that is already in good condition and has a solid IM. These cases are the most fun, because you really have to work to make an improvement that the case writer will value. This is when you will recognize that the writer/reviewer relationship is an interdependent, synergistic partnership from which both benefit.

10. Take Your Responsibility Very Seriously

Authors are depending on you to show them the way to improve their case writing. The way you teach them is the way they will teach others.

All of us succumb occasionally to the careless, hurried review of a student paper or a journal or conference submission. But every time I am tempted to dash off a fast review, especially a rejection or a revise and resubmit that requires substantial work on the part of the author, I think of my colleague and her frustration (and hurt). And I slow down and think of the possible response to my recommendations.

● ● ● ● ●

How to Write a Valuable Review

Let's start with what you do **NOT** need in order to write a valuable case review.

You do not need to have published cases in order to review them. Writing and reviewing are distinct skills and, although related, are not mutually dependent. You do not need to have reviewed cases before. Most editors are happy to pair new reviewers and experienced reviewers for your first reviews, and all journals will provide you with a set of guidelines to follow. It's the best way to become a stronger case writer, so why not try it out?

What you **DO** need is an interest in and understanding of the purpose and use of cases in the classroom. Here are a few brief guidelines for getting started:

■ If you use cases, you know exactly what you need them to do for your classes. You know what would help you teach the case (so you understand intrinsically the value of a strong Instructor's Manual), and you know what interests your students (so you know what is likely to interest the students of others).

- You need to be able to frame your comments in a positive and constructive way (you do this by writing what you, yourself, would like to hear from a reviewer), and you need to be generous with your advice (providing examples if necessary or appropriate references and other suggestions).
- You need to be willing to help others for no reward, simply because service to our profession is a noble task.

Characteristics of a "Good" Reviewer

A good reviewer:

- Has a sincere desire to improve the submission, and this desire guides all the commentary and suggestions the reviewer makes.
- Understands what appeals to students at various educational levels and is able to explain why a specific case is best geared to an undergraduate, graduate, or executive/practitioner audience.
- Is able to frame comments constructively and avoids negative, non-developmental commentary.
- Is willing to provide comprehensive suggestions to the author. This costs the reviewer nothing and adds tremendous learning value to the author.
- Is generous of spirit. Sharing one's expertise and one's valuable time to help other case writers is an act of generosity that can only be repaid by returning the favor to another author.
- Puts ego aside and focuses on commentary that will help the author rather than enhance the personal satisfaction of the reviewer. Remember— the review is not about you; it is about the case you are reviewing with an eye toward improving it.
- Has depth of content knowledge in a specified area. This content knowledge allows the reviewer to make appropriate and current references to the literature that the author may have overlooked or to suggest theoretical perspectives for analysis that might enhance student learning.

Characteristics of a "Good" Review

The following factors describe a good review:

- Thorough comments that provoke the author to think through any issues the reviewer is raising. This is the time to drive home your points rather than be subtle and hope that the author will understand what you are looking for.

■ Follow-up and consistency. Make sure that you are not contradicting in comment 17 what you may have stated in comment 6.

■ Attention to detail. If an author has made a factual error on page 2 and repeats that error on page 5, indicate this on your review.

■ Concern for the submission's readability and less focus on copyediting (the editor's job). As an editor, I ask my reviewers not to focus on copyediting; their skills are for structure and content. The copyediting is the editor's job, and it is best not to confuse the author with multiple grammar-related comments. Of course, it is very hard to read a manuscript without thinking about the quality of the writing, so you should feel comfortable either commending the quality or suggesting the need for a thorough edit. If the writing gets in the way of making sense of the case, be sure to note that.

■ Quick turnaround. You know how difficult it is to wait and wait and wait to get feedback on your work. We all feel the same way, so do your best to complete your reviews promptly.

■ Content-specific suggestions. The journal editor cannot be a subject matter expert in all areas of business. We count on reviewers to provide solid suggestions for improvement in terms of discipline-specific information and techniques.

See WS 7:6 for samples of weak reviews and good reviews.

●●●●●

Steps in Writing a Review

The most efficient way to review a case is to read the case and the Instructor's Manual concurrently. I suggest you refer back to Modules 3 and 5 (Writing the Case and Building the Instructor's Manual) for what makes strong elements in a case and IM.

Step 1: Start by Reading the Case Hook

Is the hook interesting? Is it engaging? Does it introduce us to the protagonist? Does it foreshadow the problems that the rest of the case will address? Does it avoid the trite scenario, the contrived conversation, the all-too-familiar manager looking out the window?

Step 2: Shift to the Instructor's Manual and Read the Case Synopsis/Abstract and Learning Objectives

Does the abstract (hook for instructors) describe the same general business problem as the case hook (for students)? Does it provide a brief overview, reference to critical events, and an indication of the research methodology? Do the learning objectives provide specific and measurable goals for the students?

Step 3: Read the Full Case as if You Were a Student

Read it quickly without much attention to detail.

Step 4: Shift Back to the IM and Read the Discussion Questions

Do these questions match the learning objectives? There should be at least one question for each learning objective and no questions that do not relate to at least one of the learning objectives. Do the questions make sense to you? Are they specific to the case or are they generic topical questions such as "How could a SWOT analysis help the owner?"

Step 5: Answer the Questions Yourself before You Read the Answers Provided in the Instructor's Manual

Can they be answered from the material in the case or must students do additional research to answer the questions?

Step 6: Read the Full Instructor's Manual Now

Did you answer the questions correctly according to the IM? Is the section on theory satisfactory to your standards? Is there another theory you would suggest to the author? Does the teaching method make sense? Does the epilogue provide the closure that students will seek? Would you be willing to recommend this case to your colleagues or to use this case in your own class?

Step 7: Read the Case One More Time

On a subjective level, do you like it? Why or why not? Will students be able to learn from it? Is it rich enough? Is there any suggestion you can make to the author to enhance the usability of the case further?

Go to WS 7:7 for an exercise in reviewing. Then, contact a journal editor and get started!

● ● ● ● ●

References and Readings

Van Fleet, D.D., A. McWilliams, and D.S. Siegel. (2000). "A Theoretical and Empirical Analysis of Journal Rankings: The Case of Formal Lists." *Journal of Management* 26, no. 5, 839–861.

Vega, G., B. Armandi, and T. Leach. (2007). "Case Research and Writing: Professor Moore and the Demons of Review." *The Case Journal* 3, no. 1 (February). http://emeraldinsight.com/doi/pdfplus/10.1108/TCJ-03-2006-B002

Vega, G., H. Sherman, and T. Leach. (2009). "Case Writing and Research: Professor Moore Reviews a Case." *The CASE Journal* 6, no. 1. http://emeraldinsight.com/doi/pdfplus/10.1108/TCJ-06-2009-B007

Worksheets

WS 7:1   Case Conferences (A Partial List)

WS 7:2   How to Select the Journal That Will Welcome Your Case

WS 7:3   Peer-Reviewed Journal Outlets (A Partial List)

WS 7:4   Non-Peer-Reviewed Journals and Distribution Outlets

WS 7:5   Sample Cover Letter and Responses to Reviewers for a Revised Case

WS 7:6   Sample Elements of Weak Reviews and Good Reviews

WS 7:7   Steps in Writing a Review

WS 7:1

Case Conferences (A Partial List)

The list presented here will help you identify an appropriate conference at which to present your case. All these conferences welcome international participation. All except WACRA are held in the United States.

Please note that this list is limited to case association conferences devoted purely to case presentation. Many disciplinary conferences also have a case track.

Association	Month Held	Website
CASE Association (CASE)	May	www.caseweb.org
North American Case Research Association (NACRA)	October	www.nacra.net
Society for Case Research (SCR)	July	www.sfcr.org
Southeast Case Research Association (SECRA)	February	www.secra.org
Western Casewriters Association (WCA)	March	http://cbe.calstatela.edu/wca.html
World Association for Case Method Research and Application (WACRA)	June	http://www.wacra.org/

WS 7:2

How to Select the Journal That Will Welcome Your Case

The following matrix will help you select an appropriate outlet for your case.

Journal Differentiators	Benefits	Drawbacks	Comments/ Suggestions
High ranking	The journal ranking provides additional credibility for your publication with committees that review your scholarly output.	The review process may take a considerable amount of time because of the large number of submissions at highly ranked journals.	Your decision should be guided by your institution's requirements.
Peer-reviewed or non-peer-reviewed	Acceptance at a peer-reviewed journal states unequivocally that your work is acceptable to your peers. Non-peer-reviewed journals generally provide feedback quickly.	It can sometimes be difficult to convince a peer-reviewed journal to accept nontraditional work, novel formats, and alternative styles because the review process focuses on adherence to existing standards.	Aim for peer review whenever possible.
Fast review turnaround	You will know quickly the outcome of your submission.	Speed sometimes has a negative effect on the quality and depth of the review.	Weigh the importance of a timely publication versus an extensive review.
Discipline-based	Readers of this journal are very likely to use your case in class because it speaks to their content-based interests.	Many cases can be used in a variety of disciplines; a discipline-based journal limits exposure to one group of professionals.	A discipline-based journal can be a good outlet for an advanced or highly technical case.
Pedagogy-based	People who read pedagogical journals are interested in creative teaching methods. If you are introducing something novel, this is a good outlet for you.	Your case may not reach the instructors who are content-focused rather than teaching-focused.	Pedagogy journals rarely publish "regular" teaching cases, focusing instead on methods of teaching cases.

Journal limited to cases and case-related papers	Instructors who use cases regularly consider case journals their primary source of new material.	People who do not normally teach with cases are not likely to find your case.	You will find your most avid reader here.
Online journal	Online journals have quick publishing turnarounds, few length limitations, and the ability to link directly to source material. This is the standard of the future.	Possible confusion by evaluators about the differences between online journals, open source journals (like wikis), and open access materials.	This is a great way to entice new readers to consider using your case.
Print-only journal	Print-only journals provide you with a hard copy of your work, making it easy to include in your course packs and your personal evaluation packets.	Some print journals have stringent length requirements that may limit your ability to publish a complicated case geared to term-long usage.	More traditional academics are likely to read these journals.
Available through library databases	Students can access your case easily at no cost.	It becomes very difficult to evaluate the usage your case is getting.	This provides you with very wide exposure.
Accessible through distributors	Your case is listed in an extensive directory of cases organized by topic, discipline, or course. This makes it easy for instructors to find an appropriate case for their classes.	There are many cases competing for attention at distributors. Unless your case has been published by a journal, the potential user cannot evaluate its quality.	Your case can be delivered electronically or in print, making it easy to add to course packs.

WS 7:3

Peer-Reviewed Journal Outlets (A Partial List)

Journal Name	Website	Publisher/Acceptance Rate (per journal website, where available)	Comment/Discipline
Journals (Case Journals and Disciplinary Journals)			
Asian Case Research Journal	www.worldscientific.com/worldscinet/acrj	World Scientific Publishing	Field-research or secondary sources; open access **Asian companies and companies operating in Asia-Pacific**
Business Case Journal (BCJ)	www.sfcr.org	Society for Case Research 10–12%	Decision cases and descriptive cases Field-research preferred. No fiction. **Business disciplines**
Case Research Journal (CRJ)	http://www.nacra.net/crj/index.php5	NACRA 20%	Field-researched and decision-focused cases **Administrative-related disciplines**
Electronic Hallway Journal	http://hallway.evans.washington.edu/	W. Evans School of Public Policy and Governance (U. of Washington)	Online only access to members (faculty only) but cases accepted by nonmembers **Public administration and public policy**
IMA Educational Case Journal	http://www.imanet.org/resources-publications/ima-educational-case-journal-(iecj)	Association of Accountants and Financial Professionals in Business	Fictional cases are considered. Coauthoring between academics and practitioners is encouraged. **Management accounting**
International Journal of Business and Social Science (IJBSS)	http://www.ijbssnet.com/	Centre for Promoting Ideas	Publication fee—$200 Open access **All business disciplines**
International Journal of Case Studies in Management (IJCSM)	http://www.hec.ca/en/case_centre/ijcsm/	HEC-Montreal	International cases published in English and French; fiction acceptable **All business disciplines**

International Journal of Entrepreneurship and Innovation (IJEI)	www.ippublishing.com	IP Publishing Ltd.	**Entrepreneurship, innovation**
Journal of Applied Case Research	http://swcra.net/journal-of-applied-case-research/	Southwest Case Research Association **38%**	Field research and secondary data cases. No fiction. **All business disciplines**
Journal of Business Case Studies	http://www.cluteinstitute.com/journals/journal-of-business-case-studies-jbcs/	The Clute Institute for Academic Research 21–30%	Open access. Submission Fee: $75 Publication Fee: $400—$1200 **Business and economics**
Journal of Business Cases and Applications	www.aabri.com/jbca.html	Academic and Business Research Institute 20%	Open access. Fiction OK. All case formats acceptable. Review Fee: $45.00 -$95.00 Publication Fee: $195-$395 web or $295-$495 web and print **All business disciplines**
Journal of Case Studies	http://www.sfcr.org/jcs/	Society for Case research 30%	Must present at an SCR workshop before submission. Decision-based or descriptive cases. **All business disciplines**
Journal of Cases on Information Technology	www.igi-global.com/journal/journal-cases-information-technology-jcit/1075	Journal of Cases on Information Technology	Case studies and teaching cases. **Utilization and management of information technology**
Journal of Finance Case Research	www.jfcr.org	Institute for Finance Case Research	Must be a member to publish ($57.00 annual membership) **Finance**
Journal of Information Technology Education: Discussion Cases	www.informingscience.org/Journals/JITEDC/Overview	Informing Science Institute	Open access publishing; coauthoring opportunities with reviewers. Discussion cases only. **Information systems and communication technology**
Journal of Information Technology: Teaching Cases	http://www.palgrave-journals.com/jittc/index.html		Open access Article Processing Charge: $2600 **Information systems and communication technology**

Journal of the International Academy for Case Studies (JIACS)	www.alliedacademies.org/the-international-academy-for-case-studies/	Allied Academies 25%	Must be a member to publish ($75.00 annual membership) Decision cases and articles about case usage **All business disciplines**
Marketing Education Review	www.marketingeducationreview.com	**Society for Marketing Advances**	**Marketing**
Online Journal of International Case Analysis	http://ojica.fiu.edu	Florida International University, Miami, Florida	International business issues; some non-English-language submissions accepted. Open access publishing. **All business disciplines**
Small Business Institute Journal	http://www.sbij.org/index.php/SBIJ	Small Business Institute	**Open access Entrepreneurship and small business**
South Asian Journal of Business and Management Cases	https://us.sage-pub.com/en-us/nam/south-asian-journal-of-business-and-management-cases/journal202129#description	Birla Institute of Management Technology/ Sage Publications	No fiction. **All business disciplines**
Southeast Case Research Journal	http://secra.org	Southeast Case Research Association 30%	Disguised cases OK Members-only publication ($75 fee) **All business disciplines**
The CASE Journal (TCJ)	http://www.emeraldinsight.com/journal/tcj	Emerald Group Publishing with The CASE Association <20%	Both field-research and secondary research accepted; decision and evaluative cases; no fiction **All business disciplines**
Wine Business Case Research Journal	www.sonoma.edu/sbe/wine-business-institute/wine-business-case-journal	Sonoma State University Wine Business Institute	Open access. Field research preferred. No fiction. **Wine-related business**

Note: Publication rates listed are self-reported and represent the rate as indicated by the editor for the year prior to the publication date. Not all journals keep their listings updated, so these acceptance rates may not be accurate. Any journal's acceptance rate varies wildly, depending on the year, the number of submissions received, the quality of those submissions, and the speed with which the authors return their revisions. Some rates appear low because authors have case revisions sitting in their desk drawers, while other rates appear high because authors are motivated to revise their work and resubmit it quickly.

WS 7:4

Non-Peer-Reviewed Journals and Distribution Outlets

The following outlets are not peer reviewed. Some are editorially reviewed, while others serve primarily as distributors or registrars of cases. **Once a case is registered with a distributor, you can no longer submit that case to an academic journal.** *Some of the registrars and distributors (noted in comments) accept fictionalized cases. Many of these publishers and distributors partner with one another.*

Outlet Name	Website	Location/Submission and Acceptance Information	Comment/Discipline
Darden	https://store. darden.virginia. edu/	Darden Business Publishing/U. of Virginia. Cases are written or supervised by Darden faculty members.	**All business disciplines**
The Case Centre	http://www.the casecentre.org/	Cranfield University (UK) and Babson College (U.S.)	Largest international not-for-profit distributor of case studies **All business disciplines**
Harvard Business Review (HBR)	https://hbr.org/	Harvard Business Publishing. Cases are not solicited from authors outside HBS.	**Fictionalized cases**
Harvard Business School Cases	http://www.libr ary.hbs.edu/ hbs_cases.html	Harvard Business Publishing. All cases are written by HBS faculty, research associates, and/or library staff.	**All business disciplines**
Ivey Business Journal	https://www. iveycases.com/ PublishCases. aspx	IVEY Publishing. Peer reviewed by a faculty member. You must assign your copyright to the Richard Ivey School of Business.	Available in printed and online versions **All business disciplines**
Create	http://create. mcgraw-hill. com/create online/index. html#	McGraw-Hill does not accept unpublished cases. It distributes cases from the major journals.	**All business disciplines**

WS 7:5

Sample Cover Letter and Responses to Reviewers for a Revised Case

Dear Editor and Reviewers:

Once again, thank you for the time and considerable thought you invested into the improvement of our case. Using your most recent comments and suggestions, we made substantive changes to both the case and the teaching note. The following provides a summary of the changes we made in response to your feedback. For ease of review, we repeated your comments; the italicized font provides the disposition. We sincerely hope that we grasped the essence of your suggestions. Our aim was to provide the substantive changes that would strengthen the combined value of the case and the note as a pedagogical vehicle.

Case: Reviewer 1:

The organizational chart is helpful even though it lacks "personnel" (titles and names of major decision makers). The few other charts are helpful although I would have preferred to see financial data from more than one year of the firm's operation.

The company does not use titles but rather roles in the organization. Societal practices (an artifact from an earlier era) diffuse titles, responsibilities, and formal organizational structures. Management will not release additional financial data. The purpose of the data is to provide factual support and reinforce the industry's revenue stream business model. (Animation is a promotional platform for branded products. The majority of sales and income derive from licenses and sales of branded products.)

IM: Editor:

What specific knowledge (marketing theory) should the instructor have covered before students read the case (chapters from a textbook)?

The authors listed the marketing concepts instructors should cover prior to assigning the case.

IM: Reviewer 1:

The answers to many of the questions still seem fairly short; however, the plethora of questions may make up for the shortness of the answers.

The authors revised the answers to the discussion questions to provide more robust, theory-related responses.

IM: Reviewer 2:

The case is dense with facts and gives solid detail to the events of the case. I suggest that it be reread with the objective of editing out unnecessary detail in order to increase further its readability. The IM's structure should follow categories listed in the first IM section, above. Place the detailed answers to the DQs with integrated theory and "A" and "C" answers in only one place in the IM. Don't refer the reader to other places in the IM for the answers. Exhibit E Q 4 Board Diagram is very complete. It should be located with the other DQs and their answers. Use the Board Diagram as an illustration of how to teach the various DQs in class.

Done.

WS 7:6

Sample Elements of Weak Reviews and Good Reviews

The following comments are drawn from real case reviews. For you to consider:

■ Why are the "weak" reviews weak? How can they be improved?
■ What makes the "good" reviews valuable?

Review Topic (Case)	Weak Review	Good Review
Is this case interesting? Please explain.	This case is interesting, although I'm not sure that students will find it that interesting.	The case has sufficient material of intrinsic interest to business students. The context of the case is one that most people can identify with. The manner in which the business enterprise was created—a group of founders with each bringing something of value to the enterprise—is also a common experience. The case itself is presented in a simple enough manner that it would appeal to business students, especially at the introductory levels.
Are graphs, charts, and tables adequately displayed?	Yes.	The tables look fine. I question whether all of the tables are necessary to the case. I would move tables 2, 4, 6, and 8 to the IM. I would recommend replacing one of these tables with a pie chart graph in the case.
Is the case sufficiently complete, complex, and focused to be worthy of publication?	No. It needs more work.	The case lacks complexity. The uncertainty around the event leads to fluctuation in demand and hence product price. Further, it borders on speculative economics.
Does the case present a situation, problem, or issue that is worthy of publication?	Yes.	Yes, the case involves cross-cultural management, dealing specifically with employees who perceive they are being treated unfairly.

Additional Suggestions: Weak	Additional Suggestions: Good
The case is much too long, much too detailed, and seems rather unfocused, given the cases questions in the IM. The story of the high-performing unit is a good one, but I don't know how to suggest working it into the case format.	I found the lack of a well-developed issue or decision focus frustrating and the list of questions at the end of the case (what to do next) contrived. The organization of the case followed the consultant's work plan, and this did not make for a very interesting case. Consider adding more exchanges and interactions among key principals and the consultant before and after the off-site workshops. Without this additional contextual information, the questions raised in the case seem to be too scripted and forced. Add a case hook or challenge to the introduction. Shorten the introduction and make it more focused. End the case with a return to the issue or challenges (the hooks) raised in the introduction. Consider adding additional biographical information on the main characters in the case, possibly by including a brief bio on each person in an appendix. The personality characteristics and the "characteristics of corporate culture" need further elaboration. This is especially important for this type of case, one that focuses on "process" and the values, ethics, vision, and mission-driven strategies. This additional information is especially important for a case that deals with company and managerial values and management succession. Add the code of ethics, mission, and vision statements to the case. Add raw data or comments from the various off sites to the case. This additional information would liven up the case and make it more interesting to the reader.

Review Topic (Instructor's Manual)	Weak Review	Good Review
Does the instructor's manual include all elements: synopsis, description of the fields for which the case is intended, level of student, learning objectives, relevant texts, research methodology, discussion questions and answers, teaching strategy, theory as appropriate, and epilogue, if known?	No.	The IM does not list applicable texts. The case does not supply sufficient information to address the authors' claim that the case applies to marketing and supply chain management. Although the authors claim the case involves strategy, growth, and supply chain leadership, the IM does not adequately address these topics.
Are the pedagogical objectives of the case clearly set forth? Can the case be used to meet those objectives?	Yes, with minor modifications.	Yes. It would be difficult to address all the learning objectives solely by assigning this case. For example, objectives 1 and 2 and can be taught without the benefit of this case; objective 5 cannot be met solely through the case. One does not know whether the process used and ethics code developed at this company are effective or not. The author needs to either assign additional readings along with the case or clearly state what pre-work or prior course work is needed to best meet the pedagogical objectives.

Is the instructor's manual complete? Does it cover all case objectives? Are answers complete and based on information found within the case? Is topic coverage comprehensive?	The answers are rather complete; however, I find that students could not draw on the case material to adequately answer the questions.	There is limited discussion of relevant theory in the responses to the discussion questions; too many discussion questions with limited use of case data in the responses; limited analysis of each question; there is no teaching plan; limited documentation of case use in classroom (used over 30 times, but little explanation of its effectiveness by course level is included). For example, how might "A" students handle the discussion questions versus other students? No discussion or explanation of exhibits A, B, and C in IM; no epilogue. Most of the answers to the discussion questions do not require in-depth analysis or can be addressed generally without assigning the case.
Does the instructor's manual relate case issues to current theory, practice, or literature in the fields intended for case use?	Many of the references are classics, but not recent at all.	Yes, but leaves out some of the most obvious cultural comparison literature, Hofstede and Trompenaars.

Overall Evaluation/Quality	Weak Review	Good Review
Is the case well written and suitably organized?	It's OK.	The case addresses an interesting situation. It is a little too long, and it seem disorganized. Sometimes there is repetition of words (see pp. 3, 7, and 11), and sometimes of ideas (pp. 3–5 and 12–13). The case appears slanted to the views of the protagonist.
Are spelling, grammar, and punctuation correct?	See my comments within the edited case.	Poor grammar and many violations of case writing conventions. The common mistakes were: ■ verb tense—cases are always written in past tense ■ vague time references—words like "currently" and "now" become meaningless when the reader isn't sure to what time period they refer ■ capitalization problems ■ use of slang

WS 7:7

Steps in Writing a Review

Select a case (published or unpublished) and its related Instructor's Manual for this exercise. Following the steps outlined here, write your review in the right-hand column.

Step/Action	Your Evaluation of This Case
Start with the case and read the case hook.	
Does it draw you in? Will students relate to it? Does it avoid the "manager-pondering-his-next-steps" syndrome?	
Go to the IM and read the case synopsis and learning objectives.	
Do you know what the case is about? What students are expected to learn? Are you interested in using this case or referring it to a colleague?	
Go back to the case and read it through once quickly (as students are prone to doing).	
Does it hold your attention? What additional information did you want that was not in the case? Did the case follow a logical path or were you confused? Do you know what the author expects you to do at the end of the case?	
Return to the IM and read the Discussion Questions.	
Can you answer them from the case? Is there something significant missing or are there assumptions of tacit knowledge made?	
Return to the case and try to answer the questions before you look at the answers in the IM.	
Can your students answer the questions? What do you expect they might say? Is the case written at the correct level?	
Complete your reading of the IM.	
Do the answers to the discussion questions reflect the kinds of answers you would anticipate from students? Does the author treat theory the way you would prefer? Are there key references that need to be added? Is the bibliography extensive enough? Does the teaching methodology make sense to you? Did you learn something?	
Read the case one more time.	
Is it well written? Engaging? Directed to important learning? What special advice might you give the author?	

Module 8

●●●●●

Working with Coauthors

●●●●●

Creativity and Productivity: Working Alone Together

As academics, we most often work alone. We prepare our classes alone. We go into the classroom alone. We make difficult decisions alone. We do most of our research alone. We tend to write alone. The Academy is a great place for loners—for private, introspective individuals.

But creativity is *not* a solo activity. It requires bouncing ideas off other people, listening and brainstorming, building on suggestions, leaping on an opportunity and riding it until you get to the place that expresses your vision. This cannot be done alone in a quiet sanctuary. According to noted creativity gurus Tony Buzan (1991), Edward de Bono (1999), and Michael Michalko (2001), we get most creative in the company of others.

Case research, case writing, and case analysis are creative, communal activities. We encourage our students to work in teams to analyze cases, but we most often write them alone. Writing them with others (in teams or with just one coauthor) provides opportunities for us to improve our writing, enhance our own (and our students') understanding, and develop a more useful and comprehensive product. Now might be the right time for you to put aside your reservations and connect with a congenial colleague, an individual who is knowledgeable in a related field, or an interdisciplinary team of interested academics/professionals to produce an integrated case with multiple perspectives that will challenge your students' and your own long-standing beliefs.

See WS 8:1 for an overview of the differences between writing alone and writing with others.

Writing Alone

Most of the modules in this workbook focus on case authors writing alone. In the "References and Readings" section of this module, you will find a selection of excellent academic writing guides that offer advice on structuring your individual writing processes.

Writing with One Colleague

Writing with a colleague can be a rewarding and intellectually exciting process. On the positive side:

■ A coauthored project can take special advantage of each writer's particular skills. Perhaps you are great at structuring the case narrative and your partner has a very clear handle on the theoretical issues necessary for the Instructor's Manual. Maybe your teaching expertise lends itself well to designing a classroom process, while your coauthor's organizational skill and elegance of expression is best applied to the case story. You can fuse your talents into a superior final product by combining your skill sets.

■ Simply having a partner establishes a sense of accountability and helps to avoid partially developed manuscripts languishing in your digital file cabinet.

■ A case may address two different disciplinary areas at the same time if the coauthors come from distinct backgrounds. A finance professor may marry skills with a management professor, for example, to write a case about a financial management issue in a large corporation. My personal experience in this regard resulted in the publication of a finance textbook richly illustrated with brief case examples. This text was designed specifically to meet the finance-based needs of our entrepreneurship students, and it has been well received by others with similar needs. Neither of us could have written this book alone.

■ When you are having an awful semester and cannot find the time to conduct research on your own or manage the reams of research you have already generated, your writing partner can take over with confidence, knowing that you would do the same for her.

■ When a project is simply too big to handle alone, sharing it can make it manageable.

■ Brainstorming is better when done with someone else. When you are alone, all your ideas tend to sound either excellent or worthless. Having a realistic and trusted sounding board with whom you can toss about your ideas will result in more creative and interesting possibilities than you could generate alone.

■ In a best case scenario, you have half the work and twice the productivity.

Writing with a partner can also be a nightmare:

■ If your partner is all about ego, you will end up being a junior partner rather than a true collaborator.

■ When your work styles differ dramatically, you will end up irritating each another unintentionally. Suppose, for example, that you like to get a paper drafted quickly and then work slowly to clean it up, while your coauthor prefers to craft each sentence with care from the very beginning. Your initial speed makes your coauthor nervous and anxious because he can't keep up. His "turtle's pace" drives you crazy because you can't move forward. One style isn't better than the other, but they cannot be combined easily.

- You like to plan your work ahead, set milestones for yourself, and want feedback on an ongoing basis. Your coauthor leaves all the work in her head until the very last minute, at which point she works nonstop and does not give you an opportunity to critique the direction in which she is heading.

- One or both of you are control freaks. Or one of you is a slacker.

- You can't figure out whose name goes first on the author line. Do you opt for an alphabetical listing, which—if you are a "Vega," as I am—typically makes you the second author by default? Does the person who had the idea become the lead author? Or does the person who has the skill to implement the project become the lead author? What a bother—and one that often results in resentment.

- When one author has poor writing skills and the other has a sharp editing pencil, conflict will erupt or bad feelings will fester.

- When either author becomes wedded to an idea, an expression, or a single focus, the project may never be completed.

If these things happen to you in your writing partnership, take heart from knowing that you need to finish only one project with this coauthor. You don't have to do it again.

If Your Writing Partner Is a Student

This scenario poses a different set of concerns than simply writing with one coauthor who is a colleague.

If you are writing with an undergraduate student, you should bear in mind the following:

- Undergraduates cannot write an Instructor's Manual, so you will have to undertake that task on your own.

- You will be responsible for cleaning up the writing quality, maintaining voice, and doing all the editing tasks that one might normally share with an experienced coauthor.

- There will be issues of power or influence that will arise in your relationship. As the instructor, you are in a position of power; your student is not likely to know how to rise to the partnership level without your help. Part of your overall task is to develop the student's skills and make sure she recognizes the value and importance of the coauthor role.

■ Undergraduate students frequently have a casual relationship with deadlines, but if you are writing for a conference, for example, you *must* meet the deadline or your submission will not be considered. Student excuses for late delivery of documents (I had to study for an exam, my boss called me in to work extra hours, my computer broke, the dog ate my homework, etc.) will have no impact on the conference organizers. You will have to remind the student about the deadlines many times.

What *is* the role of the student coauthor? It sounds like the instructor does it all and simply adds the student's name to the title page. What is the student bringing to the table? Here are two key contributions:

■ Almost always, the student brings the case idea, access to the company, and a good story. These are critical elements of case writing and should not be undervalued.

■ Working with a student coauthor forces you to slow down, think things through as you explain them to the student, and really focus on what you are doing so that you can be sure that the student understands the relevant processes and protocols (and the reasons for them).

If you are writing with a graduate student, much of the preceding applies. Of course, the MBA student will have greater world knowledge and experience and will certainly understand the firmness of deadlines.

If you are writing with a doctoral student, the game changes. The expectation is that you will be the senior author but that you can assign nearly any task to the doctoral student. This is one important way for them to learn and provide evidence of learning. You can treat a doctoral student almost the same way as a full colleague, with the understanding that the responsibility is still yours—you are the instructor, sharing your wisdom, knowledge, and skills (and evaluating the work of the student).

Writing with a Team

Writing with a team is different from writing with just one coauthor. It is simultaneously more complex and more straightforward. Whenever people get together to work in teams, certain traits, characteristics, and roles emerge naturally. These behaviors fall into three broad categories: task-related, social-related, and individualistic. The following list shows the emergent roles:

■ Someone will always volunteer for the task role of **initiator**, taking on the responsibility for generating new ideas. This person often becomes the **opinion seeker, opinion giver,** and **elaborator** as well.

■ Other task roles that team members will gravitate toward naturally include the **evaluator** (identifies an objective standard for the product), the **energizer** (motivates the group), the **technician** (responsible for logistics), and the **recorder** (a critical role in any team). The **devil's advocate** helps the team identify flaws that they otherwise might have overlooked.

■ Social roles are the roles that hold the team together. A key social role is held by the **encourager/harmonizer** (the peacekeeper). Without this person, the writing team will have trouble remaining productive when tempers flare. The **standard setter** keeps the team standards high and acts much the same way the **evaluator** does, but in a way that focuses on positive social outcomes.

■ Other social roles involve functions that maintain group satisfaction, such as **tension reducer, communicator,** and **active supporter**. If people fail to fill these roles, it is likely that a group will become dysfunctional and not be able to recover.

■ Individualistic roles signal dysfunction. These are the collaborators who need a lot of personal attention, block the forward progress of the group, call attention to themselves, and try to manipulate other group members. Sometimes, these are collaborators who spend a lot of time complaining, consistently attempt to gain sympathy, or attack other members of the group. If you have one in your team, you will need to set acceptable behavioral parameters early on and be prepared to remove the person from the team if the negative behavior persists.

If the team members do not take up the task and social roles on their own, the roles should be assigned. See WS 8:2 for a full description of the responsibilities that accompany each of the roles.

⬤ ⬤ ⬤ ⬤ ⬤

Benefits and Challenges of Working with Partners

Benefits

There are three main benefits to working with a partner: increased productivity, improved personal learning, and enhanced collegiality.

Increased Productivity

Changing standards for attaining various accreditations have put a heavier emphasis on both quantity and quality of publications by faculty. As discussed in Module 1, the pressure is on in many schools to produce additional publications to maintain one's academic qualifications. This is more easily accomplished when working in teams of two or more, as each team member will reap the publication benefit of each case or article that goes to press. As a noble goal, this one falls short; as a practical measure of efficiency, however, it is both sensible and rewarding.

Improved Personal Learning

Due in part to increasing demands on our time and in part to the pro-
liferation of discipline-based papers, it has become harder and harder
to remain current in our own areas of specialization. Consequently, it is
nearly impossible for us to undertake new learning in other related areas
of study, and this is where writing in a team really fills a void. One member of the team may be well grounded in the financial issues surround-
ing mergers and acquisitions, while another is particularly skilled in the
cultural aspects of merging organizations. A third might have a particular depth of knowledge about the industry in question, and a fourth
might be the one with the organizational contacts. By working together,
you will all learn new material, expand your own skill sets, and possibly
even begin to do some theory development based on your case study.
The process will certainly stimulate you intellectually and refresh your
worldview.

Enhanced Collegiality

Once you have finished teaching your classes, polishing your course
preparations, meeting with students, and handling administrative tasks
and committee responsibilities, how much time do you really get to
spend with your colleagues? In a best-case scenario, your colleagues will
become personal friends and you will develop enormous professional
respect for one another. This is good for you, for your colleagues, and
for your institutions because people who like one another and work well
together are likely to strengthen their ties with the institution and its mission. See the section later in this module that provides guidelines for establishing your own community of practice around case writing.

Challenges

Although the list of challenges is long, do not be daunted by it. Overall,
the challenges are offered more in the spirit of "things to organize" than
"factors to fear." See WS 8:3 for a checklist to help you decide if your project is better off done alone or with others.

How Do You Decide Who Is on the Team?

This is the key question . . . and the answer will determine the likelihood
of the project's success. First, think of all the teams you have served on,
both in your professional life and in your private life. Identify the people
who you would never want to work with again. Why not?

I have worked with people who don't pull their weight, who always
have to be right, who complain about things that are wrong but have
no suggestions for fixing them, who are frequently late with their work,

whose ego is even bigger than mine, who produce work of dubious quality, whose writing I have to "fix" all the time, and whose standards are not consonant with mine. I am willing to bet that your list is similar.

I have also worked with people who don't complain, who know their material, who write well, who are understanding and kind, who have a sense of humor, are willing to tolerate me and my foibles, who meet deadlines, who have ideas, and who hold standards similar to my own. I hope you have been lucky enough to work with these people as well.

Choose people from the second group to be on your team. Avoid people from the first group, even if they are your friends, because it will be an enormous strain to work with them.

Identifying the Strengths of Team Members

Of course, you must be certain that your chosen coauthors bring the strengths you need to the project. You can do this by providing a data collection form similar to the sample in WS 8:4; this tool will help you build a database of skills, knowledge, and expertise that your potential collaborators can provide. It is important to identify research interests and methodological preferences as well as skills in order to take best advantage of the available talent.

Accept, Acknowledge, Approve

Once team members have been identified and all have agreed to work together on the project, drive home the message of the Triple A: Accept, Acknowledge, Approve.

Accept: Don't argue with the ideas of the contributor who has been selected because of her expertise in a particular area. The accounting professor should not squabble with the organizational expert. The logistics guru should bite his tongue when the marketing professor talks about social media. This does not mean that people should not have their own ideas and express them; however, it does mean that your ideas are most valuable when they are in your own area of knowledge.

Acknowledge: The specialists know best in their own disciplinary domains. In order for them to provide their best possible input, the rest of the team has to acknowledge each partner's expertise, knowing that each will get a turn to excel and shine. I can happily admit that I have little proficiency in finance because my coauthor has deep knowledge of the field, and that takes a burden off me. She looks to me to provide information and suggestions about behavioral issues and organizational structure.

Approve: As each element of the case is conceived, drafted, written, and edited, make sure that each team member approves the changes. If this process is followed from the beginning, everyone will be participating at an equivalent level and you will have no surprises at the end. If you discover early on that you have a team member who can't "play well with others," get this person off the team quickly. The approval process will help you separate the real contributors from the nonparticipators.

Logistics

Dividing Up the Work: Figuring out what is fair and sensible in terms of task distribution is not a simple matter. As you are aware from your experience handling student teams and their interactions, you know that each member feels she is doing the lion's share and the others make lesser contributions. Students don't feel this way because they are young; they feel this way because they are human. WS 8:5 provides a chart that may allow you to balance contributions in an objective manner.

Mutual Availability: One of the real problems in team writing comes from timing and availability issues. I have found only one way to identify and manage this problem: Set a time and date for meetings (face-to-face or conference calls/net meetings) and stick to it. Everyone on the team must commit to participating in the meetings or this arrangement will not work. Plan to hold as few meetings as you possibly can (aside from the scheduled interviews and/or site visits); set out to accomplish most of your work electronically, through one of the many secure cloud sites that can track your document changes and permit ongoing oversight of document development. You can find some popular document management sites in WS 8:6.

Work Styles: We all have our own unique work styles, and they fall into several generally accepted broad categories:

- People who like to work alone, often in quiet and non-stimulating environments
- People who prefer to bounce ideas off others or with others around them
- People who work heads-down until they complete a task
- People who intersperse one kind of task with another, moving forward in small increments on several tasks concurrently

If you are a single focus heads-down worker and your writing partner is a multitasker, conflicts will result. If you like to work alone in a quiet place and your coauthor wants to work in the same room as you and toss ideas back and forth, your communication efforts will suffer.

One solution to this problem is to plan ahead and establish mutually agreeable ground rules. Set aside some time for joint meetings to satisfy the needs of the inveterate brainstormer and reserve other times for uninterrupted individual work. Agree to incremental work products so that the heads-down worker does not feel constrained by the task juggler and the juggler does not feel pressured by the focused concentrator. There are many instruments available online—at no cost for you and your team—that will help you determine your individual work styles and plan ahead to avoid unnecessary and potentially destructive conflict. I have listed some books and articles for you in "References and Readings" if you prefer print sources.

Accountability: Who is in charge? Picking a team leader is a critical, early task. The team leader must be someone who can hold others accountable for delivery of their work product while accepting responsibility for the project as a whole. This is the role of a project manager, and yes, academics need a designated project manager who will keep them on task and on time. Be careful when assigning this role: *do not* assign it to the "nicest" person on the team, the most easygoing individual, or the person who never seems to be able to find his glasses.

Deadlines: All team members must commit, in writing if necessary, to deliver their materials by whatever deadlines have been established. If this occurs, your project will proceed reasonably seamlessly. When even one team member is late, however, that tardiness holds up everyone else and the project soon falls behind. When it comes to conferences, there is usually no leeway for submission, and that one late person may cost the entire team a valuable opportunity.

⦿ ⦿ ⦿ ⦿ ⦿

Interviewing in Teams

Please refer to Module 2 for a full discussion of interviewing processes and techniques. These remain the same whether you are working alone or in a team. What really differs in a team is the way you manage the processes.

An interview guide is what keeps your interview on track. Without it, you are likely to lapse into a "cuppa coffee conversation," a friendly chat that does not provide the valuable information you need to write your case. The interview guide fills the gap between the topic that interests you (the research question), the literature (or background information), and the special knowledge that you seek to elicit from the interviewee (the interviewee's role in the process under investigation). An interview guide is not "just" a set of questions. It provides a method of enhancing and enriching the stories and systematizing the data collection process.

Elements of the Interview Guide

Topic Clarification

It is important to *know what you want to know*. Try to think of the interview guide as your roadmap through the research process. If you don't know where you are going, you won't know when you have arrived. If the topic of your research is a major change in technology, for example, you should be eliciting stories from the interviewee about his involvement in that change. Although it might be interesting and instructional to learn about the person's relocation from California to Iowa and how that affected his life, that information is not relevant to the topic of your research. So, right up front, include a short paragraph—a 30-second description—of the goal of the interview so that the interviewee knows what to expect. You may wish to adapt the relationship-building statement in the preceding section and include that in the introduction. Certainly, these interviews will all reflect some element of global collaboration, so that should be included in the initial statement as well.

Initial, Open-Ended Questions

You have to start somewhere. This is the place to frame your general questions and some specific ones. (See the section in Module 2 for information on question design.) Typically, these initial questions are broad and arise naturally from your research. Although there might be some similarity in the questions used for each case project, the questions must be drafted fresh with each new case. There are no "magic bullet" questions beyond the most vague, "Tell me a bit about your XYZ project. How did you get involved? What was your role?"

Designing the Preferred Flow of the Interview

Interviewers should not feel stifled by the suggested format. Think of it as a general suggestion about the natural and logical direction the interview is likely to take, not a rigid format from which the interviewer must not deviate. The flow of the interview identifies the end point—where you want to end up. You can get there any way you are comfortable traveling. Try not to waste the interviewees' time asking for information that you can get from your own basic research. Instead, develop your questions from your research and then ask for amplification, clarification, confirmation, or disconfirmation of your conclusions, always heading toward your pre-identified end point.

Technical Information

If more than one interviewer is going to follow the same general format, it is wise to provide some operational information. This might include:

1. Suggested interview length;
2. Preferred method of recording and/or taking notes;
3. Any technological protocols; and
4. Other similar items that are best handled systematically.

Roles

There are several distinct roles that team members must play during the interview process.

The Contact

One person should be designated the **contact.** This is the person who initiates and responds to all e-mails and telephone calls from the interviewee. The goal is to avoid confusion and crossed messages. All communication should go through the contact.

The Interviewer

Another person should be designated the **interviewer.** This person guides the interview throughout but does not function as the only person permitted to talk to the interviewee. The goal is to make the entire interview process as stress-free as possible for the interviewee and specifically to avoid making the interviewee feel like he is being interrogated instead of interviewed. Having one team member act as the primary interviewer will facilitate this process. Take special care to avoid having one team member talk over another; the interviewee and the designated interviewer always have the floor.

The Note Taker

The **note taker** has the primary responsibility for taking notes at the interview. This does not relieve the rest of the team from taking notes; however, the assigned note taker will probably not do much talking due to the level of concentration required for this task.

The Timekeeper

One person should be designated the **timekeeper.** This person makes sure that the interview does not extend too long, interrupting the workday of the interviewee. The timekeeper needs to monitor the interactions carefully to identify the point at which the interview should draw to a close. It pays to establish a predetermined signal or code to indicate an appropriate closing point.

When working alone, you must fill each of these roles yourself. It is a real luxury to have team members who can take the pressure off by accepting one or more of these roles.

● ● ● ● ●

Knowledge Management Protocols: The Beauty of Schedules

The Critical Path

A critical path identifies all activities that must take place to attain a specific goal, estimates the time needed to perform the activities, and documents the relationships among the activities.

Data collection begins with WS 8:7, Data Collection Responsibilities (an expansion of WS 2:6) and the key question: What do you want to find out? This is not as simple as it may sound. It is the case analog to the Instructor's Manual question: What do I want students to learn from this case? Both these questions must be answered before you begin collecting data.

> *Note:* Refer to WS 8:8, Steps in the Case Writing Process, and WS 8:9, Case Development Timeline, for a visual representation of the entire case writing critical path.

Some data are consistently required, regardless of the case content or learning objectives. These data include corporate history, industry information, background about the major players, and easily identifiable problems. Once these basics have been collected and stored, the search begins for less easily identifiable problems and issues requiring resolution. You can use WS 8:10—Materials and Corporate Access Needed—to brainstorm the sources of the data you require, then assign responsibilities for gathering the materials based on the preferences and skills of the team members.

Data collection should continue throughout the case writing process, because triangulation is the key to a solid case. Should one of you come across information that conflicts with previous findings, recognize that this information is important and valuable in the development of a credible case study and must be documented. You can assume that basic data collection will be more or less complete by the second draft of the case, but you may continue to discover important facts and relationships that can enrich your case right up to the time of publication. The assumption is that a complete case and IM written by an experienced team will be ready to test in the classroom within six to seven months, with anticipated final completion between nine and 12 months. The first three months comprise the bulk of the research collection; then, additional elements are added during the draft writing period.

Data Storage

Case writing involves enormous quantities of data. Once you have begun to collect it, either as an individual or in a team, you are confronted with the challenge of filing the data in a usable format in an accessible location. This is particularly difficult when working in an academic team because much of the teamwork is done remotely; that is, you go to your various private locations and research, think, and write. You interview either alone or most frequently in teams of two. You rarely have a central location to store data for later use (a location that is available whether you are in your offices, your homes, or the local Starbucks). In addition, even if you were to have such a "case study research room," you would still need to design a data management protocol to which you could all commit.

One way you can maintain a central filing system efficiently is via technology. I mentioned collaboration software earlier in this module, and I encourage your teams to investigate a system that will work well for you.

Storing Data in Collaboration Systems

Once you have decided on a collaboration system, you must build the initial format by setting up a Materials Folder to store all templates, protocols, data, and general information for easy access and use. All users should feel free to enter this folder and download whatever they need.

Each project undertaken should contain a file labeled Knowledge Management (KM) Protocols. The KM Protocols file found in WS 8:11 includes information such as: What We Know; What We Want to Find Out; Sources and References; Interview Guide; Topics; Discussion Board; Case Drafts; IM Drafts; and similar headings. This file should be updated and saved each time new material is added by a user so the most current version is used by all participants. This will allow all data to be captured and retained by the writing team.

Developing an Institutional Case Writing Mindset

Colleges and universities, especially those with a primarily pedagogical mission, look for ways to engage their faculty in research and scholarship that serve the needs of the institution and the students who attend it. Because business schools tend to focus heavily on teaching with cases, it makes good sense to develop an appreciation of case writing within the faculty itself. I have worked with several schools to establish a case writing mindset, and the result has been an increase in faculty engagement, a greater number of publications, and a revived enthusiasm, especially among experienced faculty, for the art of teaching and the craft of writing.

Setting Up a Community of Practice around Case Writing

There are a variety of goals around which a community of practice can be developed. Perhaps you are looking primarily for a group to discuss case writing problems or challenges in a roundtable format, such as used in case conferences. Or maybe you are actively seeking coauthors for a collaborative case writing effort. Or maybe you simply want to encourage others in your institution to learn about case writing and investigate the possibilities it may have for your faculty. Each of the following types of groups has its own internal logic and degree of commitment.

■ The Roundtable Discussion Group

Inherent in its name is the indication that this group exists to "discuss" the ongoing development of cases in progress. The commitment that members of this group make is to meet on a regular basis (weekly/monthly/four times each semester) to critique one another's work in a positive, constructive manner. Following the suggestions for group establishment earlier in this module, once you have set a schedule and formally or informally determined basic roles, each member agrees to advance his work incrementally (no specific amount of writing should be required) and share the work at least one week before the group convenes its session. Each member commits to reading the work of the others and commenting on it in writing (yes, scribbling on the paper itself is perfectly fine) in preparation for the roundtable session. At the session, each author in turn describes the advances made since the previous meeting, and all participants comment on the work presented. All members of the group should leave feeling satisfied that their work has advanced and knowing the direction they need to go to move forward with their case project.

■ The Collaborative Case Writing Effort

This group is far more formal than the roundtable group. The guidelines for this group have been the focus of most of this module. The collaborative case writing groups that I have established at several universities succeeded because of three things: there was an advocate in the dean's office to support and sustain the group; one member of the group was the initiator and "force" behind the effort; and the group members were committed to the general goals of the collaborative effort. Once launched, these groups continued to produce case after case in their newly established model.

■ The Case Exploration Group

This group is designed for the purpose of enhancing a sense of community in a school by identifying a mutual interest held by colleagues in various departments (even across the campus). In such a group, participants may share cases they have found to be useful in their classes, ideas about new ways to teach cases, suggestions for classic cases to be used in a program-development mode, or as a safe place to seek help for classroom case-related problems, teaching advice, or other collegial sharing. The primary rule of such a group is that "what happens in the exploration group remains in the exploration group."

Writing in teams creates a sense of collegiality among faculty members and develops a natural tendency by the more experienced to mentor the newer case writers. This is an opportunity for the mentoring to cross experience lines, as often the new academics are more comfortable with some of the case writing processes than their more experienced colleagues.

I urge you to launch your own case writing team using the worksheets and information provided in this manual. And, of course, you can always contact me directly for additional assistance.

● ● ● ● ●

References and Readings

Benne, K.D., and P. Sheats. (1948). "Functional Roles of Group Members." *Journal of Social Issues* 4, no. 2, 41–49.

Boice, R. (1990). *Professors as Writers: A Self-Help Guide to Productive Writing.* Stillwater, OK: New Forums Press.

Buzan, T. (1991). *Use Both Sides of Your Brain: New Mind-Mapping Techniques,* 3d ed. New York: Plume.

de Bono, E. (1999). *Six Thinking Hats,* rev. and updated. Boston: Back Bay Books.

Hammer, A.L., and E.R. Schnell. (1996). *FIRO-B® Interpretive Report for Organizations.* Report. Palo Alto, CA: Consulting Psychologists Press, Inc.

Huff, A.S. (1998). *Writing for Scholarly Publication.* Thousand Oaks, CA: Sage.

Michalko, M. (2001). *Cracking Creativity: The Secrets of Creative Genius.* Berkeley, CA: Ten Speed Press.

Myers-*Briggs Type Indicator® Team Report.* (1998). Palo Alto, CA: Consulting Psychologists Press, Inc.

Silvia, P.J. (2007). *How to Write a Lot: A Practical Guide to Productive Academic Writing.* Washington, DC: American Psychological Association.

Vega, G., and M.S. Lam. (2016). *Entrepreneurial Finance: Concepts and Cases.* New York: Routledge (Taylor & Francis).

Wenger, E. (2000). "Communities of Practice and Social Learning Systems." *Organization* 7, no. 2, 225–246.

● ● ● ● ●

Worksheets

WS 8:1   Differences between Writing Alone and Writing with Others

WS 8:2   Team Role Responsibilities

WS 8:3   Is Your Project Better Off Done Alone or with Others?

WS 8:4   Skills, Knowledge, and Expertise Data Collection Format

WS 8:5   Balancing Individual Contributions

WS 8:6   Cloud Document Management Sites

WS 8:7   Data Collection Responsibilities

WS 8:8   Steps in the Case Writing Process

WS 8:9   Case Development Timeline

WS 8:10   Materials and Corporate Access Needed

WS 8:11   Knowledge Management Protocols

WS 8:1

Differences between Writing Alone and Writing with Others

Tasks associated with case writing appear in the first column, followed by who holds the responsibility for completing the tasks.

Task	Writing Alone	Writing with Others
Identification of company	You do it	Shared
Making contact with company	You do it	Shared
Obtaining releases	You do it	Shared
Archival research	You do it	Shared
Interviewing and observation	You do it	Shared
Maintaining records	You do it	Shared
Drafting initial case	You do it	Shared
Refining case	You do it	Shared
Drafting IM	You do it	Shared
Refining IM	You do it	Shared
Testing case	You do it	Shared
Submitting to conference or journal	You do it	Shared
Revisions	You do it	Shared

WS 8:2

Team Role Responsibilities

The following table identifies roles that people perform in teams. Some of these roles will help you complete your project; others will help you develop strong positive team relationships. The last group identifies some dysfunctional roles that may hinder your team because they are focused on personal rather than team needs.

Make sure that each of the roles in the first two categories are adopted by members or assigned to members. If you notice behavior from the third category, deal with it as soon as you see it.

Role	Description	Team Member
Task-Related Roles		
Initiator/Contributor	Proposes goals, new ideas, and solutions; defines problems; suggests procedures; points out benefits	
Information giver	Offers facts and relevant information or experience	
Opinion giver	States belief about alternatives; focuses on values rather than facts	
Information seeker	Seeks clarification of suggestions based on facts relevant to the problem	
Opinion seeker	Asks for clarification of values held by the group in relation to the problem	
Coordinator	Clarifies the various suggestions, ideas, and opinions and coordinates them	
Summarizer	Summarizes and restates back to the team; draws member activities together; offers conclusions	
Clarifier/Elaborator	Interprets; gives examples; defines terms; clears up confusion or ambiguity	
Evaluator	Subjects the team's activity to some criterion— for example, practicality, logic, etc.	
Orienter	Tries to show the team the position it is now taking and may raise questions about its direction	
Procedural technician	Performs routine tasks for the group such as secretary, treasurer, timekeeper, and the like	
Energizer	Stimulates the group to action leading to closure	

Relationship-Related Roles		
Encourager	Praises good points; exhibits acceptance (the "we" feeling) and group solidarity	
Harmonizer	Attempts to mediate differences among members or their points of view; reduces conflict and tension; attempts to reconcile differences	
Gatekeeper/Expediter	Works to encourage communication, bringing persons into the discussion who have not given their ideas, keeping the discussion on point, etc.	
Standard setter	Expresses standards the group should attempt to achieve and applies them to evaluating the group process	
Compromiser	Is willing to compromise, yield his or her idea or point of view, or admit an error	
Group observer	Keeps records of the group process in action and brings as much data into the discussion as seen pertinent	
Follower	More or less a passive and accepting person; going along	
Dysfunctional Roles		
Aggressor	May express disapproval of others, joke excessively, attack the group or the problem, show envy, etc.	
Blocker	Is negativistic and resistant, disagrees and opposes beyond reasonable objections; gets discussion off on a tangent; focuses on personal concerns rather than on team problem; argues too much	
Recognition seeker	Tries to get attention; calls attention to self; boasts; exhibits loud or unusual behavior; excessive talker	
Dominator	Tries to assert authority to control team at expense of other members	
Avoider	Acts indifferently; withdraws from discussion; daydreams; wanders off, talks to others; fools around	
Playboy/girl	Does not involve self in group process but sits back and engages in horseplay, whispering, etc.	
Self-confessor	Brings in personal feelings, ideas, etc., neither pertinent nor oriented to the group	
Help seeker	Attempts to express insecurity, gain sympathy, or in other ways deprecate self	
Special interest pleader	Expresses own biases or prejudices by pleading for the minority groups within the group	

Source: Adapted from Benne and Sheats (1948).

WS 8:3

Is Your Project Better Off Done Alone or with Others?

The following chart will help you decide whether you should write your case alone or in a team.

You will need to make your decision on each specific case project, because your answers will likely change according to the content and context of the project.

	Work Alone	Work with a Team
You have a company contact who is willing to work with you.	X	
You don't have much patience for delays.	X	
You want things done your own way.	X	
You have a light course load or minimal preps.	X	X
You play a key role in one or more institutional committees.		X
The case situation revolves around an area in which you have little expertise.		X
You need an external sense of accountability to move forward on projects.		X
You like to work with other people.		X
You like writing the case but dislike writing the IM (or the reverse).		X
You want to teach a colleague how to write cases.		X
You think it would be fun to write with someone else.		X
You are uncertain how to proceed.		X

WS 8:4

Skills, Knowledge, and Expertise Data Collection Format

Provide one form for each team member or potential team member. You can develop a database from the resulting information and easily identify the right people for your team when you need them. This is especially useful to do for a business school faculty; be sure to do it well in advance of initiating a project. You can easily upload this template to an online questionnaire system to make data collection and coordination simpler.

Name: _____

Strengths/Skills	*Place a ✓ in the cells that represent your particular strengths and areas of interest*
Writing dialogue and/or descriptive material	
Performing archival research	
Talking to people	
Listening to people	
Analyzing people's actions/behaviors	
Performing quantitative analysis	
Analyzing strategy	
Developing theoretical supports for an argument	
Careful observation	
Knowing when to talk and when to listen	
Having strong intuition or insights	
Especially good in the classroom	
Identifying most salient learning opportunities	
Synthesizing various approaches or theoretical perspectives	
Diagramming, designing figures, graphical talent	
Preferences	**Place a ✓ in the cells that represent your particular preferences**
Prefer to work alone	
Prefer to work in a team	
Prefer to conduct quantitative research	
Prefer to conduct qualitative research	
No preference for quantitative or qualitative research	

I have background in the following areas:	Check as many as apply
Organizational behavior/Theory/Development	
Strategy	
Human resource management	
Accounting/Finance	
Business ethics/Corporate social responsibility	
Consumer marketing	
Produce development	
Change and innovation	
Entrepreneurship	
Information technology/MIS	
Operations management	
Other (please list)	
Other (please list)	

WS 8:5
Balancing Individual Contributions

The following chart lists and describes elements of the case and the Instructor's Manual so you can determine tasks of equivalent difficulty to distribute among team members.

Remember to include the task of overall project management, which should fall to the team leader or lead author. This person will also submit the case to an outlet and follow up with managing the revision process.

Elements of a Case	
The Opening Hook:	The beginning of the case that grabs you and makes you interested. Not an abstract, but should stimulate curiosity.
The Company Story:	The organizational history, salient features of the company, other background information.
The Industry:	A full description of the services or product, size of the industry, competition, factors that produce profit, barriers to entry, context.
The Actors:	Detailed description of the protagonists or key characters. The readers need to relate to the characters.
The Situation:	This is the problem or issue that you want to use as the centerpiece decision of the case.
Additional Information:	This is where you add complexity, subtexts, and other necessary and relevant data.
The Closing Hook:	The part that makes us want to help the protagonist and hints at what we should be focusing on. It must refer back to the problem mentioned in the opening hook.
Elements of an Instructor's Manual	
Case Summary:	Your opportunity to sell your case to other instructors. Include a brief synopsis and the challenge to students.
Research Methods Employed:	Field researched or written from secondary sources.
Audience and Placement:	Undergraduates, graduate students, or an executive education program; course(s); time in the term; selected texts and relevant chapters.
Learning Objectives:	What should students be able to do as a result of discussing this case?
Discussion Questions:	These must be answerable from the case itself—be sure to include sufficient information in the case.
Analysis and Answers to the Questions:	This may include additional relevant readings for instructor or students. Try to write answers with an A/C split.
Teaching Strategies:	These should include the time and effort necessary in preparation before class and activities during class.
Epilogue:	The outcome, if known. If not known, state that.

WS 8:6

Cloud Document Management Sites

The following list identifies some URLs you can visit to find document management software. New sites are appearing regularly via cloud computing.

To find more sites, enter these key words in your online search: content management systems; document management systems; cloud computing; document management software; enterprise software solutions.

Name/URL	Description
AuditMyPC, "Free Document Management Software" http://www.auditmypc.com/free-document-management-software.asp (accessed April 6, 2016)	Products and online tools software
The CMS Matrix, "Compare Content Management Systems" http://www.cmsmatrix.org/matrix/cms-matrix (accessed April 6, 2016)	Compare any two or more content management systems with a click of your mouse
"2016 Content Management Software Reviews" http://cms-software-review.toptenreviews.com/ (accessed April 6, 2016)	Reviews and downloads of popular content management systems
Google Drive www.docs.google.com (accessed April 6, 2016)	Free software that is compatible with most office packages; if you use Gmail, you already have Google Drive available for use
Briley Kenney, "5 Cloud Storage Alternatives to Dropbox, Google Drive, and iCloud," October 15, 2015. http://www.cheatsheet.com/gear-style/5-cloud-storage-alternatives-to-dropbox-google-drive-and-icloud.html/?a=viewall (accessed April 6, 2016).	If you want to find systems similar to Google Drive, this site provides side-by-side comparisons of five other free cloud computing systems

WS 8:7

Data Collection Responsibilities

What do you want to find out? Use the final column to assign responsibility.

Code	Data, Information, Indicator	Level of Importance*	Collection Method	Location or Source	Researcher Responsible
CH	Corporate History		Corporate website, handouts and annual reports, books and articles, archival materials	Internet, library, company archives	
IN	Industry Note		Books and articles, archival materials	Internet, library	
PI	Performance Indicators		Internal documents	Finance, marketing, production	
SF	Stakeholder Feedback		Internal documents, newspaper articles	Internet, blogs, company archives	
P^1	Easily Identifiable Problems		Interviews	Leaders, team members, stakeholders	
P^2	Less Easily Identifiable Problems		Observation, interviews, public documents, internal documents	Internet, library, company archives	
	Other Interest Areas				

*H = High Importance; M = Moderate Importance; S = Somewhat Important; N = Nice to Know.

WS 8:8

Steps in the Case Writing Process

Set dates for these tasks in each case you undertake.

Case: _____

Team Members: _____

Task	Date
Identification of company or individual	
Selection of writing team	
Background/forensic research (Module 2)	
Identify learning objectives (Module 5)	
Establish the Interview Guide (Module 2)	
Draft case outline (Module 3)	
Draft IM outline (Module 5)	
Draft #1 of case	
Draft #1 of IM	
Draft #2 of case	
Draft #2 of IM	
Test case in class	
Refine and complete final draft of case	
Refine and complete final draft of IM	
Submission to conference or journal	

WS 8:9

Case Development Timeline

Use Figure 8.1 *to estimate the amount of time your team will need to complete a full case and Instructor's Manual from the very beginning. Experienced case writers will complete this process more quickly.*

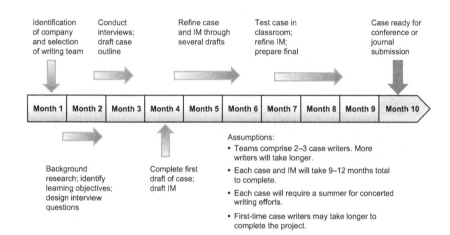

Identification of company and selection of writing team

Conduct interviews; draft case outline

Refine case and IM through several drafts

Test case in classroom; refine IM; prepare final

Case ready for conference or journal submission

| Month 1 | Month 2 | Month 3 | Month 4 | Month 5 | Month 6 | Month 7 | Month 8 | Month 9 | Month 10 |

Background research; identify learning objectives; design interview questions

Complete first draft of case; draft IM

Assumptions:
- Teams comprise 2–3 case writers. More writers will take longer.
- Each case and IM will take 9–12 months total to complete.
- Each case will require a summer for concerted writing efforts.
- First-time case writers may take longer to complete the project.

WS 8:10

Materials and Corporate Access Needed

Use this form to record materials and corporate access needed, along with the name of the individual responsible for getting each piece of information. Add or delete items as relevant to your case.

Case Name: _____

Item Needed	Person Responsible
Glossary of acronyms	
Brochures and sales materials	
The complete "solution" to the case problem (current update for use in epilogue)	
Committee notes and meeting minutes, if nonconfidential	
Financial and other projections (market considerations, etc.)	
Organization charts	
Access to specific individuals (identify)	
■ (name or title)	
■ (name or title)	
■ (name or title)	
Other (specify here)	
■	
■	
■	

WS 8:11

Knowledge Management Protocols

Establish a separate file for each case and label: KM_COMPANYNAME. This will be the first file in each case folder and will provide an overview of all materials related to a specific case. Examples appear in a different font.

Consistency in this process will make research easier, allow knowledge to be shared, provide a secure holding location for data, and ensure access for all case writers.

Knowledge Management: Sample File

Topic Code and Name	What We Know	What We Want to Find Our	Where We Can Find It	Priority	References and Sources
Draw from WS 8:7—be sure to match the codes	Links and files, named clearly	Include type of data where possible (lists, charts, tables, narrative, spreadsheets, diagrams)		High, medium, low	Use APA formatting and add all references to the master file. Attach article if possible, otherwise attach link.
CH Corporate History	corphistory_ 1990–2005.doc	■ Corporate history 2005–2010 ■ Founder's bio ■ Reporting structure 2005 (org chart)	■ Interview with founder ■ Corporate records	High	Author's last name, first initial. (date). Title in upper- and lowercase. Journal Name, volume no., pages.
IN Industry Note					
Etc.					

Module 9

●●●●●

Teaching with Cases

●●●●●

A Look Back at the IM . . . A Look Ahead to the Classroom

Once a case has reached its target—your students—the next step is figuring out how to maximize student learning. Module 5, Building the Instructor's Manual, explored the importance of teaching strategies and emphasized learning objectives and learning theory. In this module, we will focus on practical techniques to use in the classroom, both face-to-face and online, along with methods for connecting them to pedagogical theory.

As a reminder, teaching starts with learning objectives—specifically, what you want students to walk away with. Before you design your teaching strategy, make sure the case fits your learning objectives: These are specific, measurable actions that students can implement. This means taking particular care to select a case that satisfies your needs. No matter how good, how interesting, or how rich a case may be, if it does not result in student learning that is relevant to your course, the case is of no value to you.

●●●●●

The Five Ps

A simple way to organize your teaching strategy when using cases is the Five Ps: Purpose, Persona, Preparation, Problems, and Practice.

Purpose: Why Teach with Cases?

There are many reasons to teach with cases:

■ We use cases to **foster critical thinking**. Thinking clearly, logically, and analytically does not come naturally to most people; these skills must be taught and practiced before they are applied instinctively. One excellent way to teach students to think critically is to immerse them in situations where they either have to (1) make a decision or recommendation, or (2) analyze someone else's actions. Cases are the ideal vehicle to provide these challenges.

■ Cases **encourage student responsibility for learning**. Instead of requiring the instructor to teach specific skills or techniques, cases require students to discover how to apply facts and intuition to a problem. The simple transfer of responsibility engages students more deeply in the education process and supports retained learning more effectively.

■ Cases **blend affective and cognitive learning**. Combining the beliefs and emotional responses that reside in the affective domain with the facts, analysis, and applications that reside in the cognitive domain creates a complete learning experience. Short of actually experiencing a situation, cases bring the learner closer to this blending than any other method of instruction.

■ Cases **enliven the classroom**. If we are to be honest with ourselves, direct transfer of information (lecture) can be tedious in the extreme. When students have the opportunity to serve as problem diagnosticians, information detectives, solutions analysts, and recommending consultants, they are more likely to remain fully engaged in the learning process.

■ Cases help students **develop collaboration skills**. Case analysis in its many formats (see "Case Teaching Methods: How to Teach a Case—Let Me Count the Ways," later in this module) lends itself to teamwork and collaborative interactions. This is especially valuable because people rarely work alone in business, even when working from remote locations. Teamwork is the norm, and collaboration has long been shown to result in better outcomes, especially in terms of unleashing creative potential.

■ Cases **teach questioning and self-directed learning**. Instead of accepting the first idea that comes to mind, learning with cases encourages students to think a little harder, question their automatic responses, and apply tools of metacognition (thinking about the thinking about) to the problems presented in the case narrative.

See WS 9:1 to clarify what *your* purpose is in teaching with cases.

Persona: Who Are You Today?

The instructor's role comprises many responsibilities. We must:

■ provide leadership and management
■ keep the discussion orderly

- involve the entire class
- become a listener and a devil's advocate
- question and interject only to clarify and advance thinking
- abandon the accustomed role of expert
- be aware of the time
- operate at three levels

  - Participant/note taker
  - Guide to keeping the discussion on track
  - Evaluator of student performance

- and keep out of the way when the class is on the verge of discovery

Although we are by and large the same person day after day, small things can have a big impact on the way we interact with the world. If we sleep poorly, burn our breakfast toast, get a speeding ticket, or have a bad hair day, our approach to our students is likely to be less easygoing and more demanding. If we have just received good news, lost those two recalcitrant pounds, or received an e-mail from an old friend, we are likely to be more relaxed in the classroom and willing to try new things.

When stressed, our natural tendencies extend themselves and take over our relationships both with people and with inanimate objects. If we tend to be reserved, a stressful day can make us appear cold and unfeeling. If we tend toward extroversion, a lot of stimulation may make us too casual and encourage us to be "one of the guys" instead of the teacher.

Day by day, we should take a reading of our emotional and psychological condition before we enter the classroom or login to our electronic classroom to decide if today is the day we are a "Sage on the Stage" or if, instead, we are a "Guide on the Side."

The "Sage on the Stage" Is a Content and Theory Approach

This approach represents a system in which the instructor is the holder of knowledge, the wise one in the literal or figurative front of the room who tells students what they need to know. The Sage on the Stage lectures and the students take notes, preparing to feed this information back to the instructor on exams. Although this form of learning is passive, it is a very effective way to transfer information, especially if students have prepared properly and have learned the relevant theories before the class. But, as discussed in Module 1, cases are not the best vehicle for information transfer. Instead, the strength of cases lies in their ability to encourage critical thinking, analysis, and the generation of solutions. Cases lend themselves to a different kind of teaching.

The "Guide on the Side" Is a Process Approach

This approach represents an interactive form of learning in which knowledge is created within the classroom, emerging from students as often as from the instructor. When an instructor takes the role of Guide on the Side, that instructor relinquishes much of the power in the learning process and places the responsibility for learning into the hands of the learners themselves. A learner-centered classroom provides a great forum for opportunistic teaching, with the students in the lead. Theory can be formalized later and related back to the case in question. It is hard to be a Guide on the Side: You must "work without a net"—that is, you must be prepared for the unexpected and help learners discover the lessons of the case as they emerge.

A Guide on the Side also must accept the likelihood of feeling foolish or confused, of stumbling or of having to scramble to keep the class discussion focused. If this makes you too uncomfortable, perhaps Guide on the Side is not for you. However, I encourage you to select a day when your toast is perfect, your bathroom scale is your friend, and you feel good about yourself to take the risk and let your students learn, rather than insist on teaching them.

Preparation (Yours)

You need to prepare, and prepare well, before you teach a case. You cannot assume that your job has become easier because the responsibility for learning has been transferred to the student or because your students are one step removed from you in an online setting. On the contrary, your preparation for teaching a case requires a considerable amount of homework. The Instructor's Manual that comes along with the case may be of some help, but unless your goals for your class are identical to those specified in the IM, you need to start from scratch.

1. Know the case. Inside out and backwards. Know the characters. Know the facts. Know the sequences. This may require you to read the case many times. Until you have taught the case several times, you are not likely to feel comfortable in the depth of your knowledge. Remember— you have no backup in this system. You have to be ready for the unexpected.

2. Plan the discussion, but remember that your plan is just that—a plan, not a commitment. Case teaching is an instructional mode that calls for opportunistic teaching. When an opening appears that introduces a concept you had not planned on examining at that time, grab it. It's the exact time for you to follow through on that concept and solidify the student learning. You may never get such a good chance with your students in so receptive a mood. See WS 9:2 for a simple, easy-

to-follow discussion plan for a face-to-face or synchronous electronic discussion.

3. Have a list of questions handy. Do not depend on the questions that are provided in the IM, although these may be valuable and useful to you. Students will rarely answer them the way the author has answered them, and if you are fixated on those questions and related responses, you are not likely to mine the students' knowledge for insights and alternative analyses. See WS 9:3 for a list of useful questions and their learning purposes.

4. Anticipate problems. There will be problems. There are always problems. A full discussion of potential classroom problems appears in the following section. Your goal is to identify them in advance and have the solutions up your figurative sleeve before they get out of hand.

My strong personal suggestion to you is to avoid inviting a classroom visit by your own evaluator the first two or three times you teach any case, no matter how experienced you are.

Problems: Special Issues That Arise in the Classroom

There are several common problems that arise consistently in classrooms. Students have not read the assignment, students are late to class and interrupt the ongoing discussion, students have read the case in a cursory manner (see the section titled "Student Preparation" for handling some of these issues), and students spark similar classroom management problems. We have all developed our own methods to deal with these nuisances, so I will not address them here. Instead, I will focus on three common problems that occur in case discussion:

Students Ask for the Answers

It is generally accepted that the instructor knows more than the students, and students always suspect that you have some inside knowledge to which they are not privy. However, case instructors need to remember that student learning is most "sticky" (in a good way) when students discover the answers themselves rather than receiving them already processed and spoon-fed by the instructor. Although it may be tempting to share your own analysis, you must avoid being trapped into providing your insights before the students have exhausted their own resources. If your own analysis (your "answer") differs significantly from the class's answers, you can share it after the discussion is complete and the debriefing has begun.

Discussion Collapses

It happens. People run out of steam, run out of ideas, run out of interest. First, identify why the discussion is not working the way you want it to. Has it degenerated into a "he said/she said" argument or an "I'm right/No, I'm right" squabble? Have you allowed the discussion to continue beyond the point of surfacing all the ideas and perspectives? Have you made the case relate to the students' lives? For example, you might ask students to identify one or two things that they can apply to their own work experience (or school life) from the case situation to stimulate further conversation.

Try asking the question in a different way. Reframing can jog fresh thinking. Try suggesting an obviously incorrect answer. When students object, simply ask, "Why not?" This can result in a new look at the data and an alternate analysis. Sometimes you will just have to drop the question altogether. If the question is geared to elicit important information, come back to it later in the class.

The management of case discussion is a skill that takes time to build, very much like baking a soufflé. Beat the eggs one minute too long, and the soufflé dries out. Bake it one minute too little, and the soufflé falls flat and wet when you remove it from the oven. Practice your timing and close the discussion before boredom deflates it.

Few Students Participate

Lack of participation can be the result of lack of student preparation. If students have not read the case and thought about it before class, they will be unable to provide any meaningful contribution. But let us assume that the students are prepared, that they have read the case and thought about some case questions, yet they are still not participating. It is time to consider your own expectations.

We have all seen videos of case classes where students are jumping out of their seats with enthusiasm, waving their arms in the air, and breaking in on one another's statements while the instructor strolls around the room, watching and inserting the occasional wise word. If you have not taught with cases before this and you think that your class is going to behave like the one in the video, guess again. Yes, there are classes that exhibit high engagement, shouting out arguments that are both reasoned and passionate. But this does not happen every time a case is discussed, even in that enthusiastic and excited class. And the instructor is more likely to be recording the discussion on the board and making sense of the often random comments that arise during the discussion than strolling around looking wise.

Typically, participation in case discussion is the result of hard work on the part of the instructor, beginning with the preparation mentioned earlier and continuing through classroom management skill and careful questioning. The classroom management component involves creating a safe space in which students can express themselves and risk being wrong. A sense of humor on the part of the instructor can make this environment easier to create, as can sharing student laughter at one's own expense. It doesn't hurt, it doesn't cost anything, and the payback in participation is tremendous.

Practice Makes Permanent

Most new techniques are difficult to do the first few times, and introducing case teaching into your classes is no different. It is best to start slowly, but right at the beginning of the term. When selecting your cases, bear in mind the level of the students and make sure that it matches the level of the case. A case that is too complex will turn students off; a case that is too easy is simply boring. Use straightforward cases early in the term and save the complex ones for later. Gear the sophistication of the material to the students to make it easier for them to relate the case situations to their own lives and experiences.

I often hand out a short case on the first day of class and conduct an impromptu case analysis with the students. I make it clear exactly what I expect from them—the facts, identification of the main problem presented in the case, where they may have encountered an analogous situation, potential solutions, and one supportable recommendation. Everyone must participate in order to receive credit for the class period; I do not allow "tourists" in my classes. Confronted with this approach, students seem to have little trouble accepting my classroom culture: They either engage or accept the fact that they are unlikely to receive an acceptable grade. About a quarter of the way into the term, I do begin to have some classes in which students are tumbling over one another to speak. They got that way because of practice.

It is energizing and great fun to teach a class where students are engaged. If you make cases a compelling method of learning in your classes, your students will respond favorably and learn more, and you will enjoy coming to class more as well.

Practice does not make perfect; it makes permanent. If students practice case analysis with insufficient preparation or unclear instructions, they will learn to perform poorly. It is the instructor's responsibility to teach them how to analyze cases before they can pull off an insightful analysis on their own. Only with perfect practice can practice make perfect.

● ● ● ● ●

Student Preparation

Students need to know a few things before participating in case classes. They need to know how to read a case. They need to know what *you* mean by participation, what your expectations are, what comprises an A, and how to get one.

Student preparation begins with reading the case. But reading and preparing a case for class discussion involves a lot more than reading a blog, an e-mail, a novel, or even a chapter in a textbook. Students can be advised to try a technique called "The Three Reads." Try it yourself and see how it works (WS 9:4).

Student preparation also requires that students be ready to participate in case discussion, regardless of the actual teaching method you use. It pays to clarify exactly what you mean by participation. Often, students misinterpret participation to mean mere attendance in class. Clearly, students cannot participate if they are not present; however, a body in a chair does not suggest active involvement in the discussion. That calls for meaningful engagement. The instructor can accomplish this goal in several ways:

■ Students can make the notes suggested in WS 9:4 and bring them to class. When students are uncomfortable speaking in front of others, prepared notes can help ease their nervousness. This is one situation for which online classes excel; less confident students have time to formulate their responses before committing to them publicly.

■ You can encourage them to speak early in the discussion, when it may be easier to make a contribution. For example, asking a shy student to provide a précis of the case narrative can break the ice for that student. In subsequent classes, you can assign progressively more challenging questions to that student. This works especially well for students who panic when called upon in class without warning.

■ You can assign specific students to prepare answers to certain questions or to prepare a case analysis ahead of time. Then, those students become the "experts" on that case and gain confidence through this role. See WS 9:5 for a sample case analysis format that can help students prepare well for case discussions.

Some instructors prefer not to hand out questions prior to class discussion for fear of leading the students to specific conclusions. This is a calculated risk. If your questions make it appear that there is one right answer to the case, students will be misled into narrowing their thinking too much. If you frame your questions in an open-ended manner ("Provide three options for Gary," instead of "What is Gary's best course of action to keep his business viable?"), you are likely to generate better student analysis, response, and participation.

Class size can have a large impact on student preparation. It is easy to hide in a lecture hall or even in a class of 40 students. If you break your classes down into manageable groups of no more than five to seven students, each group can be assigned one case question ahead of time. The groups can then lead the class in a discussion of their question, enriching the opportunity for the insights that arise only with in-depth analysis. Or, each team can undertake the full case analysis of one case. This works well in lecture hall classes; it also helps minimize tedious repetition and allows for the analysis of a case per class (or per week).

The clearer your instructions are, the more prepared your students can be.

• • • • •

Case Teaching Methods: How to Teach a Case—Let Me Count the Ways

Teaching is personal. We are alone in the classroom with our students. No one tells us what to do. Only rarely does someone guide us in a teaching method, practice, model, or technique. Over the years, we accumulate a variety of teaching tools, developing some expertise in the ones best suited to our personal style and preferences. Here are 20-plus ways to teach cases in a traditional classroom, followed by several suggestions of ways to teach cases in an online class:

- **Traditional three-board format.** The Socratic Method is a dance of argument. Students must be well prepared and willing to take a position and defend that position to their peers. The use of carefully structured questions and follow-up questions allows for a lively classroom environment, especially at the graduate level. The "three-boards" referred to in the label allow the instructor to map the case for the students, based on questions asked, information volunteered, and linkages between protagonist, options, and recommendations. WS 9:6 provides sample board formats for several different kinds of case discussion.

- **Role-play.** In teams or individually, students take on the roles of various case characters. They then role-play the interaction that the characters are likely to have. This process can result in a negotiated exchange, a series of emotional or rational responses, a fact-finding exercise, or some other appropriate interaction.

- **Debate/structured debate.** You present a statement for debate. Students should prepare both positions before class, doing relevant research. In teams, students argue one side first and then reverse their positions, allowing them to consider both sides of a "hot" issue seriously.

- **Group discussion.** This is your opportunity to use the discussion questions from the IM (or invent your own). The questions can be provided to students ahead of time for preparation or discussed in groups during class, then presented in a large group for consideration.

- **Brainstorming.** A standard brainstorming process can be very helpful for surfacing multiple recommendations, identifying solutions, or raising concerns from an assortment of perspectives. Using traditional brainstorming protocols (such as listing all suggestions, avoiding evaluation in the early stages, carefully recording all offerings), students can surface many more options and possibilities than they could generate individually.

- **Written analysis.** From time to time, you will want students to provide analyses in writing according to a format that you have developed. Students will be graded based on their submissions (see section titled "Evaluation and Grading" later in this module).

- **Team-based analysis.** Students work in assigned teams to perform a full case analysis, either for presentation or as a written assignment.

- **Structured controversy.** The instructor identifies a controversial topic from the case about which students are likely to have strong feelings. Individuals do research outside of class, share their findings in class, and seek consensus on the issue.

- **Problem-based learning.** Students take full responsibility for the case learning process. They decide what information they need to do the analysis, determine the best strategy for research, do the research, share the findings, come up with a solution, and identify the learning.

- **Clickers.** Clickers can help you gain wide participation in lecture or large classes. Each student has a digital device. Using this device, the students "vote" for their response from among multiple choices provided by the instructor. In this way, the instructor can get a quick reading of the classroom opinion.

- **Games.** You can design a game that relates specifically to the case you are teaching. It can be a quiz game like *Jeopardy*, a scavenger hunt for case information or clues, a speed challenge, or any other kind of game that will stimulate student interest.

- **Lecture.** You know what this is.

- **Student presentations.** You know what this is, too.

- **Video clips.** YouTube is a rich source of short videos that can start conversations, enrich discussions, or generate response to a topic. In addition, many movies have scenes that illustrate situations like the one you are teaching in your current case. Visual reinforcement is a powerful learning tool.

- **Paired with an additional reading.** A reading related to the case situation can generate deeper understanding in students, especially those who have less world experience than others. Select an article from a news magazine or an excerpt from a novel, a poem, or a newspaper article for undergraduates. Select a journal article or any of the preceding choices for a graduate class.

- **Technology.** Discussion boards, Facebook, Twitter, or your classroom online management tool make discussion simple for your students—especially the more reserved students. Post an interesting question and see what happens. You can find a full discussion of the use of technology in Module 11.

■ **Guest speakers.** Ask someone from the community (a graduate of the school is often willing) to speak to your class about the case topic or industry. This will provide additional insights for your students when they do their analysis.

■ **Exams.** You can use a brief case (not more than three or four pages) as the basis for an open book exam. Identify how you want the analysis completed and let the students test their analytical skills.

■ **Updates.** Some of the great cases are the classics: cases about Nestle, Bhopal, the space shuttle Challenger disaster, and other widely used cases. Over time, they have become somewhat dated, so you can have students analyze the classic case then research updates to bring the case epilogue to currency.

■ **Mock trial.** This lends itself to cases in which the protagonists have adversarial positions. Each side selects a "lawyer" to represent it in court. A judge is appointed and a jury of class members is chosen. The lawyers make the arguments while the judge presides. The jury determines which side wins.

■ **Your own new way.** You must have many other ways to teach. Please share them with me by e-mail (gina.vega978@gmail.com), and I will happily share them with others.

■ **For online classes.** Although many of the preceding suggestions work for online classes, some additional instructor inputs will really make teaching cases easier for you and for students in your class; you may or may not already be doing this. However, many online instructors overlook the critical need to establish a learning model for students. See Worksheet 9:7 (Checklist for Online Case Teaching) for a set of guidelines for online case teaching.

  ■ Start with the very basics of team building, depending on the experience level of the community from the very first online interaction. Without a solid, safe, and comfortable online learning environment, students will not succeed at the collaborative tasks demanded by case analysis. Refer to Module 5, Working with Coauthors, for some team building basics.

  ■ Move slowly, step by step, through your expectations. Begin with very simple assignments before asking for complex analysis. PCASI is especially helpful here (see following discussion).

  ■ Be very, very clear as to what students should be doing. If there is any way that your instructions can be misunderstood, you can be confident that they will be.

  ■ Require that students interact with one another, and grade them on this interaction. We know that that which is rewarded is what will be accomplished. Rather than leave the interaction to chance, design discussion questions and groups that are engaging enough to encourage student interaction.

Do bear in mind that all these different teaching methods have the same goal: some specific learning outcome for students. A wonderful mentor that I had early in my case teaching career suggested a simple acronym to ensure that case goals were accomplished: **PCASI.** The hard-to-pronounce PCASI (sounds like Picasso but with an *ee* sound at the end) stands for **Problems, Causes, Alternatives, Solution,** and **Implementation.** This sequential format encourages students to adopt a logical method of analysis that leads to the core of the case and gives them tacit permission to disregard factors that are not relevant to a case "solution." The PCASI template should be reserved for decision cases; it will not work well for descriptive cases. See WS 9:8 for a PCASI template to use in the classroom.

● ● ● ● ●

The Best Way to Teach a Case

With so many options for teaching, how can an instructor determine the best way to teach a case? One thing is guaranteed—there is no single "best way" to teach a case. Consider the following questions before you select a teaching style for your case today, tomorrow, or next week.

Question 1: What Is Your Goal?

As a general rule:

- If content, then Sage on the Stage.
- If process, then Guide on the Side.

Question 2: What Type of Students Are You Teaching? How Many Are in the Class? How Old Are They? What Is Their Experience Level?

The younger and less experienced the student, the more creative you need to be with your teaching style. Undergraduate students enjoy games, structured assignments, digital challenges, videos, and guest speakers. Graduate students prefer debate, research, team analysis, and role-play. No one likes exams.

Question 3: What Kind of Cases Are You Using? Decision-Based? Illustrative? Iceberg (Meaning Most of It Is Under the Surface)? Application? Prediction? Controversial Issue?

You need to match your teaching style with the case style for the best outcomes.

Question 4: Where in the Term Are You? Do Your Students Know One Another? Do They Know You?

If you begin your term by introducing several of the teaching models to your students, you will soon determine the best match for your class. It is not realistic to expect students who do not know you or each other to perform role-plays or to take personal risks, so save those techniques for a little later in the term.

Question 5: How Much Time Do You Have?

You cannot rush case-based learning. I have had classes that devoted a full hour session to a one-page case and other classes that were happy doing a perfunctory 20-minute analysis of a complex case.

Question 6: What about YOU? How Fearful Are You of Looking Foolish? How Fast Are You on Your Feet? What Is the Condition of Your Ego? Are You Comfortable Not Being the Only One in the Room with the Answers?

Some of the aforementioned teaching suggestions require the instructor to take the risk of making mistakes, encouraging laughter, being wrong (gasp!), and being quiet (even harder). If you don't feel up to trying some of these methods, don't force yourself to do so.

Regardless of the methodology you use, each case teaching session must conclude with a **debriefing** period. During this period, the instructor needs to pull together the specific learning that took place, emphasizing the connections between theory and practice through the use of focused questions. The debriefing process revolves around your initial goals—the learning objectives you identified when you decided to use this case in class.

A sample debriefing might proceed as follows:

INSTRUCTOR OK. What have we learned here? What's the bottom line?

STUDENTS It seems like the owner could never figure out what direction to take or what he wanted to do.

INSTRUCTOR OK. Let's briefly reiterate his options.

STUDENTS [They provide a list of options, instructor writes them on the board. Or, if online, they are posted publicly in an open discussion location.]

INSTRUCTOR So, the class consensus seems to be that he should go with the third option. Why didn't he?

STUDENTS He was afraid that he didn't have and couldn't get enough resources.

INSTRUCTOR What analogous situations have we studied in this class? What theories did we apply to them? Can we apply that theory to this situation?

The discussion may proceed for a period of time, with the instructor taking this opportunity to reinforce the learning goals and clarifying the desired student takeaways. Try to avoid dismissing a class without taking the time to do a proper debriefing. If you do not debrief, students are likely to leave your class thinking that the purpose of the case was to tell a story by sharing one experience, rather than drawing a lesson from the case that could help them in future similar circumstances.

● ● ● ● ●

Written Assignments as Teaching Tools

We have focused most of this module on interactive teaching methods. It is important to remember that significant student learning takes place outside the classroom while they research and prepare their case presentations or written analyses. The PCASI action plan for classroom discussion applies equally well to written analyses. The same five components should be addressed in any format that makes this process straightforward for the students. You might consider simply supplying your students with the PCASI form from WS 9:8 to facilitate their case analysis.

● ● ● ● ●

Evaluation and Grading

When we talk about grading our students' output, we are actually talking about two different concepts: *summative evaluation* and *formative evaluation.*

Summative evaluation refers to giving a grade on the quality of the output. This grade is a complete evaluation and is not revisited for improvement. This is what students refer to as their "grade" on the project, exam, or course. We hope that they learn to improve their grade on subsequent assignments based on what they have learned from the grade they earned on this assignment, but despite our best efforts at feedback, summative evaluation does not guarantee improvement.

Formative evaluation has a different purpose. Formative evaluation is also a grade, but it is a grade that is designed to change for the better with each iterative submission of the same assignment. Students are given the opportunity to redo the assignment and earn a higher grade by correcting the deficiencies identified in the earlier version. An instructor who does formative grading can expect two outcomes—better quality in the final product and a lot more work in terms of evaluating each submission. Determining the kind of evaluation you do is a conscious decision on your part.

Whether you choose to grade summatively or formatively, or whether the case analysis takes place in the classroom or in a written format, the key to good grading is the clear identification of your measurement criteria. The elements that you select as important are the ones to which students will devote their energies, so take special care with this process. Some elements to consider in your grading include:

■ Did students identify the problems accurately?

■ Were the students able to identify salient facts?

■ Did the students "see" the unspoken, subtle information in the case?

■ Did the students draw appropriate conclusions from the facts and tacit information?

■ Did the students surface multiple alternative solutions?

■ Were the student recommendations logical, usable, and supported by the data?

■ Were the students able to outline an action plan for implementation of the case solution?

●●●●●

Designing Rubrics

One effective method of evaluation involves rubrics. Rubrics are scoring tools that identify the critical grading criteria and the value awarded to each criterion. Rubrics attach numerical valuations to narrative descriptions, making it simple for students to aim for the best possible evaluation they can achieve. If we provide only vague explanations of our expectations, students are often flummoxed when they try to satisfy us.

Consider this assignment:

You can earn an A by answering the questions completely. Be sure to include a full analysis and use professional writing.

What does "completely" mean? What does a "full analysis" include? What is "professional" writing? It is no surprise that students who receive instructions like these do not submit assignments that reach our desired threshold.

Now consider this assignment:

You can earn an A by answering the questions completely. A complete answer is generally one to two pages and provides a discussion of the central topic and a conclusion based on data provided in the case. Be sure to include a full analysis, incorporating the following elements: problem identification, alternative solutions, and your recommendation. Your writing should be clear and of the quality you would present to your boss.

This is better, but still not good enough. What comprises a "discussion of the central topic?" What is "clear" writing? What are your boss's expectations of good writing?

You need to provide even more guidance, and this can come in the form of a grading rubric handed out to students before they begin the assignment. The grading rubric should be as comprehensive as you can make it with categories that are clearly calibrated. The example that follows will serve as a guide to the development of other rubrics (see WS 9:9 for a blank rubric form for you to adapt).

The simple rubric shown in Table 9.1 was designed to capture the three elements listed in the preceding assignment: complete answers, thorough analysis, and professional writing. It assigns a number value to each component at each of three levels: weak, acceptable, and exemplary.

Rubrics take time to put together, but they are a worthwhile investment. When your expectations are clear, your students are more likely to be able to turn in high-quality work.

Table 9.1 Rubric Sample

	Weak	*Acceptable*	*Exemplary*
Complete answers	Answers are less than one page and/or have a limited discussion with little incorporation of data analysis. Little or no reference to relevant theories.	Answers are one to two pages in length and include both a discussion of the central topic and a data-based conclusion. The data analysis is properly conducted. Theory is applied properly.	Answers are one to two pages in length and provide an insightful discussion of the central topic. The data-based conclusion is not limited to the data provided within the case. Theory is applied creatively as we have practiced in class.
	0–20 points	**20–25 points**	**25–30 points**
Thorough analysis	Overlooks significant problems, suggests only one or two alternate solutions. No real evidence of insight in the recommendation.	Problems are identified correctly, alternative solutions are provided, and a reasonable recommendation is made.	Problems are identified correctly, issues and consequences are fully developed, alternative solutions are provided, and a creative recommendation is made.
	0–35 points	**35–45 points**	**45–50 points**
Professional writing	Many careless grammar and spelling errors that detract from the analysis could have been caught by spell-check, grammar-check, or careful proofreading. Little effort was taken in the writing process.	The analysis does not appear to have been edited beyond spell-check and grammar-check for style or expression, but the work is both readable and clear.	There are very few grammar and spelling errors, the writing is coherent, and the analysis is easy to read and engaging.
	0–15 points	**15–19 points**	**20 points**

● ● ● ● ●

References and Readings

Arter, J., and J. McTighe. (2001). *Scoring Rubrics in the Classroom.* Thousand Oaks, CA: Corwin Press.

Boehrer, J., and M. Linsky. (1990). "Teaching with Cases: Learning to Question." In *New Directions for Teaching and Learning*, ed. M.D. Svinicki, 42 (Summer). San Francisco: Jossey-Bass, 41–57. doi:10.1002/tl.37219904206

Golich, V.L., M. Boyer, P. Franko, and S. Lamy. (2000). *The ABCs of Case Teaching.* Washington, DC: Pew Case Studies in International Affairs and the Institute for the Study of Diplomacy, Georgetown University.

Gopinath, C. (2004). "Exploring Effects of Criteria and Multiple Graders on Case Grading." *Journal of Education for Business* 79, no. 6, 317–322.

Kerr, S. (1995). "On the Folly of Rewarding 'A,' While Hoping for 'B.' " *Academy of Management Executive* 9, no. 1, 7–14.

King, A. (1993). "From Sage on the Stage to Guide on the Side." *College Teaching* 41 (Winter), 30–35.

Leach, T.L., G. Vega, and H. Sherman. (2008). "Case Writing and Research: Professor Moore Looks for a Better Way to Grade Student Case Analyses." *The Case Journal* 5, no. 1, 68–96.

Mauffette-Leenders, L.A., J.A. Erskine, and M.R. Leenders. (1997). *Learning with Cases.* London, Ontario, Canada: Richard Ivey School of Business, University of Western Ontario.

Naumes, W., and M.J. Naumes. (2011). *The Art & Craft of Case Writing*, 3d ed. Armonk, NY: M.E. Sharpe.

Sherman, H., and G. Vega. (2007). "Case Writing and Research: Professor Moore Teaches a Class with Cases." *The CASE Journal* 4, no. 1. http://www.emeraldinsight.com/doi/abs/10.1108/TCJ-04-2007-B007?journalCode=tcj

● ● ● ● ●

Worksheets

WS 9:1 Is This Concept Best Learned via Cases?

WS 9:2 Discussion Plan Format and Tips for an Engaging Discussion

WS 9:3 Questions and Why We Ask Them

WS 9:4 The Three Reads

WS 9:5 Two Written Formats for Case Analysis

WS 9:6 Sample Board Formats

WS 9:7 Checklist for Online Case Teaching

WS 9:8 PCASI in the Classroom

WS 9:9 Rubric Template

WS 9:1

Is This Concept Best Learned via Cases?

Cases are not for every kind of learning or for every learning situation. This checklist will give you a fast idea about whether you should use a case to teach a concept.

Concept, Skill, or Learning Outcome	Case Appropriate	Use a Different Method
Foster critical thinking	☑	
Develop collaboration skills	☑	
Provide experience in analysis	☑	
Transfer information		☑
Teach rudimentary level skills		☑
Apply skills to situations	☑	
Improve oral and written communication	☑	
Teach specific analytical techniques		☑
Introduce theoretical concepts		☑
Acquire historical knowledge		☑
Demonstrate mastery of techniques	☑	
Performing basic research		☑
Develop comfort with ambiguity	☑	
Identify salient aspects of a complex situation	☑	

WS 9:2

Discussion Plan Format and Tips for an Engaging Discussion

The following plan is for a traditional case discussion, often used with the three-board teaching plan. You will have to adapt it for use with technology.

The Plan	
Review the case content	Ask a student to provide a brief synopsis of the case action. Focus on the story or case narrative to give the students time to get into the characters' situations and problems. Be sure to ask if anyone has anything to add or correct before you move on.
Statement of the problem	Why are we reading this case? What does the protagonist need our help with?
Collection of relevant information	Have students identify the case facts that may have bearing on the analysis and problem solving.
Development of alternatives	Keep at this until you are satisfied with the number of alternatives that have surfaced. Remind the class that "do nothing" is always an alternative to consider.
Evaluation of alternatives	A list of pros and cons is valuable here, whether in tabular format or in graphic mind-mapping format.
Selection of course of action	Students are often eager to set a course of action before they have identified the decision-making criteria. This is a good time to remind them that setting criteria precedes decision making.
Implementation plan for recommended solution(s)	This last step is frequently overlooked in class discussion. Students are pleased with their recommendation but neglect to consider whether or not it can be implemented.
Discussion Tips	
Keep your ice-breaker question simple, but open-ended (and related to the case content)	E.g., How many of you drink beer? Or, Who has ever gotten a parking ticket? Or, What's wrong with the registration process? These questions will generate a lot of buzz and laughter.
Several well-chosen questions are better than a laundry list	If you "waste" class time by asking a lot of irrelevant or far-too-simple questions, student attention will drift and you will get fewer and fewer responses.
Challenge students' assumptions	Do not allow students to think there is only one way to solve a case or only one best solution. Make them think a little harder.
All students need to participate—no tourists	Case discussion is a social kind of learning, and all must be involved in the discussion for learning to take place.

Be flexible—allow some conversational wandering	Remember—case teaching is opportunistic teaching.
Change seating arrangements to shake up the usual student coalitions	Case work requires some nonserial, partly random, and apparently disorganized conversation. Linearity does not always mark the shortest line between two points.
Remember to let students fill the silence	Your biggest challenge is to keep silent as learning emerges, and let students find their way.

WS 9:3

Questions and Why We Ask Them

There are many kinds of questions with innumerable examples of each. This worksheet provides a dozen question types and examples gleaned from multiple sources and years of classroom experience. Use them to prime your own "question pump."

Kind of Question	Examples
Diagnostic	How do key people feel about this problem?
	How high are the stakes?
Information Gathering	Which programs did you start?
	What other kinds of programs are in effect here?
Priority/Sequencing	What should be done first?
	What are the process steps you follow?
Prediction	What do you think will happen next?
	Who do you think will arrive first?
Hypothetical	What would happen if you did XYZ?
	How fast do you think an ambulance could get here?
Application	According to your job description, what should you do?
	What specific directions does the Procedures Manual suggest?
Analysis	Where else have we seen this problem?
	What analogous situations occur in other industries?
Synthesis	What impact did your prior actions have on the outcome?
	How do your responsibilities relate to the bottom line?
Evaluation	What is the optimal solution?
	How does solution A compare with solution B?
Challenge	Why do you think that was OK?
	How do those findings connect to the research?
Simple Open-Ended	What happened here?
	What is going on?
Action-Focused	What do you need to do now?
	Where can you get the information you need?

WS 9:4

The Three Reads

Student Handout

Reading and preparing a case for class discussion involves a lot more than reading a blog, your e-mail, a novel, or a chapter in a textbook. If you have not developed the case-reading skill yet, now is the time to try a new technique called "The Three Reads" model.

First Read

- Find six minutes (yes, six minutes is enough for a 10-page case) to sit down uninterrupted. Turn off your IM and mute your cell phone so that you do not get distracted during this short reading period.
- Read the hook. This may be several paragraphs long and will introduce you to the case "problem." Write the problem in one sentence in the margin.
- Read the first sentence (and only the first sentence) of each paragraph in the case. Write a keyword or two in the margin next to the paragraph.
- Read the title only of the attachments and exhibits.
- Read the titles in the reference list. What kinds of readings did the author use as references? What general content area do they cover?

That's it. Turn your IM and cell phone back on and go about your business.

Second Read

- This is the big one—reserve at least one hour for this read later that day or some time the next. Remember that if you have interruptions, this hour must be extended—let's be fair to the author! After all, the author spent upward of 50 hours writing the case, and that work deserves a fair share of your attention.
- Read the entire case, slowly and carefully. Jot notes as you go along about the characters and their behavior, the situation, and the action.

Sometimes preparing a timeline of action makes it easier to follow and remember. Be sure to include the exhibits and attachments when reading this time.

■ Jot down your own response to the situation and the characters, even if it's unsupported by theories or formal concepts. Make any connections you can to analogous situations you have experienced or read about before. What are the differences or similarities to this situation? Remember, these notes that you are making are yours alone—no one else will be looking at them. It doesn't matter if they are messy, have lines drawn all over them, or are put together in right brain or left brain style, just as long as they exist. They are meant to help you.

■ Make a list of the assumptions you are making and the information you still need before you make a recommendation. Something is always missing, or the case would be really boring. So, what is missing?

■ List the alternative solutions to the case, their pros and cons, and then select one recommendation. You always have to select one recommendation and provide a rationale for it. This recommendation should be supported by some theory, concept, or class discussion in this or some other class. Again, these are notes, not papers meant to hand in.

■ Prepare any case questions you have been assigned. These get handed in.

You should be tired at this point. Put the case away.

Third Read

■ This last read takes place not too long before class. The point of it is to make sure that the case is fresh in your mind and that you are still comfortable with your recommendation.

■ This read resembles the first read: read the beginning, the first sentence of each paragraph, etc. But this time, include both your marginal notes and the notes you have made during the second read. You will need your notes to prepare for exams and to sound "smart" in class. Remember that class participation means that you have to talk—it's okay to read aloud what you have written if you are uncomfortable talking off the cuff.

That's it! The entire process has not taken more than two hours, which is about the amount of time you should anticipate using for class preparation.

WS 9:5

Two Written Formats for Case Analysis

The formats that follow are for two different kinds of cases: decision-based cases and descriptive cases that do not require a decision.

Decision-Based Case Analysis	
Executive summary	Write this section last even though it appears first in the case analysis. The goal of the executive summary is to provide a brief overview of the main issues, the proposed recommendation, and the actions to follow.
Statement of the problem	Describe the core problem of the case and the decision to be made by the protagonist. Include the symptoms of the problem and differentiate them from the problem itself. For example, the symptom is that you have spots on your face. The problem is that you have the measles. Statement of the problem is a diagnostic process.
Causes	This section is an exploration of potential causes of the main case problem. Support your exploration by the application of relevant theories learned in this course or in other courses.
Possible solutions or alternatives	Surface as many possible solutions or alternative actions as you can. You should not limit your possibilities to what you think is easy to accomplish or logical, but rather brainstorm a wide variety of options.
Analysis of alternatives	Select criteria for determining the basic feasibility of the alternatives identified above, then consider the pros and cons of each feasible alternative. You must consider at least three alternatives in this section.
Final recommendation	What would you recommend that the protagonist do? Support your recommendation with a rationale that is based both in facts and in the appropriate theory for the problem (i.e., market analysis, financial statements analysis, the impact of organizational structure, supply chain management, or other disciplinary focus).
Implementation	What are the steps that the protagonist should take in order to make your recommendation happen? Identify to the greatest extent possible the responsibilities, costs, timeline, and measurement of success of the final implementation.
Descriptive/Analytical Case Analysis	
Executive summary	Write this section last even though it appears first in the case analysis. The goal of the executive summary is to provide a brief overview of the main issues, your analysis, and your conclusions.

The facts	This is not simply a list of case facts. You need to determine which facts are relevant and which are background information. If you are analyzing a business ethics case, for example, it probably does not matter that the action takes place in autumn. However, it may well matter that the action occurs at the end of a sales period or some other critical timing.
Behavioral inferences to be drawn	Why did things happen as they did? What else might happen as a consequence? What are the implications in terms of attitudes and relationships?
Theory-based discussion of the case action	Apply relevant theory to an explanation of actions and consequences, implications of actions and consequences, and the impact of various criteria on the decisions that were made in the case.
Options to the actions within the case	Compare the actions of the protagonist with the other courses of action that were open at the time. What might have been the logical outcomes of those actions? Determine a hierarchy of preferred actions based on your established outcome criteria.
Conclusion/Reflection	This is your rationale for preferred action. If the protagonist has done the right thing according to your analysis, explain why. If the protagonist should have done something else, explain why. Reflect on your reasoning.

WS 9:6

Sample Board Formats

Each case will require its own board format. This worksheet provides samples for several different kinds of cases that you can adapt to your own classroom needs. Your boards will be more appealing if you use a variety of colors. Consider not adding the headings until after the information appears on the board. Note that not all cases lend themselves to three-board discussions or to tabular analysis. For some cases, a mind map, diagram, or other visual tool may be preferable.

Format for an Ethics Case

Note: This format posits three boards side by side.

Board 1 (Left-hand board)

Stakeholders	Position/Influence/Power
John Doe	Owner; Decision maker
Mary Smith	Regular customer
XYZ Company	Supplier
Etc.	Etc.

Board 2 (Center board)

Options/Actions	Benefits/Positive Outcomes	Drawbacks/Costs
Sell the defective product	Gets it off his shelves Increases revenue	Damage to customer relationship Potential injury to customer Loss of customer trust
Sue the business owner	Gets reimbursement or compensation for injury	Lawsuits are expensive Emotional costs are high on the legal path
Etc.	Etc.	Etc.

Board 3 (Right-hand board)

Facts Influencing the Decision	Positive or Negative Impact
Business is slow	–
Wants to get rid of old inventory	–
Mary has been his customer for 25 years	+
John is a member of the city council	+
XYZ Company is a longtime supplier	+
Etc.	Etc.

Format for a New Product Marketing Case

Note: This format posits three boards side by side.

Board 1 (Left-hand board)

Product Features	Product Benefits
All metal casing	Hard-wearing, able to withstand abuse
Three color choices	Matches décor
Etc.	Etc.

Board 2 (Center board)

Promotion Method	Pros	Cons
Word of mouth	Contractors trust contractors' advice	Limited reach
Ads in trade magazines	Splashy ad attracts attention of potential customers	Costly
Etc.	Etc.	Etc.

Board 3 (Right-hand board)

Placement (distribution outlets)	Benefits	Drawbacks
Retail stores	Target market looks here first	Shelf space is costly
Internet site	Wide reach to young audience	Target market does not match demographic
Etc.	Etc.	Etc.

Format for a Strategy Case Using SWOT Analysis

Note: This format posits three boards side by side.

Board 1 (Left-hand board)

Pre-Launch	
Strengths (internal)	*Weaknesses (internal)*
■ Personal strength and work ethic ■ Partner had capital and contacts with VCs	■ No experience in the industry ■ No experience in small retail establishments
Opportunities (external)	**Threats (external)**
■ No competitors using the European Model ■ No stores in high-traffic areas ■ Low cost of inventory ■ Customer service orientation unique in the industry	■ Established competition ■ Potential increases in the cost of goods ■ Growth in outlets (i.e., grocery stores, warehouse clubs) ■ Potential increases in the cost of store rent

Board 2 (Center board)

2007	
Strengths	*Weaknesses*
■ Personal strength and work ethic ■ Five years' experience in the industry	■ No experience in franchising ■ No plans in place to vet franchisees properly ■ Top-heavy organization structure
Opportunities	**Threats**
■ Customer Service orientation unique in the industry ■ By 2007, the economy had recovered ■ People were spending freely	■ Other established competition ■ Increases in the Cost of Goods ■ Growth in outlets (i.e., grocery stores, warehouse clubs) ■ Potential increases in the cost of store rent ■ Franchisees did not follow the operational guidelines

Board 3 (Right-hand board)

The Immediate Competition	
Strengths	*Weaknesses*
■ Experienced consolidators ■ $30 million available to invest	■ Did not understand the industry and what the consumer wanted ■ Poor accounting systems

Opportunities	Threats
■ The similarity to the video industry in terms of size, maturity, level of fragmentation, and lack of national branding ■ Savings through economies of scale	■ The stores did not want to become carbon copies of one another; they wanted to maintain their individuality ■ They were a victim of the economy

WS 9:7

Checklist for Online Case Teaching

	Make Your Students' Work Easier and Learning More Effective—Promote Student Collaboration
	Establish "rules of engagement" that encourage civil and clear interaction
	Assign small groups (not more than five students) for discussion
	Establish private chat rooms for each group
	Appoint (or have each group select) a Reporter to upload summaries of group discussions
	Remind students of the dangers of being too fast on the "send" button without reviewing their posts
	Create many opportunities for student interaction
	Make Your Job Easier, More Efficient, and More Effective
	Limit your own online hours. Students may work at midnight, but there is no reason for you to do so.
	Remember the dangers of being too fast on the "send" button
	Tempting as it may be, do not eavesdrop or lurk in the student chat rooms
	Take special pains to both listen to and hear what the students are saying
	Provide timely extensive feedback
	Course Design for Case Learning
	Start on Day 1 with a short case
	Model appropriate case analysis processes
	Provide rubrics, analytical structures, and other tools to facilitate student learning
	Make sure you are clear in your instructions
	Plan to repeat yourself or link to earlier posts
	Assign a variety of case types (one paragraph, critical incidents, full length cases, video cases, etc.) to generate sustained engagement

WS 9:8

PCASI in the Classroom

This action plan provides an outline of case goals. Use it when prepping to teach your case and when debriefing the case discussion. You can even provide it to students for their own case preparation and analysis.

P	**Problems.** List the case problems	
C	**Causes.** Identify the causes	
A	**Alternatives.** Specific actions that address the problems	
S	**Solution.** The preferred recommendation	
I	**Implementation.** Responsible entities, short- and long-term implications, costs and benefits, potential negative consequences	

WS 9:9

Rubric Template

Adapt the rubric to match your own desired criteria, evaluation categories, and descriptions.

Suggested Criteria	Poor/Weak/ Needs Improvement	Satisfactory/Acceptable/Good	Outstanding/Exemplary/ Excellent
Thoroughness	One or more required section is missing or treated perfunctorily	All required sections are addressed to a great extent	All required sections are addressed completely
	X points	**X points**	**X points**
Theoretical Relevance	The analysis does not incorporate relevant theories	Addresses theories and course concepts appropriately	Addresses theories and concepts appropriately and insightfully
	X points	**X points**	**X points**
Quality of Analysis	Does not suggest careful thought or provide insights	Analysis suggests both effort and understanding of the material	Detailed analysis that offers careful and logical inferences
	X points	**X points**	**X points**
Conclusions	Unsupported or missing arguments that overlook salient issues	Supported arguments that capture main issues	Supported arguments that address both main issues and subtle problems
	X points	**X points**	**X points**
Writing Quality	Careless writing, many grammatical and spelling errors, poor organization	Clear writing, few grammatical and spelling errors, organized presentation	Flawless writing, clear organization, correct grammar and spelling
	X points	**X points**	**X points**

Module 10

• • • • •

Student Case Writing

The Case Research Study Model for Undergraduates and the Graduate Student Model

• • • • •

Why Teach Students How to Write Cases?

This module is meant to help you design a case writing project for classroom use with graduate or undergraduate students. It contains materials to help you guide students through the complexities of qualitative research, case design, case writing, and case analysis and includes some of the guides I use for my own classes—guides that have received good feedback from student users.

It is simple to understand why we want our graduate students to write cases. The experience of researching a company problem, identifying relevant information, and preparing it for presentation in a coherent and well-written format is a valuable learning exercise. It forces students to think objectively about real situations and real problems similar to those they encounter in their daily work lives. Graduate students should have sufficient command of theory to be able to put together a rudimentary teaching note that focuses on appropriate learning methods and applies theory to practice.

But why bother teaching undergraduates to write cases? Don't students have enough challenges simply analyzing existing cases? Research has shown that students benefit in some surprising ways from writing cases. Writing cases helps students to:

■ strengthen their ability to think, write, and make presentations;
■ identify problems and analyze information selectively;
■ build confidence and develop composure;
■ relate concepts to real situations and solve problems;
■ learn to deal with ambiguity and work with incomplete knowledge;

- learn to reflect and reframe challenges;
- identify critical incidents;
- apply theoretical principles to practical learning;
- learn to distinguish between the significant and the trivial;
- become better written communicators and increase their observation skills;
- become more motivated and interested in the course; and
- expand their professional networks.

This chapter will focus first on the Case Research Study Model for undergraduates and then will move to a simplified method of case writing for graduate students. You may find that many of the elements of the Case Research Study Model can be applied successfully to your graduate classes as well.

● ● ● ● ●

What the Case Research Study Model Is All About

The Case Research Study Model is a very different sort of case from the teaching cases we have addressed in other modules because it combines elements of a teaching case and Instructor's Manual with elements of a research case. It results in a project that allows the student to perform extensive interviewing and observation (practicing qualitative research skills) and to apply relevant theories and concepts to specific organizational challenges (practicing analytical and consulting skills). This model is appropriate for undergraduate students to give them a taste of the real purpose behind learning the multiple theories and perspectives with which they have had to wrestle in their business school programs. It is also useful for less experienced graduate students as an integrating exercise in the early stages of their program. I do not recommend this model for executive education classes nor for doctoral programs.

One strong predictor of a positive outcome when assigning student projects is the degree of clarity provided vis-à-vis instructor expectations. A common failing is a tendency to write instructions that are unclear because of the instructor's unarticulated assumptions or vague performance expectations. To help ensure student success, you will find worksheets with instructions for students in narrative form, in template form, in suggested PERT charts, in grading rubrics, and in self-grading rubrics—all of which appear as worksheets in this module. Encourage students to refer to these items prior to submitting their cases. In addition, provide samples of both high-quality and low-quality work for students to evaluate against the rubrics so that they can refine their understanding of your expectations. Students have reported that the samples were most helpful in understanding what their final projects should look like.

As a major term deliverable, this assignment is complex and demanding. Nonetheless, students usually are enthusiastic about the project, in part because it differs so dramatically from most of the other term papers they've done and in part because of the built-in opportunity to interact with business owners and managers on a professional level. See WS 10:1 for a student handout that describes the project and WS 10:2 for a timeline of deliverables and major assignments for the instructor.

●●●●●

Elements of the Case Research Study

There are 11 distinct elements that comprise the Case Research Study. The following sections provide a description of each element and a brief sample drawn from student projects completed over several years (see the "References and Readings" section for a list of student projects).

1. The Hook

The hook is the beginning of the case. It must grab the reader and generate interest in reading further. It should not be an abstract or synopsis of what is to follow. Instead, it should stimulate interest or curiosity in the reader for what is to come.

Excerpt from a Student Project

> *Above the door of the Howling Wolf Taqueria is a sign that says "Feed your good wolf." This sign refers to a Cherokee legend about the fight between two wolves, the evil one and the good one. These two wolves represent the two sides of every human being. The question of which wolf will win is resolved by the one you feed. Pat and his partner, Matt, want the Howling Wolf to be a place where people can feed the good wolf inside themselves. But without much experience in restaurant ownership, they fear they may not be up to the challenge.*

2. The Industry

An abbreviated industry note includes a full description of the services or product in question, the overall size of the industry in the region, identification of the primary factor that produces profit within the industry, major barriers to entry, competition, and any other information that will be helpful in understanding the context of the business.

Excerpt from a Student Project

> *The barriers to entry in the ambulance service industry are extremely high, especially for emergency services. Some obstacles include having to develop a history of swift response and providing quality care. In addition, there is the high cost of vehicle maintenance, the difficulty of recruiting qualified personnel, and government restrictions, all of which make it difficult to compete in the industry. The requirements for certification and regulations are stringent. Paramedics must be state-certified and there are federal regulations to comply with.*

3. The Company Story

The company story is an organizational history—when the business was founded, who founded it, how big it is at present, the most salient features about the business at this time, and similar background information.

Excerpt from a Student Project

> *In a little town in Italy, Mr. C's grandfather farmed and sold horses. When the family moved to the United States in the 1950s, Mr. C's uncles first worked in a bicycle shop, then started a motorcycle sales and repair shop in Cambridge. After his father lost his engineering job, he went to work with his brothers in the motorcycle industry, and the family soon opened three other dealerships. Mr. C. dreamed of owning his own auto showroom: "My grandfather sold horses, my father sold motorcycles, and I will sell cars . . . three generations of transporting souls." The dealership flourished for years until 2008, when the economy dipped badly. Early in 2009, Mr. C.'s franchise with Chevrolet was eliminated.*

4. The Business Owner or Manager

The description of the business owner or manager should be vivid and detailed enough for the reader to actually visualize the person. Use as much of the owner or manager's language as possible to help the reader hear the way the protagonist might react or respond to a given situation.

Excerpt from a Student Project

> *Fitzroy was born in the Caribbean and came to the United States at the age of sixteen. He lived in a commune, and it was there that he developed his love of bread, as it was his responsibility to bake for the other members of the commune. He said, "I came to this country when I was only 16 years old, willing to learn new things. And look at me*

now. Leaders are born. And I am a leader. Now watch me crush my competition!"

5. The Problem

Write this in the P-voice (from the protagonist's perspective) to the greatest extent possible. (P-voice and R-voice—the latter standing for the researchers' voice—will be explained in greater detail later in this module.) Use the narrative format (storytelling format) so that it sounds like fiction, even though it is factual. Some of this section will have to be reproduced by the student researcher based on observations made during data collection; it is unlikely that the protagonist will spell out in quotable language the human interactions that the student researcher observes. Note that the problem as identified by the protagonist may not be the same as the problem that the student researcher perceives.

Excerpt from a Student Project

> *"This company (a printing firm) was run before in a way that wasn't scalable," said Kevin, leaning back in his chair. "Every company has peaks and valleys to balance out and keep people on their toes and also give a break when needed. For my business it is always huge peaks and huge valleys." Kevin ignored three phone calls and declared, "Right now we are at our hugest peak of the year, election time, and after elections is our largest valley." Kevin smiled and ignored a few more calls. "I basically sleep in my office during the election period, but after elections I relax and golf. A steady flow of work is something I would like to strive for in the future outside of the political campaigns in order to keep myself busy."*

6. Commentary

Use the R-voice to comment, provide analysis and identify theories, or connect concepts or learning that might explain the protagonist's behavior. Be as specific as possible when making these identifications.

Excerpt from a Student Project

> *Diversity and making his brand stand out are the strengths of the company. The owner spent a great amount of time showing us around and identifying what made the company different. He understands the theory of branding, that a strong brand is made by the image of the company and represents the company when a*

person is not present. He told us the importance of image to him—
the uniforms that his crews wear are different from any other crews
in the industry. They would stand out, and standouts get remem-
bered.

7. Alternating Sections of P-Voice and R-Voice

Write about the protagonist's personal business history, most satisfying
business experience, advice for new managers, or other stories, alternating with discussion/commentary by the student researcher. Try to apply
at least one theory or concept to each P-voice revelation.

Excerpts from Student Projects

■ *The second tip that Elizabeth had for new entrepreneurs was: "Never*
depend on others when buying an existing business. Once you sign a
contract and the business is yours, the previous owners will either help
or you'll never hear from them again."

■ *One of the first things we learned in Introduction to Business was lia-*
bility. The owner of the store is liable for any problems, so when buying
a business it is important to research the company for any trouble they
might be in. Once the business is purchased, the previous owner is no
longer liable and you are left with all the problems.

8. Alternatives

Propose at least two recommendations to solve the protagonist's problem. Discuss them with pros and cons.

Excerpt from a Student Project

> *One possible option is to consider ceasing all commercial work for*
> *the time being and focusing entirely on residential jobs. Commer-*
> *cial jobs have a much lower profit margin, and payment for work*
> *often takes over a month to collect. The jobs themselves take longer*
> *to complete, but the great thing about residential jobs is getting paid*
> *quickly, often before you even leave the job site. Another possible op-*
> *tion is to consider a marketing strategy that focuses more on com-*
> *mercial work to generate higher profits. They could expand their*
> *area of operation and bid on jobs outside their current service area.*
> *This strategy would provide greater revenue and exposure, which*
> *in turn would give the company the chance to increase its overall*
> *workforce.*

9. Final Recommendation

Make one firm recommendation and explain why you have made this recommendation.

Excerpt from a Student Project

> *We strongly recommend that Michael look into raising capital for his business. He lacks education in management and finance, but he can work with his accountant for guidance. We recommend that he seek out debt capital; for his kind of small niche company, equity is not a favorable way to raise funds. The benefits to debt financing are that he will maintain control over his business, the cost of such capital is generally low, and there are tax benefits available to him. The drawbacks are less significant, relating primarily to the need to make payments regardless of profits.*

10. Methodology

How did you collect the research for this case study? How did you get to know the protagonist? How many interviews did you conduct? Where did you hold the interviews? What forensic research did you undertake? Which websites did you visit? How many drafts did you complete? How did you and your research partner interact?

Excerpt from a Student Project

> *Before meeting Mr. Schultz, we visited the restaurant to observe what it was like on a regular day. We tried the food and beverages and relaxed in the comfortable atmosphere. Later, we had three weekly interviews with Mr. Schultz on Monday afternoons. Before each meeting, we developed questions to ask him. After the first interview, we realized how difficult it was to interview and take notes at the same time. Consequently, for the second and third interviews, we brought along a recorder. But when we went back to listen to the recording, we found it difficult to understand and very time-consuming to retrieve the information. Looking back on the project, it may have been better to interview at different times and days to get a better idea of how the restaurant is at busier times. Using the company website, Census Bureau data, and Ibis World, we were able to research the industry, finding the background, NAICS code, size and other industry information.*

11. A Final Word

A final word is a personal reflection on the process of researching and writing the case research study. What have you learned by doing this project?

Excerpts from Student Projects

■ *It isn't just about gathering information; it's about gathering the correct information.*

■ *I had a great time interviewing and working with my group members throughout this semester. I really enjoyed listening to Jonathan talk about forming relationships with different business entities and elaborating on his job as a relationship manager. It introduced me to a different side of business I wasn't previously familiar with.*

■ *I feel I really improved on listening to other group members. Every single time we met, I learned something new or heard a different idea, and I believe my writing improved because of listening to the others. The case was a reminder of how hard work pays off in the end. It seemed like a mountain to climb in the beginning of the semester, but little by little we accomplished our goal.*

● ● ● ● ●

Elements of the Graduate Student Case Study

Graduate students can be held to a more standard version of a case study—one that resembles a traditional teaching case. They can write a full case, following the directions and suggestions in Module 3, using the Worksheets in that module. The major difference between a graduate student case and a "real" teaching case is the appearance of a teaching note instead of an Instructor's Manual. As we saw in Module 5, an Instructor's Manual contains eight main elements: overview/synopsis/ abstract; intended audience, recommended courses, and placement; learning objectives; discussion questions; teaching strategies; literature review/theory/recommended readings; answering discussion questions; and epilogue. Unless our students are business professors, they are not likely to be able to do a credible job on several of these pedagogical elements, and therefore I recommend that the student teaching note should include the following:

■ Overview/Synopsis/Abstract
■ Research Methodology
■ Learning Objectives
■ Literature Review, Theory, and Recommended Readings
■ Discussion/Analysis
■ Recommendation
■ Epilogue

Full descriptions of the overview/synopsis/abstract, learning objectives, literature review, and epilogue are presented in Module 5. Several of the worksheets will prove helpful to students in this project, specifically WS 5:1 (Writing a Synopsis), WS 5:3 Learning Objectives), and WS 5:7 Writing the Epilogue). You can find two formats for case analysis and recommendations in Worksheet 9:5 (Two Written Formats for Case Analysis). You may already have your own preferred case analysis style and assignments for students—perhaps you will be willing to share them with me and the rest of the case writing community.

Note that this style of teaching note will allow the student to provide a solid analysis that allows the instructor to evaluate the quality of student learning and the student's ability to apply theory to practice appropriately. For the evaluation of student work, you may consider the rubrics I have provided in Worksheets 10:13 (Self-Grading Rubric) and 9:8 (Rubric Template).

⊛ ⊛ ⊛ ⊛ ⊛

Helping Students Get Started: An Introduction to Project Management

Students often have trouble organizing their projects and keeping those projects moving forward. You can help them by spending a little time early in the term introducing them to elements of project management, referring to student handouts WS 10:3 (Managing Your Projects) and WS 10:4 (Timeline of Case Deliverables and Major Assignments), amended to fit your own preferred schedule.

⊛ ⊛ ⊛ ⊛ ⊛

The Importance of Relationships

Business is about relationships; therefore, it pays to consider the relationships between the case protagonists and the instructor, the case protagonists and the student case writers, and the links within the student teams.

Case Protagonist and Course Instructor

The relationship between the case writers and the protagonist of the case is established at the first contact between protagonist and the course instructor. It is the responsibility of the instructor to locate appropriate business owners or managers and gain their agreement to participate in the case writing project long before students become involved. It is not difficult to locate willing participants; you'll find that many business owners and managers like to play a role in university projects and "give back" to the academic community from their own experience. You can reach them readily through local umbrella organizations such as the Chamber of Commerce, the business development council, or your own institution's alumni association.

The instructor must clarify the role of the business participants in the case writing process. Make it clear to them that it will involve (1) setting aside three to four hours over the course of a term to be interviewed by a student team; (2) allowing this student team several hours to watch their operations and observe the actions/behaviors of employees; and (3) attending the case presentation at the conclusion of the term. Business participants must also be willing to sign a consent form prior to the beginning of the project that describes the project, its potential benefits and harms (if any), and clarifies their role in it. This form should be approved by the school's institutional review board (IRB) for everyone's protection. See WS 10:5 for a Sample Informed Consent Form.

Student Researchers and Case Protagonists

When writing a field-researched case study, the researcher has a unique relationship with the protagonist of the case. Rather than the expected role of "research subject," the protagonist is considered the "coresearcher"—a full partner with the case writer. Because of this relationship, it can become difficult for the inexperienced writer to separate his or her opinions from the facts of the case. Undergraduate students in particular may find it challenging to differentiate between their opinions and the facts of the case. The next section of this module is designed to help guide students in the early stages of case writing on this path.

Relationships within the Student Teams

The need to establish and manage student teams increases the level of difficulty of this project for the instructor as well as for the students. Students often reject the idea of working in teams because of the prevalence of free riders and the likelihood of uneven participation and varying work quality. It is important to provide working guidelines and set parameters for engagement that clarify your own expectations regarding issues of participation and grading. If students are encouraged to do some of their work in class (where you can see them), you can forestall some of the problems that become obvious in the student interactions. It is helpful to have students write a contract with one another to avoid some of the most frequent problems they encounter: tourists (students who are "just passing through"), late assignments, unreachability, not responding to e-mails or text messages, "forgetting" to complete assignments, and the famous homework-eating dog.

●●●●●

Shifting Voice: A Powerful Means of Expression (Used in the Case Research Study)

Differentiating between facts and opinions requires the case writer to shift between the voice of the protagonist (P-voice) and the voice of the researcher/student (R-voice). The story or narrative is written from the protagonist's perspective, the "P-voice"; the theories and commentaries are written from a researcher's analytical perspective, the "R-voice." This method is based on a two-column exercise in which one column is reserved for facts (direct observations, protagonist statements) and the other is reserved for the researcher's insights, perceptions, and attitudes.

One of the common concerns shared by undergraduate instructors is that students tend to learn in silos; that is, they rarely transfer what they have learned from one course to another. The current emphasis on multidisciplinary teams in business that has trickled down to the business schools themselves is evidence of the difficulty of integrating knowledge. Students often struggle to analyze situations in a management class even though they have learned the relevant theories in an accounting or marketing class (or earlier in the term in the management class itself). The two-column approach can help in a case writing context. The interviews are recorded by the researcher in the two-column format although the case research study itself takes a more traditional written form. The following example shows how the P-voice and the R-voice provide a rich description by encouraging both fact and perception to play a role in the case study.

Narrative in the P-Voice

This woman came into the restaurant with a child hanging off her hip and two other kids running around her. This was the woman's second time in the restaurant and she knew the layout of the restaurant and how it operated but seemed preoccupied by all the kids. Because of the kids she didn't pay attention to what she was ordering and ordered flour tortillas. The woman was a celiac, a person allergic to flour. Because of her unfortunate experience at the restaurant she gave the Howling Wolf a one star rating and wrote up a bad review. How do I counter that? It was apparently her mistake because of her lack of attention. My general manager was able to resolve the issue with the customer and we thought that was the end of it.

Student Researchers' Opinions in the R-Voice

Restaurants can live or die by a few online reviews now that the majority of food connoisseurs are taking to the Internet before they decide where to dine. With so many different places to write reviews online, it can be a nightmare to try to keep up with even half of them. Pat is looking for nothing more than to associate the restaurant with good food and a good place.

In the more traditional case study for graduate students, the P-voice appears frequently in the case and the R-voice is reserved for the analysis in the teaching note.

The process of researching and writing a case research study requires the writer to connect the narrative to previously learned material. Ultimately, the shifting and reintegration will guide students in making a recommendation that helps the protagonist solve the problem at the core of the case. The resulting integration of logical analysis and emotional or intuitive understanding can be most helpful in providing both valid information and valid evidence of learning.

●●●●●

Building Blocks of the Case Research Study

Data Collection: Valuing the Ordinary Using the R-Voice

There are two sides to the process of data collection—the forensic/archival research and the live interview/observation. Both are necessary to get a clear picture of the phenomenon at the core of the case research study. It is important to begin with archival research so that the student-researcher is prepared when meeting the protagonist. See WS 10:6 for guidance on conducting the research process.

Begin with the assumption that undergraduates have little or no knowledge of how to use library databases effectively or where to search for relevant information. Schedule a visit from the business librarian very early in the term (the second or third class meeting) to introduce students to the resources of the library and the Internet and guide them in preparing industry papers. For the purposes of the case research project, an industry paper is brief (no more than three pages) and provides concrete and specific information about the industry in question. It includes such things as the size of the industry nationally and locally; identification of the primary profit center within the industry, as well as the industries upon which the one in question depends; barriers to entry; opportunities for growth; competition; major challenges; and other relevant information. It can also be helpful at this time to have students read WS 10:7, How to Read a Case, to prepare them for class discussions of other cases they will be preparing.

Qualitative data collection is more challenging for undergraduate students to understand because they probably have no history with this style of research. They need to have clear guidelines and research protocols to help them direct their own research appropriately. The instructor is responsible for developing these protocols using any format that makes sense for the specific course content. The goal is not to provide a set of transactional dos and don'ts for students; rather, the goal is to suggest research parameters and behavioral guidelines that will yield high-quality learning. You can introduce qualitative research methods early in the term by practicing simple interviewing processes and simple observation techniques. (An example of the latter involves two lines of standing students facing each other; one line of students makes some minor change in their individual appearance, and the facing student must identify the change made—such as eyeglasses on or off, hair parted differently, sleeves rolled up or down, etc.) Spend time teaching students how to design open-ended questions, role-play scenarios, and design semistructured interviews for the protagonists of the cases you are studying in class.

One important message that the students need to internalize is that qualitative research requires concurrent data collection and sense-making (more on this in a following section), because their tendency is to separate these two processes as in quantitative research. This combined process can make data collection more complex-sounding than it needs to be. The concept of using oneself as a data collection tool and participating actively in the research process is alien to most students; however, once they understand the value of their role and recognize that they are respecting the ordinary by giving voice to "regular people," their creativity becomes liberated and they succeed in telling the protagonist's story.

Storytelling: Expression in the P-Voice

The emphasis in semistructured interviews is on identifying interesting stories about the protagonist, the company, or the situation being studied. Stories bring life to business situations and create impressions of people that make their descriptions more well-rounded and realistic. When we hear a story, the natural tendency is to want to hear more, and that is the foundation for these undergraduate case research studies. You can test this hypothesis yourself by reading the two short statements in Table 10.1.

The sample on the left exhibits all the characteristics of a good story—it is concrete, identifies real people, is common knowledge to the employees, is believable, and describes a social contract, the way things are done in this organization. The sample on the right is a simple statement without evidence of its truth or falsity. Ho hum . . . Hank is cranky. This is no way to convince anyone to read further! But in the left-hand sample, we have learned a lot. We have learned that (1) the organization has at least four salespeople; (2) there are both men and women in the same job title; (3) the boss has periodic meetings with the staff; (4) the boss is a difficult man to deal with; (5) there is general dissatisfaction within the organization; and (6) the boss's people skills leave something to be desired. The left is rich with dysfunction; the right tells us nothing.

Table 10.1 Expression in the P-Voice

Suzanne and Peter stormed out of the conference room, red-faced and scowling. Hank remained behind, but his angry words followed Suzanne and Peter into the hall. Karen and Jackie waited anxiously for their turn in the hot seat for their weekly sales meeting. "I can't take too much more of this," said Suzanne. "If it keeps up, people are going to start looking for other jobs. This time, he really went too far . . . "	Hank's bad temper unsettled everyone who worked for him.

Stories can be far more enlightening than we expect. This focus on evocative description is important for all types of cases.

"Tell Me about a Time When . . . ?"

Everyone has stories to tell, even the boss; especially the boss when we're doing research about her business. Asking questions like, "Can you tell me about a time when . . . ?" opens the door to a story. Organizational stories feature a person in a certain situation, and the narrative about that situation has a beginning, a climax, and a resolution. These stories are constructed with five main parts: the setting, the sequence of events, the crisis, finding out what the central character learned, and the moral. Incorporating several of these stories within the case enlivens it and provides solid qualitative data for analysis. It is a good investment to spend some class time having students tell stories to one another, prompted by questions starting with "Can you tell me about a time when . . . ?"

Designing the interview questions is part of the storytelling process. Asking weak questions will result in listless stories or responses that verge on irritation such as, "Whaddya mean a story? I don't have time for stories." Such a response can easily intimidate the inexperienced researcher. Instead, it pays for students to design a series of questions that are more likely to spark a detailed response. These questions should focus on specific events or situations. ("Can you tell me a story about a time when your deliveries didn't come in as expected and you had a shipping deadline to meet?" or "Was there a time when sales fell off so sharply that you couldn't make your payroll?" or "What keeps you up at night?")

Or, the researcher can focus on standard organizational audit questions but shift them into a storytelling format. For example, instead of asking how "innovative, risk-taking, and proactive" a venture might be, one might ask the business owner to tell about a time when she had to take a risk. The researcher can follow up with questions about how that felt, how employees responded, and similar evocative secondary queries. Or, instead of asking about "the dominant management style in the company," the researcher can ask about a time when everything seemed to be going wrong, then follow up depending upon the response. Other questions that are pretty much guaranteed to generate a story are: "Tell me about a time when you failed"; "What happened the last time you tried to make a major change within the company?"; and "What do you think is the biggest problem you have faced in this business?" Of course, all of these questions require follow-up. Emphasize to students the importance of preparing questions in comfortable language, not in academic jargon. The latter will turn the interviewee off completely. See WS 10:8 for ten basic rules for successful interviewing and WS 10:9 for some sample interview questions and an introductory observation chart to get students started. These worksheets will work at both the undergraduate and graduate levels.

●●●●●

Sense-Making and Expression in the R-Voice

According to the rules of *quantitative analysis*, once the interviews are complete, notes are clarified, observations are decoded, and stories are collected, it's time to make sense of the data amassed. In fact, if the *qualitative* researcher waits until the end of the interview process to begin the sense-making process, he has waited too long. Sense-making takes place within elements 5, 6, and 7 of the case research study (The Problem, Commentary, Alternating Sections of P-Voice and R-Voice). You can refer to the sample of the 11 elements in this module for examples of how this sense-making works.

Qualitative analysis is an iterative operation and needs to be conducted concurrently with data collection. The marginal notes the researcher makes in the field notebook serve this pre-analytical role. Ultimately, the researcher may decide that those notes are useless or biased, but without them, there is no place to begin sense-making. Inasmuch as the researcher is the research tool and participates in the research process actively, sense-making must be part of the research. So, where is a student to start?

Asking questions of oneself while asking different questions of others is not an easy task, nor is it easy to describe this process to students unless they have been prepared with a thorough grounding in the P-voice/R-voice concept. One of the goals of a solid education is to improve upon the learner's ability to think critically. This critical thinking requires that one think about something while engaging in a meta-process of "thinking about the thinking about":

> *What is the protagonist really saying? What does she mean by that? Wait a minute—someone just came in to ask her a question that seems very elementary, even to me. But didn't she say that she believes in empowering people to make their own decisions? That doesn't match the situation that I saw. What does that mean?*

And further,

> *What theories might I apply to this behavior? It seems familiar—what class did I learn that in? Where else have I seen that? My own boss does that, doesn't she? It's all very confusing when it happens to me . . . I wonder how that employee feels.*

This process of decoding behavior precedes the analysis, which takes place completely in the R-voice, and is a much more logical procedure.

Analysis in the R-Voice

The goal of the analysis is to come up with alternatives for action and subsequently to select one recommendation to make to the protagonist. Assuming that undergraduate students have internalized many complex business theories is unrealistically optimistic. Generally speaking, few students like theories or show any respect for them. Frequently, they make comments like, "That's just common sense," or "Who is going to go through all this trouble just to confirm what you already thought?" Because students often believe that theories are "just academic," they are surprised when they hear that business owners really do perform situational analyses, pay attention to the financial ratios, and think through their marketing campaigns before releasing advertisements.

As we know, theories are not "just academic." The goal is to ensure that students learn how to apply the (otherwise useless) theories in the world outside the classroom. One way to reinforce learning is to require students to identify the theories they are using, where they learned them, how to apply them, and the pros and cons of each. What are the likely consequences of various alternatives? Which stakeholders will be affected? Which important criteria should be used to determine if the alternative will likely prove successful? Which alternative would the student recommend? Why? See WS 10:10 for a handout that helps students identify appropriate theories to use for their business problems, either in the case research study or in the more traditional case study teaching note.

● ● ● ● ●

How to Write Up the Student Research as a Case Research Study

The key to writing a case study from firsthand research is to remember that the case writer is telling a story and is in complete control of what to share with the audience. This means that the student needs to draw a line between being too parsimonious with information and overwhelming the reader with data. Be selective and discriminating—but not miserly. See WS 10:11 for a student handout that provides suggestions for what to share and what to withhold when writing up a case, and WS 10:12 for guidelines for structuring the write-up itself.

How Long Should the Case Research Study Be?

The case research study should be as long as it needs to be to tell the story. It is difficult to be more specific than this. Most case research studies are between five and 15 pages—long enough to cover the subject but not long enough to bore the reader. It is hard to imagine completing the project thoroughly in fewer than 10 pages, plus any appendices, exhibits, or attachments that are needed for illustration. The same limitations (or lack of limitations) hold true for the graduate case study.

Some Language and Formatting Conventions for Case Research Studies and Traditional Case Studies

The list that follows will provide some guidance to students:

- The "story" part of the case is **always** written in the past tense, even when it sounds funny to your ear, because the action has already taken place. The analysis, personal commentary, recommendations, and other elements should be written in the present tense.
- Use headings and subheadings to make it easier for the reader to locate the various elements.
- It is perfectly acceptable for students to use the first person—that is, "I"—when they are discussing their analysis, recommendations, etc. Use "he" or "she" when referring to the protagonist in the storytelling part of the case.
- Dialogue should appear between quotation marks.
- Remind students that they know a lot more about the case than the reader does; they should not hold back important facts that seem "obvious" to them but may not be obvious to the reader.

● ● ● ● ●

Grading the Assignment

Grading traditional case analysis is always challenging; grading the writing of a case research study is even more difficult. For that reason, it is wise to provide students with a self-grading rubric (WS 10:13), as well as a rubric for grading the final deliverable (WS 10:14). The self-grading rubric serves as a wake-up call to students when they evaluate the quality of the work they are about to hand in. They should attach this rubric to their case draft (due week 12) as well as to their final project (due week 14).

The grading rubric for the final project serves as a thorough explanation of instructor expectations. As one student told another when she thought I was not listening, "Just give her what she wants and you'll get a good grade." If only delivering what the instructor wants were as easy as this student was suggesting! It isn't easy because often we are not clear in explaining what we want; grading is subjective, and we cannot hide from that fact. But the more we try to attain some level of transparency in our grading procedures, the likelier we are to get work that we perceive as a model of good quality; our students will also recognize it as high-quality work because of the grade it receives. Note that there is a category in the rubric that addresses writing quality; writing is important to project success.

Presentation

If you wish to incorporate a presentation into your assignment, the following brief guidelines may prove helpful. The goal of the presentation is both to share student work with the rest of the class and the businessperson who has been interviewed, as well as for students to gain practice in presenting and defending their ideas.

The typical presentation is 20 minutes long, broken down approximately as follows:

5 min.   A brief overview of the industry and the company, as well as background information about the protagonist.

2 min.   A description of the methodology the student researchers followed.

5 min.   A discussion of the kinds of problems that the company has experienced and the main problem of the case.

4 min.   Student alternatives for solution and final recommendation, with its rationale and theoretical support.

5 min.   Q&A.

Students should prepare a PowerPoint presentation to assist them in illustrating their comments and to give them practice in business presentation processes. The PowerPoint slides should be prepared as follows:

■ Keep it simple—leave plenty of white space so the audience is not distracted.

- Use headers that describe the slide contents.
- Keep slides free of grammatical errors. (Proofread, proofread, proofread!)
- Do not include "bells and whistles" like fly-ins, clapping hands, or marching type; keep it businesslike.
- Try to avoid using more slides than necessary. It is better to talk more about each slide than to flip slides constantly.

WS 10:15 is a student handout that provides hints for a successful presentation.

Conclusion

The process of writing cases is demanding for academic researchers. It is even more difficult for undergraduate students to grasp the concepts and understand the underlying theory that makes cases valuable learning tools. At first exposure, students may not see case writing as an extraordinarily interesting and worthwhile pursuit. They may not be willing to deal with the many challenging experiences they are likely to encounter during the course of the case writing project. When you question the wisdom of pursuing this demanding work with students, remind yourself of its many benefits for student growth. The "big six" benefits for students are:

- extension of insight and originality;
- integration of theory and practice;
- improved communication skills;
- enhanced ability to deal with ambiguity;
- development of qualitative skills; and
- development of interpersonal skills.

Additional benefits, no less important, include the development of personal and professional networks, increased motivation and interest in coursework, and an opportunity to role-play their potential future professions.

The projects that are described in this module can be adapted easily to specific academic disciplines, all of which surely have among their desired learning outcomes the benefits we have outlined here.

⬤ ⬤ ⬤ ⬤ ⬤

Note

Some of the material in this module was drawn from Vega (2010).

⬤ ⬤ ⬤ ⬤ ⬤

References and Readings

Argyris, C., and D.A. Schön. (1954). *Theory in Practice*. San Francisco: Jossey-Bass.

Ashamalla, M., and M. Crocitto. (2001). "Student-Generated Cases as a Transformation Tool." *Journal of Management Education* 25, no. 5, 516–530.

Bailey, J., M. Sass, P.M. Swiercz, C. Seal, and D.C. Kayes. (2005). "Teaching with and through Teams: Student-Written, Instructor-Facilitated Case Writing and the Signatory Code." *Journal of Management Education* 29, no. 1, 39–59.

Berkowitz, S. (1997). "Analyzing Qualitative Data." In *User-Friendly Handbook for Mixed Method Evaluations*, ed. J. Frechtling, L. Sharp, and I. Westat. Document No. NSF97–153, August. Arlington, VA: National Science Foundation. http://nsf.gov/pubs/1997/nsf97153/chap_4.htm (accessed September 21, 2011).

Burtis, J.O., and L.K. Pond-Burtis. (2000). "Students Writing Case Studies of Group Dysfunction." Presented at the National Communication Association Convention, November. Available on ERIC, Record 453 565. http://www.eric.ed.gov/ERICWebPortal/search/detailmini.jsp?_nfpb=true&_&ERICExtSearch_SearchValue_0=ED453565&ERICExtSearch_SearchType_0=no&accno=ED453565 (accessed November 10, 2016).

Forman, H. (2006). "Participative Case Studies: Integrating Case Writing and a Traditional Case Study Approach in a Marketing Context." *Journal of Marketing Education* 28, no. 2, 106–113.

Greenawalt, M.B. (1994). "Student-Written Case Studies: The Benefits to the Internal Audit Curriculum." *Managerial Auditing Journal* 9, no. 2, 3–7.

Jones, K.A., and E. Woodruff. (2005). "Using Student-Written Cases to Enhance Competency-Based Assessment and Diagnostic Skills." *Social Work in Mental Health* 4, no. 1, 49–69.

Katz, J. (2004). "Reading the Storybook of Life: Telling the Right Story v. Telling the Story Rightly." In *Narrative and Discursive Approaches in Entrepreneurship*, eds. Daniel Hjorth and Chris Steyaert. Northampton, MA: Edward Elgar, 233–244.

Kvale, S. (1983). "The Qualitative Research Interview: A Phenomenological and a Hermeneutical Mode of Understanding." *Journal of Phenomenological Psychology* 14, no. 2, 171–197.

Little, V., R. Brookes, and R. Palmer. (2008). "Research-Informed Teaching and Teaching-Informed Research: The Contemporary Marketing Practices (CMP) Living Case Study Approach to Understanding Marketing Practice." *Journal of Business and Industrial Marketing* 23, no. 2, 124–134.

Mitchell, R. (1997). "Oral History and Expert Scripts: Demystifying the Entrepreneurial Experience." *International Journal of Entrepreneurial Behaviour and Research* 3, no. 2, 122–137.

Morgan, S., and R.S. Dennehy. (1997). "The Power of Organizational Storytelling: A Management Development Perspective." *Journal of Management Development* 16, 494–501.

Pinkus, R.L., and C. Gloeckner. (2006). "Want to Help Students Learn Engineering Ethics? Have Them Write Case Studies Based on Their Research/Senior Design Project." Online Ethics Center for Engineering, National Academy of Engineering. http://www.onlineethics.org/Education/instructguides/pinkus.aspx (accessed November 10, 2016).

Polanyi, M. (1998). *Personal Knowledge: Towards a Post-Critical Philosophy.* London: Routledge. First published in 1958 by the University of Chicago Press.

Rae, D., and M. Carswell. (2000). "Using a Life-Story Approach in Researching Entrepreneurial Learning: The Development of a Conceptual Model and Its Implications in the Design of Learning Experiences." *Education + Training* 42, no. 4/5, 220–227.

Ragin, C.C., J. Nagel, and P. White. (2004). *Workshop on Scientific Foundations of Qualitative Research.* Report, July 11–13, 2003. Arlington, VA: National Science Foundation. http://www.nsf.gov/pubs/2004/nsf04219/nsf04219.pdf (accessed November 10, 2016).

Senge, P., C. Roberts, R.B. Ross, B.J. Smith, and A. Kleiner. (1994). *The Fifth Discipline Fieldbook.* New York: Doubleday Currency.

Vega, G. (2010). "The Undergraduate Case Research Study Model." *Journal of Management Education* 34, 574–604.

Whitt, J.D., and M.R. Grubbs. (1991). "Case Development with a Local Basis: Opportunities and Responsibilities for Students." *Journal of Education for Business* 66, no. 6, 342–346.

Student Cases (Used with Permission)

Alcantara, Manuel, Linda Brown, Kaitlyn Foley, Ashley Freccero, Malinda Maiy, and Michael Williams. "A Case Study of Traditional Breads."

Barrera, Rose, Danny Duval, Barbara Ly, and Anthony Vivace. "JC Landscaping: Mowing and Plowing Its Way through the Struggles."

Barrett, Stewart, Daniel Gibbon, Robin McCarter, and Kaitlyn Zaino. "Lifeline Ambulance."

Borseti, Cara, Marshall Jutras, Vicki Pero, and Megi Theodor. "The Seagull."

Bradley, Kyle, Neal Dike, Matt McCann, and April Gordon. "Media Spoon."

Chesson, Michael, Samuel Gordon, Jennifer Hamond, Brian McAdams, and Christopher Titus. "Howling Wolf Taqueria: Marketing the Good Wolf."

Everson, Mike, Bob Hirst, Tim LeBlanc, and Mike Muller. "Cranney Companies."

Goodreau, Stephanie, John Maliawco, and Marina Natale. "Connolly Printing."

Hendry, Sarah, Nick Luz, Jeff Nelson, Shane Shepard, and Derek Spencer. "Chevy-Hill Crest."

• • • • •

Worksheets

WS 10:1

Case Research Study Project

Student Handout (25 Percent of Your Term Grade)

A case research project can give you deep insights into behavior and attitudes, helping you to understand what may make a manager, business owner, or employee act in a specific way. What makes a manager do what he does? What makes a small business owner get up every day and perform all the challenging tasks required of him? You will interview a manager or business owner (selected from a group of volunteers) and will observe the operations of the organization to determine **how this manager or business owner overcomes obstacles**. The Case Research Study focuses on questions in the following areas:

- Personal history related to business ownership or management
- Most satisfying experience related to business
- Most challenging experience related to business and how it was solved
- Advice offered to other managers or owners

The Case Research Study comprises 11 distinct elements, all of which must be addressed in the written deliverable. We will practice each of the elements in class so that you will feel confident in your work. It is important to integrate what you have learned in this class and in your other business classes in terms of theory and concepts into the Case Research Study in order to gain the most value from this project (and to get the best grade possible).

The body of this paper should be approximately 10 double-spaced pages in length, plus any relevant appendices and a cover page with an abstract. The following timeline for deliverables also identifies the point value of each item to be handed in (out of a total of 100 points). Please hand in both a hard copy and an e-mailed copy of each element listed in the following table on or before its due date.

Week #	Points (out of 100)	Deliverable
5	5	Hand in three interview dates approved by your company contact
6	10	Hand in industry notes and draft questions (at least 10 questions)

9	15	Hand in copy (not the original) of your field notes, including observations and reactions
12	20	Hand in draft #1
14 (a)	5	The final challenge
14 (b)	45	Final case research project due + self-grader + contribution forms
15		Presentations + contribution forms

WS 10:2

Step-by-Step through the Project

A timeline of deliverables and major assignments for a 15-week term.

I = Instructor responsibility

S = Student responsibility

Week	Deliverables and Major Assignments
Pre-Term	Instructor lines up business owners and/or managers who are willing to participate and has them sign a consent form (WS 10:5) **(I)**. You can easily find small business owners in the community surrounding your institution who will be glad to have students write a case about them. I have also had good success working with the SBDC and the local Chamber of Commerce in identifying willing participants. It is really quite easy to find people who want to help students learn. It is important to have these participants sign a consent form, both for the satisfaction of your IRB and also to clarify their commitment.
1	Introduce project (WS 10:1) **(I)**.
2	Establish student teams/dyads **(I)** and match business owners/managers with student teams **(I)**. You can match these groups by providing some teasers about each company and allowing students to form their own teams based on their interests, or, if you have more time and easy access to the owners or managers, you can invite them to the class and allow them to be interviewed by the group. Introduce qualitative research processes **(I)**.
3	Visit with business librarian. Business undergraduates frequently need guidance in doing research on existing organizations. Each institution has a different set of databases for such purposes, but readily available government and public sources on the Internet are burgeoning. It pays to invite the librarian in for a visit to bring students up to date on the latest legitimate research sites. Read: How to Read a Case (WS 10:7) **(S)**. Nothing is more frustrating for a case teacher than an unprepared class; this handout will help.
4	More on qualitative research—the role of the researcher and relationship with the coresearcher; maintaining a research notebook **(I)**. Read: Ten Rules for Conducting Successful Interviews (WS 10:8) **(S)**.
5	Lesson on interviewing and question design **(I)**. Submit interview dates (actual interviews to be completed by the end of Week 9) **(S)**.
6	Go over case template and sample **(I)**. Hand in industry note and draft questions **(S)**.
7	Practice writing hooks **(I) (S)**.
8	Find a speaker who fits into your programming **(I)**.
9	Interviews complete. Students hand in copies of their field notes **(S)**. Go over these notes with the students and give them feedback on their attentiveness, objectiveness, connection to what they have learned in classes, etc.

Week	Deliverables and Major Assignments
10	Read: What to Share and What to Withhold (WS 10:11) **(S)**. Adjust this handout to fit your own specific criteria. Read: How to Connect the Problem to the Theories (WS 10:10) **(S)**. Go over grading rubrics (WS 10:13 and WS 10:14) **(I)**.
11	Writing practice. Read: Hints for a Successful Presentation (WS 10:15) **(S)**.
12	Case draft #1 due **(S)**. Presentation outline due **(S)**.
13	Challenge students to review their cases from the perspective of some other individual (such as their grandmother, their little brother, Oprah) or come up with a different solution and evaluate whether the new solution is a more or less workable one.
14	Papers due **(S)**.
15	Presentations with owners/managers present **(S)**. It is important to have the protagonists in the room when the students present the cases. It increases the value of their work, and it requires them to find language to describe uncomfortable situations in a mature way. Plus, the owners and managers really enjoy listening to student presentations and often provide very good feedback.

WS 10:3
Managing Your Projects

Student Handout

You can use these guidelines for projects in any class or at work.

Step 1: Begin at the End

In order to complete a large project on time, you will need to establish a schedule that starts with your destination and works backward. This will allow you to structure both your roadmap and your timing so you arrive at the conclusion of the project in time to meet the due date.

1. Identify the date that the project is due.

   Project Due Date: June 1

2. List all the elements you need to have in place when you hand in the project. The Case Research Study has 11 such elements, and they are all listed on the project assignment. Projects may include additional elements as well. Your list will look something like this:

   a. Hook

   b. Industry

   c. Company Story

   d. Protagonist

   e. Problem

   f. Commentary

   g. Alternating Sections in P-Voice and R-Voice

   h. Alternatives

   i. Final Recommendation

   j. Methodology

   k. A Final Word

   l. Bibliography

   m. Interviews

   n. Online Research

o. Personal Experience

p. Proofreading for Writing Quality

q. Reviewing Your Final Product

3. Describe the actions you will have to take to complete each of these elements. These may include (but should not be limited to):
a. determining the topic;

b. locating someone to interview and setting up an interview schedule;

c. collecting data in person, online, at the library, etc.;

d. visiting the college's Writing Center early in the process; and

e. producing at least two written drafts.

Step 2: Figure Out Where the Beginning Is by Using the Timeline Provided in WS 10:4

1. Determine how long it will take you to do all of the project actions required (in hours). Take your time figuring this out. Try not to underestimate the amount of time each activity will take, as things often take longer than we think. If anything you are doing depends on someone else (i.e., you have to interview someone), you must include extra time to coordinate with that individual's schedule. (Don't be surprised to discover that you may not be the interviewee's top priority.) The number of hours required to complete each task will be connected with a calendar time frame when you actually establish your schedule.

2. Figure out which actions you can perform concurrently. For example, you might be able to do some library or online research in the same general time frame as you've established for crafting your interview questions.

3. On a calendar, mark the specific dates on which you are willing to work on the project. For example, if you have no intention of working on Saturdays, don't include them in your calendar dates. You can download a free calendar template from http://office.microsoft.com/en-us/templates/default.aspx. There are many styles available; select the one that's best for you.

4. Count up the hours the work will take you, add 10 percent to cover normal delays, and determine how much time you are willing to devote to the project on the days on which you have already agreed to work.
a. If you agree to work on March 16, how many hours can you devote on that day?

b. Do this for all the days and mark it on the calendar.

5. Now, it's a matter of division. Link the work you want to do on a day or days in which you have enough time to complete that element and

identify it on the calendar. This is called a milestone. You have just committed to completing that element by the day identified.

6. Working backward from the project due date, identify your milestones and determine your start date (the day by which you **must** begin working on the project in order to meet the deadline). Of course, you may choose to begin earlier.

7. Keeping your personal commitments will guarantee that the work is done when due, which is a good thing because, in general, employers and instructors do not accept late assignments.

WS 10:4

Timeline of Case Deliverables and Major Assignments for the Case Research Study and the Graduate Case Study and Teaching Note

Student Handout

Assign due dates for each deliverable and major assignment. Add in additional assignments where needed. Use this table when managing your project.

Week #	Date	Deliverables and Major Assignments	
		Case Research Study Project	*Case Study Project*
2		Establish student teams/dyads Match business owners or managers with student teams	Establish student teams/dyads Identify company for case study and contact for approval
3		Read WS 10:6, How to Research an Industry Read WS 10:7, How to Read a Case	Perform background research on industry and company Using WS 10:8, draft interview questions
4		Read WS 10:8 Ten Rules for Conducting Successful Interviews Submit name of team contact person to instructor	Determine interview dates (to be completed by the end of Week 7) Conduct interview #1
5		Submit interview dates (to be completed by the end of Week 8)	Conduct interviews and draft case outline
6		Hand in industry note and 10 draft interview questions	Refine case outline and design any follow-up questions
7		Review grading rubrics	Complete any interviews and write draft case, using WS 10:11 and 10:12 as guidance
8		Interviews complete—hand in copies of your field notes	Share draft case with company and obtain final approval of any direct quotes and accuracy of information
9		Read WS 10:12, How to Write Up Your Research	Draft teaching note, following WS 5:1, 5:3, 5:4, and 5:7

10		Perform your final challenge	Complete the analysis and recommendations for the teaching note, following WS 9:5 or other instructions provided by your professor
12		Case draft #1 due, including sign-off on quotes by protagonist	Have colleagues (NOT the company) read the case and teaching note and provide you with feedback
13		Presentation outline due	Spellcheck and fact check on more time
14		Papers due	Papers due
15		Presentations	

WS 10:5

Sample Informed Consent Form

This form should be adapted for your students' projects and printed on your institution's letterhead for additional credibility.

Informed Consent Form

Case Study: _____
[*Insert name of company in space above*]
I am asking you to participate in a case study about your organization.
The purpose of this study is to learn more about [*insert whatever you want here*]. If you agree to participate, I will [*observe you as you work during several morning or afternoon periods over the course of a month, will interview you several times, and will take notes on our conversations, or whatever you intend to do*]. Some of the interviews may be audio- and/or videotaped.
There are no major risks involved in this study.
No one other than the researchers will have access to your recorded interviews. Transcribed sections of interviews may appear in the case, and your name and company will be disguised if that is your preference.
The case study may benefit you.
Potential benefits to you are those associated with a collaborative research project—an opportunity to gain insight that can lead to improved conditions and effectiveness.
Your participation is totally voluntary.
You are free to terminate your involvement with this project at any time, for any reason. You can reach me at [*insert your telephone number and e-mail address*]. I will be glad to answer any questions you may have.
I have read and understood the information above and consent to participate in the case study.

_____   _____   _____
Name (please print)   Signature   Date

_____   _____   _____
Student Researcher's Name (please print)   Signature   Date

WS 10:6

How to Research an Industry

Student Handout

An industry paper should be prepared for the industry with which your manager or business owner is involved. This paper is meant to familiarize you with the manager's area of expertise and help you develop insightful questions to ask.

An industry paper should provide concrete and specific information, including:

- a full description of the services or product in question;
- the industry's overall size in the United States/in your state/in your locality;
- identification of the primary factor that produces profit within the industry (How do you make money if you own a business within this industry?) and the industry upon which this one depends (i.e., if the industry is glass manufacturing and the specific company produces windshield glass, success is dependent upon the automobile industry);
- barriers to entry;
- opportunities for growth;
- biggest challenges;
- amount and kind of competition; and
- other information that you deem helpful in understanding the context of the business.

Your business librarian is a good resource for help in your searches. The following information was provided by Nancy Dennis, business librarian at Salem State University.

Step 1: Identify the SICS or NAICS Code of Your Entrepreneur's Business.

The federal government assigns SIC (Standard Industrial Classification) and NAICS (North American Industry Classification System) codes to all products and services to expedite searching in the U.S. Census site and many library databases. SIC codes are composed of two and four digits; NAICS, between two and six.

- SIC: http://www.osha.gov/pls/imis/sicsearch.html (U.S. Department of Labor, Occupational Safety & Health Administration, Statistics & Data: SIC Manual)

- NAICS: http://www.census.gov/eos/www/naics/ (U.S. Census Bureau, North American Industry Classification System, Introduction)

Step 2: Become Acquainted with Your Entrepreneur's Industry.

Key Source: IbisWorld (www.ibisworld.com). This research database provides overviews of industries in the United States and access to global reports. IBIS facilitates searching by keyword or NAICS code. A typical report includes key statistics; market segmentation; market characteristics; industry conditions; key industry factors; key competitors; industry performance, and industry outlook.

Key Source: Industry association statistics and overviews.

Some industry reports are fully accessible in Google. Search for your product and service and the term "association." Example: commercial bakeries and associations.

Some industry reports, such as those by the National Restaurant Association, are available in university libraries.

Step 3: Find Local Data on Your Industries.

- American FactFinder provides data on industries by zip code and county. Go to http://factfinder2.census.gov/faces/nav/jsf/pages/index.xhtml.

    The American FactFinder's "Business and Government" link provides data on industries by NAICS codes that can be narrowed to geographical areas.

- County Business Patterns provides data for counties, zip codes, and metro business areas. Go to http://www.census.gov/programs-surveys/cbp.html.

Step 4: Research Your Entrepreneur's Customers.

- The New Strategist "Who's Buying Guide" is a multivolume reference series that analyzes consumers of various products and services. Separate volumes include data on such variables as age, gender, race, and geographic region, and cover products such as beverages, health care, apparel, entertainment, groceries, pet care, information technologies, and household furnishings. Consult your university library or ask a Reference Librarian to identify specific titles and their call numbers.

- TableBase Users should ask their library for access to TableBase by Gale (http://assets.cengage.com/pdf/fs_table.pdf), is a library research database available that indexes data tables from a wide spectrum of sources.

- Global Market Information Database (GMID; http://www.euromonitor.com/) is a research database that provides reports and statistics on many consumer goods. To search, enter a subject in the "Text" box under the "Search" tab that appears at the upper left of the search screen. Click on results, or refine your search by consumer groups and geographical areas.

Step 5: Research the Demographics and Psychometrics of the Geographical Location of Your Entrepreneur's Business.

- Claritas.com (https://segmentationsolutions.nielsen.com/mybestsegments/Default.jsp?ID=20): You Are Where You Live. Utilizes the unique Prizm software to profile consumers within cities and towns. Nonsubscribers have access to basic but immensely helpful data in the "You Are Where You Live" module. To enter the free module, click on the round "You Are Where You Live" icon on the right side of the web page.
- *2009 Community Sourcebook of Zip Code Demographics*, 23rd ed. (Vienna, VA: ESRI, 2009). Reference Book.
- *2009 Community Sourcebook of County Demographics*, 21st ed. (Vienna, VA: ESRI, 2009). Reference Book.
- *2013 Community Sourcebook of Zip Code Demographics* by chegg com EAN: 9781589481688 Manufactured by chegg com http://upcdatabase.website/upc/9781589481688
- *2013 Community Sourcebook of Zip Code Demographics* by chegg com EAN: 9781589481954 Manufactured by chegg com http://upcdatabase.website/upc/9781589481954

Step 6: Research the Competitors of Your Entrepreneur.

- Google Maps.
- Reference USA research database is an electronic directory of local businesses that provides basic company data. After entering the "Businesses" section, set custom search criteria to search by NAICS code, sales, employee size, and geographical locations.
- Websites of competitors.

Step 7: Research What Your Entrepreneur Does.

- Search for articles on your industry/product/service in trade publications. Search for your industry/product/service in the library database Business Source Premier to identify articles on logistics, "insider" views, and trade secrets. Another good database to try is LexisNexis.
- Search for websites of associations for your industry/product/service in Google. Some sites will let all visitors view articles and data, while others limit access to members.

Step 8: Check out the Larger Regional and National Economic Picture.

Your business owner's success will be significantly influenced by state and national economic, political, and social trends. For economic forecasts and data, see:

Federal Reserve Bank of Boston, "Summary of National Economic Data." https://www.bostonfed.org/data/data-tools/national-economic-data-summary.aspx

Federal Reserve Bank of Boston, "Regional Economy." http://www.bos.frb.org/economic/regional/index.htm

U.S. Bureau of Labor Statistics, "Economy at a Glance" [by state]. http://www.bls.gov/EAG/eag.[INSERT YOUR STATE'S TWO-LETTER ABBREVIATION].htm

U.S. Census Bureau, "State & County Quick Facts." http://quickfacts.census.gov/qfd/states/25/25017.html

YOUR STATE.gov, Labor Force and Unemployment Data. For example, for Massachusetts: http://lmi2.detma.org/lmi/lmi_lur_a.asp. To find the data, select the desired geographical parameter (town, county, etc.); specific geographical name; and time period.

WS 10:7

How to Read a Case

Student Handout

Reading and preparing a case for class discussion involves a lot more than reading a blog, your e-mail, a novel, or even a chapter in a textbook. If you have not developed the case-reading skill yet, now is the time to try a new technique called "The Three Reads" model.

The First Read

■ Find **six minutes** (yes, six minutes is enough for a 10-page case) to sit down uninterrupted. Turn off your IM and mute your cell phone so that you do not get distracted during this short reading period.

■ Read the hook. This may be several paragraphs long and will introduce you to the case "problem." Write the problem in one sentence in the margin.

■ Read the first sentence (and **only** the first sentence) of each paragraph in the case. Write a keyword or two in the margin next to the paragraph.

■ Read the **title only** of the attachments and exhibits.

■ Read the titles in the reference list. What kinds of readings did the author use as references? What general content area do they cover?

That's it. Turn your IM and cell phone back on and go about your business.

The Second Read

■ This is the big one—reserve **at least one hour** for this read. Remember that if you have interruptions, this hour must be extended—let's be fair to the author! After all, the author spent upward of 50 hours writing the case, and that work deserves a fair share of your attention.

■ Read the entire case, slowly and carefully. Jot notes as you go along about the characters and their behavior, the situation, and the action. Sometimes preparing a timeline of action makes it easier to follow and remember. Be sure to include the exhibits and attachments when reading this time.

■ Jot down your own response to the situation and the characters, even if it's unsupported by theories or formal concepts. Make any connections you can to analogous situations you have experienced or read about before. What are the differences or similarities to this situation? Remember, these notes that you are making are yours alone—I will not be looking at them. It doesn't matter if they are messy or have lines drawn all over them, just as long as they exist. They are meant to help you.

■ Make a list of the assumptions you are making and the information you still need before you make a recommendation. What is missing? Something is always missing, or the case would be really boring.

■ List the alternative solutions to the case, their pros and cons, and then select one recommendation. You always have to **select one** recommendation and provide a rationale for it. This recommendation should be supported by some theory, concept, or class discussion in this or some other class. Again, these are **notes**, not papers meant to be handed in.

■ Prepare answers to any case questions you have been assigned. These get handed in.

You should be tired at this point. Put the case away.

The Third Read

■ This last read takes place not too long before class. The point of it is to make sure that the case is fresh in your mind and that you are still comfortable with your recommendation.

■ This read resembles the first read: read the beginning, the first sentence of each paragraph, etc. But this time, include both your marginal notes and the notes you have made during the second read. No one will collect your notes (except for case questions you may have been assigned), but you will need them to prepare for exams and to sound "smart" in class. Remember that class participation means that you have to talk—it's okay to read aloud what you have written if you are uncomfortable talking off the cuff.

That's it! The entire process has not taken more than two hours, which is about the amount of time you should anticipate using for class preparation.

WS 10:8

Ten Rules for Conducting Successful Interviews

Student Handout

	Things to Remember	Things to Do
1	The interview is centered on the person you are interviewing, not on you.	Put interviewees at ease, make them comfortable, and gain their trust.
2	People are interesting, and their stories are interesting. When you find people interesting, they are more likely to share their stories with you. Nonetheless, most people are likely to think that their stories are nothing special.	Make sure the interviewees understand that their stories are not only special but also important to you personally. This is "revealing the ordinary." Remember that people's everyday stories are important research.
3	The theme of the research is the focus of the interview, not the general life history of the interviewee (no matter how interesting that part really is).	All the other questions you ask should culminate in the most important one of the interview. Do not ask it right up front; instead, work your way up to it by asking other, simpler questions.
4	A good way to start your questions is to keep them specific; get the anecdotes you are looking for by asking: "Can you tell me about a time when . . . ?" and filling in that blank with the topic. For example, "Can you tell me about a time when your deliveries didn't come in and you had customers that you had promised items to?"	Ask open-ended (not yes/no) questions.
5	Keep the interview on the level of description, but listen between the lines. People rarely say everything they mean or mean everything they say. Try to understand the meaning of the words, pauses, facial expressions, body language, etc. when interviewing. You may make an incorrect interpretation, but if you have recorded the facts of the interview accurately and your own subjective assumptions parenthetically, you will be able to draw some fairly appropriate conclusions.	It is perfectly acceptable to confirm with the interviewee whether or not your assumptions are correct. Sometimes, this will even help the interviewee to reconsider his own assumptions.

	Things to Remember	Things to Do
6	Develop a preferred method for taking your notes. Maybe use a regular notebook with the pages folded in half vertically. On one side of the page, record the answers to your questions, direct quotes in quotation marks and paraphrased answers simply written down. On the other side of the page, write your questions (or a code for the questions—like #1 when the question is the first on your list), your observations of the environment and of the way the interviewee behaves, looks, etc., and your personal interpretations.	Be careful to bracket or underline the interpretations, so you do not confuse them with facts or direct observations. Once you develop a system, stick to it!
7	Be sure to differentiate opinions from facts.	Pay very close attention to physical cues.
8	Determine your own presuppositions or assumptions—that is, opinions you may have about the subject or the subject matter before you have conducted your interview.	Personal reflection is necessary, and personal reflection takes time. This investment of time is worth the effort, as you will see once you begin interviewing.
9	Do as much of your archival research as possible before the interview. This will help you develop some sensitivity to the stories the interviewee is telling.	Show respect to the interviewee through your extensive preparation.
10	Remember that the interview experience is supposed to be beneficial to both the interviewer and the interviewee. It is a rare occurrence for people to be invited to share their personal history including triumphs and failures with someone who is giving them undivided attention. The interviewee will value this process. You must make it clear to the interviewee that you respect her privacy as well as her willingness to share with you, and that you will benefit greatly from the time spent.	Say "Thank you!"

Sources: Kvale (1983); Mitchell (1997); Rae and Carswell (2000).

WS 10:9

Sample Interview Questions and Some Things to Observe and Note

Student Handout

Add your own questions to the end of these lists. Record the answers in the blank spaces provided.

Q#	Question	Interviewee's Response
1	What motivated you to start your own business?	
2	Please describe the steps you took before actually starting to serve customers.	
3	Please describe your first year in this job. Can you talk about the highs and the lows of the position?	
4	Please describe the response from your family and friends when you decided to go into this particular industry.	
5	How risky is it being in the position you hold in this industry? How has that changed since you became a . . . ?	
6	How did you raise money for your business? Can you describe your successes and failures at fundraising?	
7	Can you describe your general experience in your current position: how hard do you work, how stressful is it, how much fun, what are the best and the worst parts?	
8	What business mistakes have you made? What would you warn others about?	
9	Would you do it again if you could go back in time? What would you change?	
10	What advice would you give young people thinking about going into your business?	
Things to Observe		
What kind of building is the business in? Age? Size?		

How many people work there? Age? Gender?	
What are the offices like? Technology? Sounds? Smells? Color? Use all your senses!	
How do people talk to one another? Are they friendly? Noisy? Unnaturally quiet?	

WS 10:10

How to Connect the Problem to the Theories

Student Handout

During the time you have spent in the business school, you have been exposed to a great many theories and concepts. Every class you have taken has introduced you to theories that relate directly to the course material. Now is your chance to integrate those theories and make real use of them. The case research study project is not about learning new theories; it is about considering the theories you have already met and using them to demystify actual business behaviors and situations.

The theories and concepts you have learned in management, accounting, finance, marketing, and technology can all be applied to your case research study. However, it is likely that many of these theories have run together in your mind, or that you forgot them once the course in which they were presented was over. The big challenge for you is to reconnect with these theories and organize them in such a way that you will be able to select the appropriate one to apply to the specific problem you are studying.

One way you can do this is to design a matrix similar to the following brief sample. If you have forgotten the names of the theories you learned or the names of the theorists who proposed them, you can refer to your old texts (if you haven't sold them), the syllabi of courses you have completed, or your old course notebooks. If these items are no longer available to you, simply find someone who is taking a course you have already taken and ask that person to lend you the text for a short time so you can refresh your memory. You might even ask a professor if you can sit in the office and thumb through the current text. Sometimes, just a glance at the Table of Contents will be enough to jog your memory.

Theory/Concept (list and use a keyword to identify each theory as in the following samples)	Course in Which the Theory Appeared	Situations in Which the Theory Can Be Applied
Motivation theories Maslow (Hierarchy of needs) Herzberg (hygiene and motivators) Adams (Equity theory) Vroom (Expectancy theory)	Organizational Behavior, Management	Making choices when presented with different alternatives; length of time or amount of effort a person puts forth

MBO	Management	Planning and goal setting
Market segmentation	Marketing	Who is the customer?
Acid test (quick test) ratio	Accounting	Ability to pay off current liabilities

WS 10:11

What to Share and What to Withhold

Student Handout

Do **Share the Following:**

- Organizational history
- Industry information and background
- A clear, rich description of the protagonist
- An evocative description of the environment
- The facts about the problem that is the core of the case
- Any direct quotes that help the reader to understand the protagonist, the environment, the relationships, or the problem at hand (dialogue makes a case lively and fun to read, and it brings the characters to life)
- Data that you can make available, such as budgets, balance sheets, lists of products, service areas, etc.
- Your analytical perspective, insights, and personal opinions
- Your alternative recommendations and the final recommendation
- The methodology you used to research and write the case research study
- What you learned from doing this project

Do Not **Share the Following:**

- Facts and descriptions meant to mislead the reader
- Too many clues that point the reader to a single, specific conclusion before you have identified the pros and cons of your alternatives
- Irrelevant material
- Any suggestions that an answer is "right" or "wrong"
- Anything that the subject of the case has said is confidential

You may find it helpful to write an outline based on the project requirements. Then, fill in the blanks. Once you have something down on paper, you can amplify or delete, clean it up and polish it, tone it down, or formalize it a little.

Remember that the case study is about a **manager** or **business owner**— it is not about the business itself. It is important to tell us enough about the business that we can understand the context of the protagonist's behavior, but we don't need to know detailed levels of information about internal operations unless they are relevant to the problem/challenge you are presenting. The case is about the biggest challenge a manager or business owner has faced and how he or she has handled it. That should guide what you write about the organization and about the person.

Two Final "Rules"

- Have fun with this.
- Remember that you are doing research with real people with whom you have developed a trusting relationship. Do not violate that trust.

WS 10:12

How to Write Up Your Research

Student Handout

The key to writing a case study from firsthand research is to remember that you are telling a story, and you are in complete control of what you share with your audience. This means that you have to draw a line between being too stingy with information and overwhelming people with data. Be selective and discriminating, but not miserly.

How long should the case be? As long as it has to be to tell the story. I know that's not a "fair" answer, but it's difficult to be very specific on this. Most cases are between five and 15 pages—long enough to cover the subject but not long enough to bore the reader. If you look at the 11 case elements, it is hard to imagine completing the project thoroughly in fewer than 10 pages, plus any appendices, exhibits, or attachments you may have.

Some language and formatting conventions:

■ The "story" part of the case is **always** written in the past tense, even when it sounds funny to your ear, because the action has already taken place. The analysis, personal commentary, recommendations, and other elements should be written in the present tense.

■ Use headings and subheadings to make it easier for the reader to locate the various elements.

■ It is perfectly acceptable for you to use the first person plural when writing up your case—that is, "we," when you are discussing your analysis, recommendations, etc. However, be sure to use the second person singular—"he" or "she"—when telling the story part of the case.

■ Dialogue should appear between quotation marks.

■ Try to remember that you know a lot more than the reader does; don't hold back important facts that seem "obvious" to you.

■ Before you submit your first draft, be sure to get the entrepreneur's sign-off on direct quotes.

■ Refer to WS 10:11 ("What to Share and What to Withhold") for more information.

If you'd like to know more about writing up stories as research, you might want to read:

Dennehy, Robert F. (1999). "The Executive as Storyteller." *Management Review* 88, no. 3, 40–43.

Morgan, Sandra, and Robert F. Dennehy. (1997). "The Power of Organizational Storytelling: A Management Development Perspective." *Journal of Management Development* 16, no. 7, 494–501.

WS 10:13

Self-Grading Rubric

Student Handout

Please complete and attach to your draft case research study and to your final project.

	Something is Wrong	Everything is Correct	Student Comment Here
Presence of all required elements (refer to original assignment)	What is missing? Add it.	In the column to the right, list the items that appear in the Table of Contents.	
Issues	Some primary or secondary issues are missing.	All the primary and secondary issues have been dealt with and prioritized.	
Adequacy of discussion of consequences, depth of data analysis, application of theory	Weak in one or more of the listed areas.	Issues are fully developed— alternatives are given, consequences are spelled out clearly, data analysis is comprehensive, and theory is applied correctly.	
Quality of expression	I have not run spell-check or grammar-check. I have not had someone else proofread my work.	My work has been proofread by someone else and all errors have been corrected.	
Would I be willing to turn in this report to my employer?	If no—fix it!	If yes, you're done. Hand it in, along with this evaluation sheet.	
What grade would you give this project?	C or less	A or B	

WS 10:14

Grading Rubric

Use this rubric to grade the final case research study. You can easily adapt the point values of each section to your preferences.

	Weak	⟶	Exemplary
The Hook	Missing.	Is an abstract or synopsis.	Makes the reader want to read further.
Points	**0**	**1**	**3**
The Industry	Talks about the industry in vague terms or is missing.	Talks about the industry in terms of two or three of the suggested areas.	Talks about the industry in terms of all the requested areas to provide full context.
Points	**2**	**3**	**6**
The Company Story	Provides very little background information about the company.	Provides limited information about the company history and/or facts about current operations.	Provides a full history of the company, as well as complete information about current operations.
Points	**1**	**3**	**4**
The Entrepreneur or Small Business Owner	The reader can form only a very limited mental picture of the entrepreneur or the entrepreneur's behavior.	The reader has a general idea of who the entrepreneur is and how the entrepreneur behaves.	The reader is able to picture the entrepreneur and can anticipate the entrepreneur's future actions.
Points	**2**	**5**	**10**
The Problem or Situation	The key situation in the case is unclear.	The key situation in the case is clear, but it reads like a report.	The key situation in the case is fully elaborated and complete. It reads like a story.
Points	**1–6**	**7–10**	**11**
Commentary	No explanations or theories that explain the entrepreneur's behavior are provided.	An attempt is made to provide theories that explain the behavior, but the theories are not specific.	Theories that explain the entrepreneur's behavior are identified and applied correctly.

	Weak ⟶		Exemplary
Points	1–6	7–10	11
Alternating Sections P-Voice and R-Voice	Other stories beyond the key situation are missing, along with their relevant theories.	Other stories or situations are presented, but relevant theories explaining them are missing or limited.	Two additional stories or situations are included in the appropriate voice, along with commentary, theory, and application.
Points	1–7	8–12	13–15
Alternatives	One alternative is provided, consequences not identified, insufficient data analysis, theory not applied properly.	Two alternatives are provided, consequences are not accurately identified, data analysis not properly conducted, weak theory application.	Three alternatives are fully developed, consequences clearly spelled out, data analysis is comprehensive, and theory is applied correctly.
Points	0–5	6–10	11–15
Final Recommendation	The final recommendation is missing.	The final recommendation is missing its rationale or does not make sense in the situation.	The final recommendation and the rationale make sense.
Points	0	1–4	5–6
Methodology	The discussion of methodology is cursory.	The discussion of methodology does not cover several of the important areas.	A complete discussion of methodology exists, including reference to all suggested areas.
Points	0–1	2–3	4–5
Final Word	No reflection or no learning identified.	Some learning has been identified.	Learning has been identified and specific examples provided.
Points	0–1	2–4	5–6
Writing Quality	Many careless grammar and spelling errors exist that could have been caught by spell-check or grammar-check (or careful proofreading).	The case does not appear to have been edited beyond spell-check and grammar-check for style or expression.	There are very few grammar and spelling errors, the writing is clear, and the analysis is easy to read and engaging.
Points	0–2	3–5	6–8
Comments:			

WS 10:15

Hints for a Successful Presentation

Student Handout

Your Appearance

Rightly or wrongly, we are first judged by the way we look. For that reason, you should present yourself in the best possible light. Here are some typical errors that students make in appearance when making a presentation. Some of these may apply to you, and others will not, but you should be aware of all of them and avoid them:

- plunging necklines
- exposed midriffs
- belly-button rings showing
- flip-flops
- drooping pants
- shirt hanging outside of pants
- sloppy sneakers
- t-shirts
- dressing for the club instead of the classroom

Fear of Public Speaking

Many students (and faculty as well) claim to be afraid of presenting in front of a group. Actually, it would be more surprising if you weren't a bit nervous. Here are a few suggestions to make your presentations easier to face.

If you find that you make any of these common mistakes, know that you are not alone; however, do try to avoid them. Speakers sometimes

- get a case of the "ums," "uhs," or "ers."
- put their hands in their pockets or on their hips—or in their hair.
- fidget a lot, scratching and tossing their heads. It is not necessary to stand still; in fact, moving around is a good idea as long as there is a reason to move around.
- read directly from a paper, cards, or slides, and the paper or cards shake, distracting the listener.
- speak too softly.

- speak only to the instructor, forgetting about the rest of the class or audience.
- make up answers to questions when they are not sure of the "real answer." A better solution is to say, "I don't know. I'll check and get back to you." And then, do it (after you leave the front of the room, of course).

Some Pre-Presentation Tips to Make the Whole Ordeal Less Painful

- Practice your presentation with your team. Several times.
- Practice your presentation alone. Several times plus one.
- Worry less about memorizing your presentation and focus more on really understanding what you are saying. That way, you will not get lost even if you get distracted.
- Sometimes (but not always) a handout will help nail down your point. Plus, it will give the audience a place to make notes.
- Remember to breathe. Practice this often.

Module 11

• • • • •

Special Formats and Delivery Systems

• • • • •

Back to Basics

Throughout this workbook, I have addressed primarily traditional cases—that is, full-length cases (with or without a decision focus) delivered in paper or electronic formats. There are other options we should consider, both in terms of unique formats and alternative delivery systems.

But before we discuss special and unique case formats and delivery systems, it pays to review what a case is. Referring back to Module 1, a case is a **story** that describes a **factual** series of actions that occurred in the **past**. Using this simple, basic definition as our guide, you may wonder why I have emphasized in this manual that a case should follow a particular set of protocols. After all, you can tell a story in many ways. Fairy tales, nursery rhymes, and lullabies are our first interactions with storytelling, and each of these also follows a prescribed format that signals how we, as children, are supposed to interact with the story.

"Once upon a time" is the phrase that starts most of the best-loved fairy tales, and when we hear these four magic words we know that a good story is about to come. We prepare ourselves physically (snuggle into the sofa, cuddle up to a parent, pull the covers up to our chin), emotionally (thumb in the mouth, teddy bear or doll in our arms), and intellectually (listen carefully, look at the pictures, watch the reader's face, and pay close attention to the reader's voice). We know that the fairy tale is going to leave us thinking about something, and, depending on the time of day, we may fall asleep thinking about the story or take the book ourselves and pretend to reread it again and again, learning by repetition and review.

Nursery rhymes serve a similar but not identical purpose. Through nursery rhymes, we learn an appreciation for language, cadence, and humor. We have some of our earliest lessons in memorization (who does not know the line that follows, "Three little kittens have lost their mittens and . . .) and in morality tales ("Georgie Porgie pudding and pie, kissed the girls and made them cry"). Emotional impact plays a key role in nursery rhymes, and we learn at a very young age that actions have consequences and we must be prepared to pay those consequences.

Lullabies have a slightly different purpose. Their primary goal is to soothe both the child and the singer and convince them both, through rhythm and cadence, that all will be well if the child will simply relax and go to sleep. Again, repetition plays an important role, as does learning that behavior has an impact on outcomes (going to sleep means you will wake up energetic and happy, ready to play, drink a bottle, have a nice diaper change). Reinforcement of peaceful themes via lullabies sets expectations based on previous experience.

These goals differ very little from the generic learning goals of cases. We use cases to

- facilitate student learning about life. (What happens when your lamb follows you to school? What is the best way to take care of a pet?)
- practice considering the actions and behaviors of protagonists. (How did it happen that the three little kittens lost their mittens?)
- identify alternative behaviors that may have preferable outcomes. (How might Georgie Porgie modify his behavior so as to not make girls cry?)
- recognize analogous situations to which the current situation might relate. (Is the goal to clean up the neighborhood or is the goal to keep strangers like Goldilocks out of our unlocked houses?)
- evaluate risk to determine appropriate actions. (Was Humpty Dumpty's decision to sit on a wall a wise one, considering the risk of falling and potential damages?)

Most of the nursery rhymes and fairy tales enjoyed today originated in the early to mid-1800s, so for more than 150 years we have depended on these varying vehicles and methods to teach important lessons to our children. All methods of telling these stories have been widely accepted (consider the popularity of Disney cartoon variations on traditional stories), and television shows have repeated the lessons for half a century, perhaps changing the way the characters look but not the way they behave. Comic books, picture books, storytelling circles, primers, and modern versions (Harry Potter, for example) reinforce the same lessons in terms our children can understand.

All these variations share the characteristics of a good story: a beginning, a middle, and an ending; evocative language; characters performing some action resulting in an outcome. This is not so very different from the definition of a case. As long as we adhere closely to our case definition—a factual narrative that occurred in the past—we are not constrained in our method of delivery or in our format.

● ● ● ● ●

Some Alternative Case Formats: Paper-Based

Some alternative case formats are familiar to us, while others are less well known. We have focused on teaching cases that can be published in traditional journals and/or distributed as standalone entities, but there are other frequently used kinds of cases that do not appear in most journals. These cases are published primarily in textbooks and are focused very specifically on one topic. (For information on journals that publish in some alternative formats, see WS 7.2 and WS 7.3.)

Textbook Cases

Textbooks use four basic kinds of cases: critical incidents, vignettes, case exercises, and end-of-section cases. The descriptions that follow reflect an emphasis on usage and the length of the case situation rather than any other factor.

Critical Incidents

Critical incidents are very brief (less than one page) situations that raise an issue, present a problem, describe a turning point, or depict a moment of surprise for the protagonist. In textbooks, critical incidents are often boxed mini-cases that follow the theme of the chapter and are meant to illustrate the concept under discussion.

Vignettes

Vignettes are brief (one to two pages) descriptive portraits of a company or a commonly encountered situation. They appear most frequently as the introductory element of a textbook chapter and are meant to engage the reader with the problem or the tool that is the focus of the chapter. Vignettes also appear at the end of chapters, at which time they present an abbreviated decision-based problem or descriptive situation for students to analyze after they have absorbed the theoretical content provided in the chapter. Often, textbook authors introduce a chapter with a vignette, follow that case throughout the chapter, and conclude with another vignette about the same company. The goal of this usage is to demonstrate the application of chapter concepts by following one extended example interspersed with more abstract material.

Case Exercises

Case exercises are complete, short cases (two to five pages) that conclude with a formal set of instructions to the student about how to proceed. These instructions are not to be confused with the discussion questions that appear in the Instructor's Manual. Instead, the exercise will require the student to do something specific—research a topic, perform a SWOT analysis, design an action plan, prepare a debate, or conduct some other activity derived from the case narrative.

End-of-Section Cases

Textbooks often include a full-length case at the end of a multichapter section. These cases are of the same kind and quality you will find in a journal. In fact, they are often reprinted (with permission) from journal cases and serve the same purpose as does any full case.

A/B Cases

A/B cases are multipart, complex cases that provide several decision or analysis points for students to address. Part A is a full case that includes all relevant elements and concludes with a decision point or a prediction point. Students are challenged to make a recommendation for action or a prediction as to outcomes at the end of Part A. The reason to break up a case into distinct parts is the potential impact a decision in one part may have on actions that follow in the next part. As a result, several discrete learning goals obviate presenting the case in one unit. From time to time, a case epilogue provides a rich opportunity for students to perform a secondary analysis, and a Part B can be developed from this material by the instructor.

Part A of an A/B case can stand alone, but subsequent parts generally require students to have read Part A in order to have sufficient background to perform an insightful case analysis.

Choose-Your-Own-Action Cases

Another format that is intriguing is the choose-your-own-action case. This kind of case is based on the popular choose-your-own-adventure series in which children are encouraged to select an action from a range of actions. Their choice directs the next chapter in the book and leads to a different ending.

The way a choose-your-own-action case works is similar. A complete case is presented and a decision point reached. The reader selects from among a series of possible decisions and follows the story along the path that corresponds to the selected action by reading the follow-up as distributed by the instructor. At the end of the "path," the student performs a traditional analysis of the action taken and its resulting consequences. This is similar to a simulation.

This model is suitable for students just beginning the process of learning with cases because the simplified decision-making process acclimatizes students to the concept of case analysis. It is also suitable for cases in which the protagonist tried several different solutions before settling on the one that worked in the actual case situation. And it is fun, both to write and to analyze.

Graphic Novels or Photo Diaries

When a case requires a lot of information about a manufacturing process or a technical procedure and the case audience is not composed of professionals or even people with a small amount of knowledge in the area, the case exhibits can become confusing, heavy, and—to be brutally honest—boring. For these reasons, students may gloss over the complex exhibits or even disregard them completely. This puts them at a disadvantage when it comes to performing the analysis or making a sensible recommendation to the protagonist.

Instead of writing a tedious description of a series of difficult-to-envision processes, it may be preferable to incorporate a series of photos or drawings much like the action drawings that appear in graphic novels. You can provide the necessary explanations in brief captions that extend for no more than a paragraph each and that lead naturally into the next photo or drawing. Students will retain more information because they are both reading text and seeing an illustration (as well as enjoying the novelty of the format). See WS 11:1 (Graphic Novels or Photo Diaries) for an abbreviated example.

Alternative Case Formats: Technology-Based

None of the preceding formats requires technological facilitation, although all of them can benefit from technology. The graphic novel can come to life by presentation in a video format. Choose-your-own-action can keep the reader "honest" by presenting only the material accessed through the selection process. The Part B of an A/B case can be released electronically only after the Part A decision has been made and justified.

But technology can do more than provide digital enhancement of traditional delivery systems. The general consensus seems to endorse the use of technology to the greatest extent possible when teaching with cases. This means having video, multimedia, simulations, smartphone apps, and any other technology-enhanced method at one's disposal to engage today's learners more actively with the material at hand. Current research has shown that students who use a lot of computer technology have greater success in active learning environments. See Lowerison et al. (2006) for a full discussion of this research. A more recent government study (Means et al., 2009) indicated that students learning in online environments achieved more than students in purely face-to-face environments. This helps to move learners from a passive learning state into a more assertive and engaged model of learning, one of the stated goals of learning with cases. Valuable outcomes such as thinking in new ways about the material, increasing student confidence, and fostering more active engagement with the learning process tempt us to extend the concept of "computer technology" to the "use of technology overall," especially because instructors and students function only rarely without technology.

Nonetheless, despite the ubiquity of technology and the apparent beneficial results of using technology to learn, the cases being written and widely used today do not differ significantly in presentation or format from the cases that were initially introduced in the beginning of the last century. Students read text-based descriptions of scenarios supplemented with static graphs, financial statements, and the rare photograph. Although most of us carry significantly more computing and communication capabilities in our pockets (our smartphones) than were used in controlling the Apollo spacecraft, little of this technology has had an impact on case delivery. Technology changes quickly, but humans change slowly.

Some of the ways we can introduce more technology into our cases are as follows.

Video Cases

Video cases often take the format of a network feature news story. The video medium is used to communicate the case scenario, background information, and decision maker interviews. Students either watch the video in class or on their own prior to class discussion. Printed background materials or industry notes may accompany the video presentation.

Mixed-Media Cases

This type of case combines the traditional text-based case with one or more alternative forms of media. Short video clips may be embedded in the text to demonstrate visual aspects of the manufacturing process or to demonstrate usage of the product. Interviews with key players are also often incorporated through video or audio. Smartphone applications might utilize different formats and platforms to communicate case information integrating a variety of mixed-media components.

Multimedia Cases

Multimedia cases use computer technology to present text, graphics, audio, and video via links and tools for navigation and interaction. Multimedia cases are distinguished from mixed-media cases through the incorporation of tools that allow students to gather, process, and communicate information and ideas. Multimedia cases not only allow students to choose from a variety of media in gathering information but also permit them to utilize an embedded expert system or decision support system in analyzing the case or in developing or evaluating alternative solutions. The expert system uses analytical or decision tools to assist students by structuring their thinking processes through software applications.

Case/Simulation Hybrids

This type of case combines traditional text-based cases with computerized simulations of decision outcomes. Students study the decision-based case and then input values into a simulation program to see the results of their recommended course of action. Many publishing houses offer simulations for business students, and they have been well received for their learning value. Simulations are often used in lieu of a so-called "live case," or a case situation that proceeds in real time as students observe.

Nonconventional Cases

This category includes any technologically based case format limited only by the producer's imagination (and perhaps monetary and temporal budgets). Examples of possibilities in this realm include the use of virtual environments such as Second Life or video games to simulate a decision-making scenario.

For a descriptive or analytical case, the case author/producer can put together a script and upload it to one of the many free or low-cost programs available (such as "xtranormal.com") that will turn the script into oddly accented audio combined with cartoon-style characters that interact with one another. The resulting video can easily be uploaded to YouTube and viewed anytime, anywhere by students at no cost to them.

●●●●●

Getting Started with Technology: Advantages and Drawbacks

Before you dive enthusiastically into technology-facilitated cases, consider the parties and their interests. Just as the best business decisions are those that satisfy the needs of all stakeholders, so too the best teaching and learning formats satisfy the needs of the stakeholders: case writer, instructor, and students. See WS 11:2 (Case Stakeholders and Their Needs) for an overview.

Students

Frequently called "Digital Natives," today's students are not only technologically savvy but also immersed in more kinds of gadgetry, software applications, and electronic-enabled information than any previous generation. Their perspective demands "free" access to the intellectual property that earlier generations have fought to protect. Their easy and apparently innate ability to work technology that comes without instructions (earlier generations swore by manuals) and their willingness to connect with one another, openly disregarding earlier attempts to protect individual privacy, all make for frequent disconnects with the Baby Boomers and Gen Xers who are their instructors in the classroom.

The classroom? Even that has changed for the post-Millennial generation (sometimes called Generation Z). They often find themselves learning through distance programs, online courses, and hybrid structures that remove them from face-to-face communication with peers and faculty. Working alone, coupled with uniquely high access to technology via the Internet, creates an environment that is conducive to technologically mediated learning processes.

Post-Millennial learners are accustomed to rapid acquisition of information and have little patience with the more labor-intensive methods of knowledge acquisition that have been the mainstay of the Boomer and Gen X classrooms. They claim that the ever-increasing presence of mobile devices and tablets, along with continuously improving wireless technology, has decreased at least some of the need for laptops or desktop computers. Today's learners tend toward a vastly different learning style than students of only 20 years ago. In the language of David Kolb's (2005) classic learning theory, current students show dramatic increases in Divergers and Accommodators and parallel decreases in Convergers and Assimilators. Simply stated, today's learners prefer to learn via concrete experimentation, imagination, and intuition rather than the abstract conceptualization and logical application of information preferred by earlier generations. The evidence seems clear: We cannot depend indefinitely on our old comfortable teaching methods, content delivery mechanisms, skills, and settings to achieve effective learning results with a different population.

Students like to learn with technology because:

- It is convenient. Most students in developed nations have continuous Internet access no matter where they are. They do not have to carry books or even notebooks when their lessons are online. It is inconceivable to them to be without web access—if not at home, then certainly at school.
- It encourages self-paced learning. No one is rushing you to finish your reading or your analysis. You can do a week's worth of work at one sitting or you can spread the work over a full week, working several

hours a day. Because online learning is mostly asynchronous, pressure is reduced.

- Many students prefer to write their responses instead of speaking in class. Some students process information more slowly than others, and the sometimes hectic pace of classroom participation keeps them from doing their best work. This is particularly important for students who speak and write English as a second language.
- The visual reinforcement provided through technology facilitates learning and makes remembering easier for the student who is a more visual learner.
- Technology can fill in gaps in understanding, as embedded hyperlinks encourage students to research terms, concepts, and processes with which they are less familiar.
- Images are simply easier to remember than text.

The main complaint students have about learning with technology is that it can be difficult to maintain focus and concentrated thought because of the ongoing temptation to visit related sites, check e-mail or social media, and respond to instant messages.

Instructors

The incorporation of technology into our teaching is appealing on several levels.

- It is fun. Traditional methods of instruction can become tiresome over time, and new methods spark our interest and recharge flagging enthusiasm. Instructors are in the business of teaching because we love learning, and if something generates learning, we tend to be in favor of it.
- It is controllable. We can limit access to some links simply by deleting those links from the text. We can incorporate our own preferred sites for student access. We can release half a case if we do not want students to read ahead.
- It provides the perception of active and engaged learning. It certainly looks like students are learning when they watch video—they appear to be engaged in the action on the monitor, and their faces show visible responses to what is happening. Students address simulations as if they were games, and they appear to enjoy the challenge.
- We think our students want it. We want very much to be current, to appear up to date. One way to do this is to incorporate things that matter to students rather than limit ourselves to the things that matter only to us. We are told that students love technology, ergo we will incorporate technology. *Q.E.D.*

Not All Fun and Games

It is important to remember that technology is not all fun and games—the use of technology "just because we can" is not a good enough reason to change a system that already works well. Instructors are concerned about the perception of learning value that derives from the transition from paper cases to digital cases.

Their first concern is about user expertise. The users in this situation may be the instructors themselves. No sooner do we learn one technology than things shift and we are expected to learn another. Conventional wisdom suggests that older people have a harder time adapting to new technologies than younger people; however, the data do not bear this out. The use of all kinds of technology is pervasive across the demographic spectrum, and instructors all have a certain comfort level with the minimal technologies required to manage their classes. It is natural to resist change, but that is not a sufficient reason to reject advances in pedagogy.

Instructors are also concerned about some more substantive issues: How will they be able to debrief their case discussion effectively if they are conducting them online or conducting them in a traditional setting without a hard copy to which they can refer? It can be more difficult to connect theory to practice when there is a disconnect between the delivery of one and the discussion of the other. How will they monitor student reactions? Will students become distracted by the special effects or the actors' clothing and engage with the material on a more superficial level? Will students be able to transcend the "story" part of the case and focus on the "lesson" part?

These are all valid questions, ones we should ask ourselves every time we design a lesson plan. But they are red herrings thrown in our path in this discussion by people who are reluctant to take a risk and try something different. When using paper cases, we cannot see our students' reactions; they are working at home or in the dorm or elsewhere, not directly in front of us. Many students never do get past the story to the lesson, regardless of the delivery system. No matter how challenging it is, we have to find a way to connect theory and practice or we are not doing our job properly.

A very important thing for us to remember is that the instructor, not the student, creates the perception of learning value. A significant part of our job is to convey this value to the students and direct their focus to what we want them to learn. If video, simulations, clever digital tricks, smartphone apps, or other technology interventions can spark learning, we should find a way to incorporate them.

Case Writers

The advantages of enriching cases via technology are obvious—it both associates learning with fun and provides an opportunity for us to collaborate with colleagues and advance innovative instructional methods.

The disadvantages of using technology to design cases are also obvious—issues of functionality can get in the way of usage, and the frequent use of links throughout a case make our role more directive than subtle.

The core of the discussion about technology and cases relates to the challenges inherent in the creation of materials. These issues fall into two broad categories: **resources** and **validity**.

Resources

There are three potential resource constraints we encounter when developing cases that incorporate technology to a significant degree: *tools, technical support*, and *time*.

Tools: There are myriad tools available to develop online games, manage projects, and design video presentations. A simple Google query for "online development tools" returned 650 million responses in a six-tenths of a second. How many of these tools do you know how to use? How long do you suppose it takes to develop expertise in any one of them? How many do you have to use in order to develop a case that is rich in technological enhancements yet maintains its academic integrity?

For most of us, the best we can do with this plethora of arcane tools is to put together something that looks like a sweater our elderly Aunt Delores knit, with her failing eyesight and shaking hands. This product will not impress our students. Instead, it will likely reinforce the belief that we "don't understand" today's students and their needs.

Technical Support: Although some schools are fortunate to have strong technical support available to their faculty, many schools are struggling to remain up to date without taking on the additional burden of providing instructional technology that is dedicated to just one kind of teaching. Resources are currently dedicated to enhancing and expanding learning management systems as schools jockey to position themselves on the forefront of distance learning, remote access, and alternative class models. Often, there is not a lot left for experimental projects.

In addition, the quality of network connectivity varies dramatically from institution to institution. Of particular concern is the variability of connectivity available to commuter students and students learning in remote environments. This means that programs may run slowly or may fail to operate smoothly. Students may have trouble accessing the bells and whistles that you have optimistically added to your cases, and the resulting skeletal version of the case is far less appealing than a rich, text-only case would be.

Time: How long does it take you to write a traditional text-only case? Not including the research, I suspect it would be difficult to write a full length case in less than 50 hours. How much time might be added to this estimate if you have to develop a short video, write a graphic novel, create functional spreadsheets with embedded formulae, develop an online searchable bibliography, or create some other useful enrichment element? Do you have this time available to you?

Perhaps more critically, can you find a partner in your institution's media department or elsewhere who can help you develop what you are not able to do on your own? Do you teach in an environment that encourages such cross-disciplinary collaboration? Does your school support activities such as these or will you be seen as a dilettante, playing with technology without serious intent? Even in the twenty-first century, this is not a minor consideration in some institutions for faculty seeking tenure.

Validity

The issue of validity is qualitative and somewhat more difficult to resolve, as it revolves around *assumptions* and *perceptions*.

Assumptions: We tend to make some erroneous assumptions about technology. The first is that our students have a level of expertise that few of them actually attain. Their actual skills may be far more limited than we realize. What should be self-explanatory ("Use CTRL + click to access this file," "Save documents in. docx format," "Download the latest version of Java to run this program," and similar instructions) often stymies our students. Their unfamiliarity with commonly used programs and their lack of skill in using them limits our own ability to incorporate advanced elements in our cases.

A second faulty assumption we make is that "all" our students are using smartphones or the equivalent. We think they "all" tweet. They "all" have social media accounts that they update constantly. In certain environments, these assumptions are fallacious. The students with whom I am in contact in my university rarely tweet. Only about half of them have smartphones. Most do have Facebook accounts (recent surveys estimate 90 percent of college students maintain Facebook, Instagram, Pinterest, or other social media accounts), and most students update them daily. Web 3.0 and its applications are a growing influence in the life of college students—this assumption is not faulty.

Social networking sites can provide ease of access for students and encourage them to participate more actively in their learning processes, according to some academics. Facebook makes it easy to set up special web pages, upload video, incorporate IM boards and other communication links for classes, for cases, or even for textbooks. Some say these processes are easier to manage in Facebook than in typical learning management software.

Perceptions: While we, as instructors, make assumptions and can manage those assumptions, we are not in control of the perceptions that others hold about our activities. The first perception we need to counter is the perception that technologically enhanced case writing is not a scholarly activity, especially in terms of academic rewards. We need to be able to build a case for the pedagogical value of the incorporation of technology into cases to counteract the misperception that a video clip or a YouTube link is just "fun."

Because we spend so much time in the academy working in silos, we tend to overlook the benefits of cross-disciplinary development of learning tools. The goal of all faculty members in all institutions is a shared one—we want students to learn. Sharing tools across disciplines enhances our ability to facilitate learning. That alone should deter critics of advances in technology-supported cases. Refer to Module 8 for information about working with coauthors and establishing communities of practice.

The last hurdle to overcome in this context relates to the fear that a focus on visuals will supersede a focus on content. We want to take care to avoid chipmunk behavior—that is, collecting clever tools in our academic cheeks (emphasizing ancillaries) to the exclusion of concentrating on the learning message. It is tempting to try new things, to play with new technologies, to experiment with the latest toys, but overemphasis on these generates suspicion about their value. We need to maintain our focus on our academic goals while continuing to develop and refine the most accessible learning processes for our students.

● ● ● ● ●

The Value of Technology: Making the Substance Clearer

In the interest of keeping current on pedagogical trends, the temptation to incorporate technology into our teaching can be overwhelming. Whether or not this is a good idea remains an individual decision. Here are some considerations:

- Video, audio, and other types of links can help to clarify case content. For example, if you are writing a case about a complex medical or engineering process, students are likely to understand the steps in the process more easily if you can show them an action video that moves them from one step to the next.

- If you are writing a marketing case, it is possible that letting students see specific commercials would help you to make clear various advertising strategies. Be aware, however, that commercials are copyrighted materials, and you must obtain permission directly from the corporation to use them. This is not an especially difficult task because most companies like the additional exposure to new audiences; however, obtaining permission is time-consuming and there is no guarantee of the continued availability of the commercial itself.

■ In a finance or accounting case, it may be helpful to include a formatted table that will perform specific calculations for students. This can only be accomplished if your case is available electronically; hardcopy cases cannot provide this functionality, but you can make visible the formulae necessary to free students from having to develop their own spreadsheets. Of course, this is of little value if your goal is to teach students how to actually develop the appropriate spreadsheet formulae.

The main element to remember is that any video you incorporate directly into a case should be integral to your students' understanding of the case. Otherwise, the video becomes a "nice to know" piece, but does not advance student learning.

● ● ● ● ●

Guidelines for Incorporating Links into Cases

One important consideration for incorporating technology into cases is where to place the links. The location of the links drives their usage, as discussed in the following list.

■ If the link appears in the case, this suggests that students must click on it (or enter it directly into their browser) in order to understand the case fully.

■ If the link appears in the Instructor's Manual, this suggests that the decision to use the link lies with the instructor. You may choose to use the link in the IM under the following circumstances:

   ■ You are not sure that the link will remain viable indefinitely.

   ■ You have several links that provide similar information, and the specific perspectives presented on the sites vary.

   ■ Your link is to a long video element, and you do not wish to require students to watch a 30-minute video for just five minutes of important or enlightening information.

   ■ Your links are for "nice to know" rather than required information.

If you are including electronic interviews or downloadable content and making it available in the case, present the link just as if it were a standard exhibit (e.g., see https://help.edublogs.org/how-to-insert-links-in-your-post/ for instructions that show this process).

• • • • •

Some Caveats

The Internet is a dynamic environment, and websites come into existence and disappear on a frequent and unforeseeable schedule. For that reason, it is wise to limit the extent of dependence on technology to make your cases more generally usable.

Each time you decide to include a link in your case or in your IM, consider the following:

■ Can the case stand on its own, without access to the specific web link you have provided? If the case does not work without the web link, you are limiting your potential audience to those who want to incorporate technology into their case teaching.

■ Is the link likely to remain available indefinitely?

    ■ If the link is from a news source (such as a newspaper, television news, or Internet news connection) or a government source, you can have confidence in its continued availability.

    ■ If the link is a corporate connection, you cannot be certain that the specific page will remain available, especially if the link is to an interview with a corporate employee who is no longer with the company.

    ■ If the link is an interview that is housed on your own university server and you have permission for use by the person being interviewed, go ahead and use the link as long as you can guarantee its continued availability.

The key to creating successful technology-facilitated cases is to remember that a case is a case is a case—they all are **factual stories** that took place **in the past**. Anything that supports learning from a case is valid. Keeping to those basic guidelines will result in useful and interesting cases that enhance student learning.

• • • • •

References and Readings

Hofstetter, F.T. (1993). "Design and Construction of a Multimedia Technology Case." *Techtrends* 38, no. 2, 22–24.

Junco, R. (2011). "The Relationship between Frequency of Facebook Use, Participation in Facebook Activities, and Student Engagement." *Computers & Education* 58, 162–171.

Kolb, A.Y., and D.A. Kolb. (2005). "Learning Styles and Learning Spaces: Enhancing Experiential Learning in Higher Education." *Academy of Management Learning & Education* 4, no. 2, 193–212.

Liedtka, J. (2001). "The Promise and Peril of Video Cases: Reflections on Their Creation and Use." *Journal of Management Education* 25, no. 4, 409–424.

Lowerison, G., J. Sclater, R.F. Schmid, and P.C. Abrami. (2006). "Are We Using Technology for Learning?" *Journal of Educational Technology Systems* 34, no. 4, 401–425.

Lundberg, C.C., P. Rainsford, J.P. Shay, and C.A. Young. (2001). "Case Writing Reconsidered." *Journal of Management Education* 25, no. 4, 450–463.

Mauffette-Leenders, L.A., J.A. Erskine, and M.R. Leenders. (1997). *Learning with Cases*. London, Ontario, Canada: Richard Ivey School of Business, University of Western Ontario.

Means, B., Y. Toyama, R. Murphy, M. Bakia, and K. Jones. (2009). *Evaluation of Evidence-Based Practices in Online Learning: A Meta-Analysis and Review of Online Learning Studies*. Washington, DC: U.S. Department of Education.

Munoz, C.L., and T.L. Towner. (2009). "Opening Facebook: How to Use Facebook in the College Classroom." Presented at the 2009 Society for Information Technology and Teacher Education Conference in Charleston, SC. http://www46.home page.villanova.edu/john.immerwahr/TP101/Facebook.pdf (accessed March 13, 2012).

Naumes, W., and M.J. Naumes. (2011). *The Art & Craft of Case Writing*, 3d ed. Armonk, NY: M.E. Sharpe.

● ● ● ● ●

Worksheets

WS 11:1 Graphic Novels or Photo Diaries

WS 11:2 Case Stakeholders and Their Needs

WS 11:1

Graphic Novels or Photo Diaries

This abbreviated version of an involved process uses photos and short paragraphs to simplify a complex procedure and make it easy to understand. Cover the photos on the left and try to understand the instructions on the right without visual assistance. You can find the full set of instructions at TheCleverCat, "Vegetarian Arroz con Gandules: A Modern Take on Puerto Rican Rice and Beans," http://theclevercat.hubpages.com/hub/Vegetarian-Arroz-con-Gandules-A-Modern-Take-on-Puerto-Rican-Rice-and-Beans.

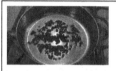	**Step 1.** Heat the oil in a large, heavy pot or caldera. Add the achiote seeds and heat for about three minutes over medium heat. The achiote will flavor and color the oil a warm orangey-red and this is what you will use to cook the sofrito (seasoned vegetable base). Strain the oil or scoop out the achiote seeds with a spoon and discard.
	**Step 2.** Add the onion and green pepper and sauté until soft and translucent, about five minutes. Then add the adobo, black pepper, garlic, oregano, Sazón, and vegetarian bacon bits. Stir to coat with the oil, and cook over low to medium heat for another 3 or 4 minutes, stirring frequently. The veggies will turn a deeper orange and smell ever so slightly smoky.
	**Step 3.** Add the rice and fry, stirring occasionally, until the rice is slightly opaque, about 4 minutes. Then add the water. It will sizzle! Add the canned goods: the tomato sauce, gandules, olives and pimientos, and brine. Stir several times, making sure nothing is stuck to the bottom.
	**Step 4.** This is the right type of boil. See the size of the bubbles? They are about 1/2–3/4 inch in diameter. Stir once more, very gently so as not to disrupt the boil. Cover it and simmer 25–40 minutes or until the rice is dry. Do not lift the lid, or your rice will turn out gummy. When ready, the rice will be fragrant and the beans will have risen to the top.

Source: TheCleverCat, "Vegetarian Arroz con Gandules: A Modern Take on Puerto Rican Rice and Beans," http://theclevercat.hubpages.com/hub/Vegetarian-Arroz-con-Gandules-A-Modern-Take-on-Puerto-Rican-Rice-and-Beans.

WS 11:2

Case Stakeholders and Their Needs

Use this table to identify the stakeholder needs your proposed case format and delivery system will address. Is your focus on the appropriate stakeholder? Note that both students and instructors benefit from innovation . . . Are case authors holding them back?

Stakeholder	Needs	Traditional (T) or Innovative (I) Format or Delivery System	
		Traditional	Innovative
Students	Easy access	T	
	Convenience	T	
	Stable/durable content	T	
	Engaging material		I
	Links to theory		I
	Links to additional information		I
	Interactive learning tools		I
	Hands-on materials		I
	Visual reinforcement		I
Instructors	Ease of debriefing	T	
	Familiarity	T	
	Currency	T	I
	Control		I
	Engaged students		I
	Connection of theory to practice		I
Case Authors	Adoptions	T	
	Ease of development	T	
	Short time from start to completion	T	
	Need for limited resources	T	
	Guaranteed durable accessibility	T	
	Being taken seriously	T	
	Access to creative ancillary materials		I

About the Author

Gina Vega, PhD, is the owner of Organizational Ergonomics, an academic consulting firm that focuses on case writing skills in faculty environments. She is past Professor of Management at the Bertolon School of Business, Salem State University (MA) and is widely published in academic journals. She has written seven books and more than 30 cases. Professor Vega is a Fulbright Specialist (Russia 2010, UK 2012), past president of the CASE Association, a CASE fellow, past editor *of The CASE Journal* and past associate editor of the *Journal of Management Education.* She has received numerous awards for case teaching, case research, case writing, and mentoring of case writers.

Index ● ● ● ● ●

Note: figures and tables are denoted with italicized page numbers.

Printed in the United States
By Bookmasters